BUMPER COOK

Susan Campbell & Caroline Conran

M

ISBN: 0 333 23856 7

First published 1978 by

MACMILLAN LONDON LIMITED

*4 Little Essex Street London WC2R 3LF
and Basingstoke
Associated Companies in Delhi, Dublin,
Hong Kong, Johannesburg, Lagos, Melbourne,
New York, Singapore and Tokyo*

Original graphic design by Peter Kindersley
Illustrations by Susan Campbell

This book is derived from *Poor Cook*
(Macmillan, 1971) and *Family Cook*
(Macmillan 1972) and contains
approximately eighty per cent of the recipes
and diagrams from *Poor Cook* and fifty
per cent of the recipes and diagrams from
Family Cook. The introduction has been
specially written, and other small
amendments and alterations have been made.

Printed in Great Britain by
BUTLER AND TANNER LIMITED
Frome, Somerset

Acknowledgments

To butchers Frederick Lovell and the late Sidney Norwood
for their help with meat diagrams; to Helen Whitten, Ivy
Bright, Carol Amos, Patricia Moran and the late Emily
Spencer for practical help and moral support; to
fishmonger Steve Hatt (Essex Road, N.1) and Inspector
G. R. Watkin (Billingsgate) for their considerable help
with the fish section; to Fred Knock of
Simpson's-in-the-Strand for his demonstrations and
expert advice on carving, to Lina Stores (Brewer Street,
Soho, W.1) for information on pasta; to the successful
competitors of *The Sunday Times* good cheap recipe
competition; to all our friends who contributed recipes and
ideas; to *The Sunday Times* and *Nova* for allowing the use
or recipes written for their readers and to Habitat for the
loan of many of the utensils illustrated.

BUMPER COOK

FOR ROBIN AND TERENCE
AND OUR CHILDREN

Contents

Diagrams

Types of pasta 43 Types of fish 62–3 How to fillet a round fish 69 How to fillet a flat fish 76–7 How to prepare and dress a crab 82 Making a raised pork pie 91 Making Cornish pasties 92 Boning a breast 95 Cuts of beef 100–1 Cuts of pork 102–3 Cuts of veal 104 Cuts of lamb 104–5 Carving a wing rib or sirloin 107 Carving a leg of lamb or pork 118–9 Carving a shoulder of lamb 120–1 Carving a saddle of lamb or mutton 123 Making a guard of honour 125 Stuffing pork fillet 131 Carving a hand of pork 133 Trussing a chicken 156 Boning a chicken or duck 158–9 Carving a turkey, large chicken or capon 163 Carving a duck or goose 167 Making apple strudel 209

Introduction

This is a collection of all the best recipes and all the most useful information and diagrams from our two previous books, *Poor Cook* and *Family Cook*. Economy was the chief motive behind those two books; it is still the main reason for this one. Why buy or publish two books when the best of both can be combined in one?

In the early 1970s, when *Poor Cook* and *Family Cook* first appeared, the practice of economy, especially in the kitchen, was not thought to be nearly as important or as necessary as it is now, after more than half a decade of non-stop inflation. Moreover, the astronomical rise in the price of food means that the era of 'cheap' food is quite definitely over. Steaks and chops have *had* to give way to best end and brisket. Originally, we wrote the books to encourage people to stick to the good old homely recipes which used humble ingredients. They were, it seemed to us, in danger of being completely forgotten as a tide of lavishly advertised convenience foods swept into supermarkets, which were themselves replacing the traditional butchers, grocers, fishmongers, greengrocers and bakeries. At the other end of the scale there were plenty of new cookery books, for those still interested in cooking, but these concentrated mainly on the sort of elaborate food which could only be served at extravagant dinner parties.

Little did we know, as we lovingly revived recipes for bread and butter pudding and found out how to skin a rabbit, that a knowledge of these things was going to be even more useful in the years to come than it was when we first began writing. What we wrote in 1971 and 1972 now seems almost prophetic. Today, also, people are much more informed and concerned about the ecological problems besetting food production and tend to be wary about what they eat, thanks to their increased respect for both health and diet. As well as giving recipes for a more wholesome approach to saving money and eating well we want in this compilation, as in the two original books, to show that economical cooking need not be dreary and unexciting, but can be as much fun to plan and prepare as it is to eat.

Storecupboard

Cheap **butter** for cooking
A large tin of **olive oil** (cheaper by the gallon)
A large tin of **arachide oil** for deep frying. Keep
  separate bottles, one for fish and one for other
  things, and always strain the oil before it goes
  back in the bottle, or it will not stay fresh
Dripping, lard, margarine and **cooking fat**
Large chunks of **Parmesan** and **Gruyère** cheeses
Streaky bacon in a piece, **Salami, Salt Cod**
Tins and tins of Italian peeled **tomatoes**
Tubes or tins of **tomato purée**
Packets of **pasta** and **semolina**
Pounds of dried **haricot beans, kidney beans,
  flageolets, lentils, chick peas, dried peas**
Rice: long-grain for curry, Italian for risotto,
  round for puddings
Large bag of **dried mushrooms,** better than
  tinned and cheaper
Spices: coriander, cumin, turmeric, cardamom,
  chilli, paprika, allspice, mixed spice, cloves,
  cinnamon sticks, mace, nutmeg
Herbs (do not keep them too long) : bay leaves
  on a branch, rosemary, thyme, oregano, basil,
  marjoram, sage, tarragon. Keep parsley, chives
  and mint fresh in polythene bags in the refrigerator
Caraway seeds, **fennel** seeds, cheap
  sherry, brandy, port and **cooking wine**

Garlic
Stock cubes: chicken and beef. Maggi are best
Tins of **tunny fish, anchovies** in oil, **sardines,
  pimentoes, capers** in wine vinegar
Dijon **mustard, mustard powder**
Sea salt, peppercorns
Olives: buy them loose and keep them in a jar
  of oil
Plain flour and **baking powder,** so you do not
  have to worry about self-raising flour
Porridge oats and **wheatgerm** for muesli
Gelatine
Home-made **pastry-mix** (margarine or cooking
  fat rubbed into twice its weight of flour)
Dried yeast, or fresh yeast from the baker
  which keeps for up to a week in the refrigerator
Demerara, granulated, soft brown, caster and
  icing **sugar**
Golden Syrup, honey
Cooking chocolate, cocoa powder
Vanilla sugar: keep a pod of vanilla in a jar of
  caster sugar, and top it up as you need to
Wine vinegar
Dried fruit, whole **almonds**
**Saffron, pine nuts, pistachio nuts, juniper
  berries** and **truffles** are all cheaper bought
  abroad

Temperatures

Electricity and Solid Fuel	Gas	Degrees Fahrenheit	Centigrade
Cool	$\frac{1}{4}-\frac{1}{2}$	250	121
Very Slow	1	275	135
Slow	2	300	149
	3	325	163
Moderate	4	350	177
	5	375	190
Moderately hot	6	400	204
Hot	7	425	218
Very hot	8	450	232
	9	475	246

The Metric System

Conversion tables for measurements and temperatures.

Weight

1 oz —	28·35 g	1 kilogramme —	1000 g — 2 lb 3 oz	approx
2 oz —	56·7 g		500 g — 1 lb 1½ oz	,,
¼ lb —	113·4 g		250 g — 9 oz	,,
½ lb —	226·8 g		125 g — 4¼ oz	,,
12 oz —	340·2 g		100 g — 3½ oz	,,
16 oz —	453·6 g		25 g — 1 oz	,,

Liquids

¼ pt (1 gill) — 142 ml
½ pt — 284 ml
1 pt — 568 ml

1 litre —	1000 g —	1¾ pt — 35 fl oz	approx
½ litre —	500 g —	¾ pt plus 4½ tablespoons	,,
¼ litre —	250 g —	½ pt less 2 tablespoons	,,
1 decilitre —	100 g —	6 tablespoons	,,
1 centilitre —	10 g —	1 dessertspoon	,,
1 millilitre —	1 g —	a few drops	,,
5 millilitres —	5 g —	pharmaceutical teaspoon	,,

Meat Roasting Table

Meat	Quick Roast	Slow Roast
	For good quality meat. Sear at Reg 8/450° for 15 minutes. Reduce to Reg 5/375° for the remainder of the cooking time.	Best for poor quality joints. It helps make them tender. Roast at Reg 3/325°.
Beef	15 minutes per lb plus 15 minutes for rare roasting. 20 minutes per lb plus 20 minutes for meat well done.	40 minutes per lb plus 45 minutes.
Lamb	25 minutes per lb plus 25 minutes.	45 minutes per lb plus 45 minutes.
Pork	35 minutes per lb plus 35 minutes.	Not suitable.
Veal	30 minutes per lb plus 30 minutes.	50 minutes per lb plus 50 minutes.
Chicken	20 minutes per lb plus 20 minutes.	Over 4 lb, 25 minutes per lb plus 25 minutes.
Turkey	8-10 lb bird 2-2½ hours 10-14 lb bird 2½-3 hours 14-20 lb bird 3½-4 hours	8-10 lb bird 3-3½ hours 10-14 lb bird 3½-4 hours 14-20 lb bird 4½-5 hours

N.B. Bone is a good conductor of heat, so meat with the bone in does not need the extra minutes over. Stuffing on the other hand is a poor conductor of heat, so joints that are stuffed need perhaps fifteen minutes extra, depending on the thickness of the stuffing. You should always judge by the shape of the joint that is to be cooked. If it is a long thin piece of meat it will obviously need less cooking than a compact thick piece. So use the chart as a general guide, supported by your own judgment.

Soups

It is really easy to make home-made soup, and it's very odd how few people bother considering how much nicer it tastes than any out of a tin. The rustling of packets and clank of tin-openers may be a welcome sound from Tiger Bay to the Wash, but what appears in the soup-bowl a minute later has very little to do with the piping hot, delicately flavoured and beautifully coloured bowlful, with its handful of sizzling croûtons or swirl of cream, that is your own vegetable soup. And the money saved by the manufacturers in buying vegetables by the ton is spent on packaging and massive advertising, so ready-made soups are not particularly money-saving and should be kept for emergencies.

If you have a liquidiser, the making of soup is simply a question of cooking the right ingredients to the right degree of tenderness and then giving them a quick whizz, to purée them. If not, a Moulin-Légumes (or mouli), a small, inexpensive food mill for sieving soft fruit and cooked vegetables, is invaluable.

One of the vital ingredients for good soup is stock. Many cookery writers between the two wars decided stock should not be used in vegetable soups, because it overpowered the flavour of the vegetables and had a certain sameness to it that robbed the soup of its delicacy and freshness. It is certainly true that if you use a strongly-flavoured or not altogether fresh stock you will end up with an awful failure. So use your own simple, freshly-made stock, obtained by putting chicken carcasses and bones in cold water, with a few carrots and an onion, plus a sprig of parsley, peppercorns and a bay leaf, and letting the liquid simmer and reduce incredibly slowly while you just go away and leave it. You can do the same with meaty beef or veal bones, freshly bought from the butcher; try to get marrow bones if you can, and remember to ask him to chop them up for you. Strain the stock, keep it in the refrigerator and use it within a day or two, then make a fresh lot. Or if you have a deep-freeze, you can keep a reserve of concentrated stock always available. The day of the never-ending stock-pot to which a procession of old left-overs made its way daily is dead and gone; we don't like having that dreary, soggy-smelling dishwater in our kitchens any more, and anyway there isn't room for it. For vegetable soup chicken stock really is the best, and if you haven't any it is perfectly feasible to use a stock-cube (Maggi tastes less of monosodium glutamate than others) but dilute it much more than it says in the directions or you will find that good old packet-soup flavour lurking in your own lovingly-made soup. Chicken broth, as well as being the best stock, makes a marvellous basis for clear soups, and is a staple of many Italian kitchens, although one doesn't all that frequently get chicken to eat there. To it you can add pasta, poached eggs, marble-sized dumplings, finely sliced vegetables (which should be barely cooked when they are served), or a handful of rice and some egg-yolks beaten with fresh lemon juice. Do not, however, attempt a complicated mixture of different things or you may well end up with an indifferent sort of wet Russian salad.

The more filling soups, made with pasta and beans, meat and pearl barley, split peas and ham bones, should be served either as a meal on their own, with cheese and fruit afterwards, or before a very light, simple main dish such as an omelette or a salade Niçoise.

If you grow your own vegetables, you can use practically anything you have too much of to make a wonderful first course: French beans coming too fast to their best, lettuces that are getting ready to bolt, peas that have grown too fat, spinach you can't keep pace with, carrots, Jerusalem artichokes, reproachful turnips, beetroots or monstrous regiments of celery, disintegrating under the attack of vitamin-hungry slugs. If you don't have a vegetable garden you can still make use of gluts, and when the whole market is suddenly flooded with cheap tomatoes, that is the time to make tomato soup.

The beauty of a very humble soup, like carrot or turnip, or of any home-made soup in fact, is much more evident if you don't plonk it onto the table in a saucepan. A traditional china or earthenware soup tureen makes it look ten times more glorious. And having spent only a few pennies on the basic ingredients, the extra expense of a shilling on egg-yolks and cream can lift even quite a boring plain soup into luxuriousness, making it rich and velvety and lustrous, and a great compliment to the cook.

Consommé

2–3 lbs beef or veal shin bones sawn up and with
    some meat on
2 pig's trotters split in four
3 onions
4 carrots
2 stalks celery
bouquet garni
6–7 peppercorns
salt
1 egg white
white wine, lemon juice or sherry (optional)

Consommé is gelatinous stock strong enough to form a jelly, which has been clarified to make it specklessly clear. It is useful for all sorts of dishes; they taste much more interesting with home-made rather than tinned consommé, and cost much less. Jellied eggs, a tarragon chicken in jelly, jellied cream cheese, all need a good stiffish consommé. Pigs' or calves' feet contribute quite enough gelatine for a home-made consommé to stand up on its own, but if the weather is very hot, or you want it even stiffer than it is, you can add gelatine out of a packet at the very end. Put the bones and the pig's trotters in a large pan. Cover with 2 quarts cold water and bring slowly to the boil. Skim and add the vegetables cut in pieces, peppercorns and herbs. Simmer for 3–4 hours, covered; then add a *little* salt, simmer for another half-hour, strain and completely cool the stock so that the fat can be removed to the last speck, and you can see how strongly jellied your stock is. Return it to the stove and boil until it is reduced to the required amount to make it set. A glass of white wine or a dash of sherry at this stage is a good addition. Drop in the white of an egg beaten to a soft peak, and whisk it in. Boil it up until the froth rises in the pan, remove it from the heat and whisk again. Repeat the boiling and whisking twice more to make sure the egg white is cooked. Put a cloth wrung out in hot water over a colander with a large wire strainer on top. Pour the stock through. The sediment will be caught in the egg white leaving the stock crystal clear. Add more sherry, lemon juice and salt to taste and heat. It will set to a beautiful jelly when cold.

Chicken Broth with Butter Dumplings

2 pints very good chicken broth
1½ oz butter
1 small egg
1½ oz plain flour
½ oz self-raising flour
salt
chopped parsley
½ teaspoon grated lemon peel

Soften the butter and cream with the egg. Add the flour (both kinds), salt, parsley and lemon peel. Add a little more plain flour if the mixture is too wet. Make little balls the size of a pea with the mixture. Drop these one by one into the simmering broth, cover and simmer ten minutes. The dumplings will swell nicely and be light as a feather.

☐ *These dumplings should be tiny and not at all filling.*

For 4

Egg Soup

½ pint very good clear stock (use chicken or beef cube if necessary, or use the consommé recipe, page 4)
1 slice crustless white bread
butter
1 egg
1 dessertspoon grated Parmesan if liked

Before you start, heat a soup-plate as much as you safely can; then, while the bouillon or stock is heating, fry the piece of bread golden on both sides in butter. Try to finish it just as the soup comes to boiling point. Put it quickly on the hot soup plate, break an egg on to the fried bread and pour the boiling liquid slowly on to the egg. Let it stand for three to four minutes before eating. The egg should be extremely lightly cooked by the combined heat of the plate, bread and soup. Sprinkle with cheese if liked.

□ *A marvellous soup for convalescence or hangovers.*

For 1

Kidney Soup

6 lambs' kidneys
½ oz butter
3 pints very good, but not salty, stock (you can improve your stock by boiling with chopped onions, carrots and turnips)
2 oz flour
bouquet garni of thyme, parsley and bayleaf
1 blade mace
1 stick celery
6 peppercorns
salt to taste

Skin and halve the kidneys, removing the cores. Fry them in the butter in a saucepan until well browned, add the stock and bring gently to simmering point. Add the bouquet garni, mace, celery and peppercorns. Cover and simmer gently for one hour. Strain the liquid into a clean saucepan, remove the herbs, peppercorns and celery, and chop the kidneys finely.

Mix the flour in a large bowl with a little cold water, and add the reheated liquid just before it comes to the boil, stirring carefully to avoid lumps. Return it to the saucepan (through a sieve if it is lumpy in spite of everything), add the chopped kidneys and simmer, stirring, for five to ten minutes. Check seasoning, and serve with hot toast.

□ *This is one of the best meat soups, thoroughly British and very rich.*

For 5–6

Scotch Broth

1 lb neck or breast of lamb
2 carrots
1 onion
2 leeks
½ small cabbage
1 stick celery
1 small turnip or slice of swede
2 tablespoons pearl barley
bunch parsley
salt and freshly ground pepper

Put the neck or breast of lamb in a large pan and cover with plenty of cold water. Bring to the boil and skim carefully. Throw in another cupful of cold water, bring to the boil and skim again. Simmer the meat while you clean all the vegetables and chop them small. Throw them and the pearl barley into the pan with the meat, add salt, pepper and half the parsley, and simmer gently, covered, for about two hours.
Remove the meat (if it is breast you can use it for epigrams, page 126) and keep it hot to eat with a caper sauce. Sprinkle a handful of freshly chopped parsley into the soup, taste for seasoning and serve.

☐ *A great, filling winter soup.*

For 4–6

Stracciatella

2½ pints good clear chicken stock
2 eggs
2 tablespoons grated Parmesan (optional)
1 tablespoon semolina (optional)

Beat the eggs very well and add the cheese and semolina. Dilute with a cupful of cold stock. Heat the rest of the well-seasoned stock and as it approaches the boil gently pour in the egg mixture. Stir it with a fork in a clockwise direction rather fast. Turn the heat really low and leave the soup slowly spinning for two to three minutes. Ideally the egg should form long, thin soft threads, but more often it looks like yellow snowflakes; never mind, it tastes the same.

☐ *A very good soup for convalescents and delicate stomachs.*

For 4

Artichoke Soup

2 lbs Jerusalem artichokes
1 onion, peeled and sliced
parsley
1 pint stock, water or bouillon made with a cube
1 pint milk
nutmeg
salt, freshly ground pepper
butter
croûtons *or* diced fried bacon

This is a very easily made and delicious soup. The only boring part is peeling the artichokes, and if they have only just come out of the ground you may not have to. But if they are already brown on the outside it is worth taking the trouble to do so as your soup will have an infinitely better colour and flavour. Peel the artichokes and put them immediately into cold water acidulated with a dash of vinegar or lemon juice. Put the sliced onion and artichokes and a bunch of parsley tied with a thread into a large pan, cover with the stock and cook until tender, about 30 minutes. Take out the parsley. Sieve or liquidise finely, stir in the milk, reheat and add a large knob of butter, a grate of nutmeg and salt and pepper as needed. Serve with croûtons or diced fried bacon.

For 4–5

Cabbage Soup

1 large onion
1 oz butter or lard
1 cabbage (about 1 ½ lbs, either white or Savoy)
½ lb soaked haricot beans *or* 2 cubed potatoes, *or*
   ¼ lb haricots and 1 cubed potato
4 cloves garlic, peeled
3 pints fresh stock
large bunch parsley
hefty pinch thyme
salt and freshly ground pepper
2 large skinned tomatoes

Chop the onions and fry in butter or lard in a large, heavy saucepan. Add the chopped cabbage, soaked beans and/or potato cubes, garlic cloves, parsley, thyme and cold stock. Don't add salt yet. Bring it slowly to the boil; skim, and simmer gently, uncovered, for three hours. Add salt, pepper and the skinned, chopped tomatoes 30 minutes before the end. Serve with chopped parsley. It is really a glorious filling sort of stew, brown and very warming.

For 6

Lemon Spinach Soup

1 small onion or shallot
1 lb spinach
1 ½ pints stock
½ lemon
2 egg yolks
salt
handful rice (optional)

Chop the onion finely and the spinach coarsely.
Simmer in the stock, uncovered, for about 20
minutes until tender. Sieve or put through a mouli.
Pour the soup back into the pan. Beat the egg yolks
in a bowl and add two tablespoons of the hot (not
boiling or even simmering) soup. Add this to the
soup in the pan with the juice of half a lemon.
Season and heat very, very gently but don't simmer
or it will curdle. Serve very hot.
No garnish is necessary.
If you want a more filling soup you can add a handful of rice, boiled and still hot, with the egg and
lemon juice.

For 4

Tomato Soup

1 ½ lbs tomatoes
½ oz butter, dash of oil
1 medium potato, peeled and chopped
1 medium onion, peeled and sliced
2 teaspoons sugar
1 teaspoon salt
1 ½ pints water
sprig of parsley
bayleaf, or, if available, some basil
1 tablespoon tomato purée (optional)

Chop the tomatoes roughly but leave the skins on.
Melt the butter in a saucepan with the oil and cook
the potato and onion until they start to soften.
They tend to stick so stir them with a wooden spoon.
Add the tomatoes and let them soften. Add salt,
sugar, pepper, herbs and water. Simmer uncovered
until the potatoes are cooked. Remove the bayleaf,
and sieve, mouli or liquidise everything else. Reheat
just before serving, correct seasoning. Add tomato
purée if it is too pale, which will depend a lot on the
tomatoes you use. Anyway it won't be a fierce
orange like tinned tomato soup but a much prettier
soft orangey red. Stir a little cream into each plate
as you serve it.

☐ *This soup is much more delicate than it sounds.*

For 6

Turnip Soup

5 medium turnips, peeled and coarsely chopped
2 tablespoons butter
1 large onion, finely chopped
2–3 pints boiling water
4–5 slices bread
2 egg yolks
¼ pint thin cream or top of the milk
salt, freshly ground pepper

Cook the turnips and onion in butter, in a large
pan, until they start to soften, but not to brown. Add
boiling water and seasoning and crumble in the
bread, crusts removed. Simmer gently until the
vegetables are tender (25–30 minutes). Sieve or
liquidise. Beat the egg yolks with the cream and add
to the re-heated soup, away from the heat. Stir over
a low heat until smooth and creamy, without boiling
or even simmering, and serve with a nut of butter
in each bowl.

For 4–6

Two of Everything Soup

2 medium-sized leeks
2   „   „   carrots
2   „   „   potatoes
1½–2 pints boiling water
salt
milk, if necessary
knob of butter
croûtons for garnish, if liked

Into a large saucepan put the potatoes and carrots
cleaned and cut into inch-square pieces, and the
leeks, including all the good green parts, cut in
inch-long slices. Pour on enough boiling water to
cover the vegetables by half an inch. Add ½ teaspoon
salt. Cover the pan and simmer the soup for three-
quarters to one hour, or up to two hours or more
if you want to go out, but it must cook very gently.
Put the soup through the mouli or liquidiser, return
it to the cleaned pan, bring it back to the boil and
simmer it gently for five minutes. If it is too thick
add a little milk; if too thin, cook a little longer. It
should be the consistency of thin cream. Taste for
salt, add a knob of butter and serve plain or gar-
nished with small croûtons of fried bread.

For 4

Vichyssoise

1 lb leeks
2–3 medium potatoes
1 onion
parsley
1 pint chicken stock
1 pint creamy milk
salt and white pepper
chives
thin cream (optional)

Clean and chop the leeks, peel and slice the potatoes and onion. Put the vegetables in a pan with the parsley tied in a bundle, and cover with the stock. Simmer until all the vegetables are tender. Remove the parsley, then sieve the vegetables, helping them through the sieve or mouli (finest disc) by moistening with milk. Add the rest of the milk, just enough to make a thinnish creamy soup, season with salt and a little freshly ground white pepper, and chill. Serve cold with chopped chives and a thread of cream if you have it. This tastes very good hot if the weather suddenly turns cold.

☐ *A well-known mid-Atlantic soup.*

For 4

Watercress Soup

2 bunches watercress
2–3 large potatoes
1 onion
1½ pints stock (or stock cube and water)
1 pint milk
salt and freshly ground pepper
knob of butter

Put the potatoes and onion, peeled and roughly chopped, into a large pan. Add cold stock, bring to the boil and simmer for 15–20 minutes; now throw in the washed watercress, stalks and all, and cook until it is tender but still a good green. Sieve all this, helping it through the mouli by moistening with the milk. If you want a green-flecked soup, use a coarse disc for your mouli; if a uniform green, use a finer disc. You can do either with a liquidiser by adjusting the timing. Now add enough milk to make the soup a good consistency. Return the soup to the stove, season and heat through. Serve with a nut of butter and a sprig of watercress in each plate.
If you sweat the watercress and onion in butter before adding the potato and stock, you make a slightly richer soup. The watercress looks best very coarsely chopped to make large green flecks.

For 6

Chick Pea Soup

6–8 oz chick peas
olive oil
1 clove garlic, chopped
1 onion, peeled and sliced
1 green pepper, de-seeded and chopped
3 anchovy fillets, chopped
3 tomatoes, skinned and chopped
pinch rosemary
4 oz short macaroni (or long macaroni broken up)
salt

Soak chick peas overnight, or all day. Put in a large pan, cover with plain cold water and bring slowly to the boil. Simmer gently, adding more boiling water if necessary, for two to three hours until tender. Add no salt yet. Cover the bottom of a sauté pan with olive oil and sauté the onions, garlic, peppers and anchovies over a moderate heat until tender. Add the tomatoes and a pinch of chopped rosemary. Simmer five or ten minutes more, then add this mixture to the chick peas and their liquid. Season with salt at this point and bring to the boil. Add the macaroni and cook the soup until the macaroni is tender. It should taste as though it is made with a really good beef-broth — the anchovies, though they seem to disappear completely, make this contribution to the soup.

☐ *This is a coarse soup with a marvellous earthy flavour.*

For 4

Dutch Pea Soup

1 lb dried peas (split green ones)
1 knuckle green bacon, soaked overnight
1 fresh pig's trotter (if salt, soak overnight)
2 onions, peeled and chopped
2 leeks, cleaned and cut up
2–3 sticks celery
4–5 frankfurters
butter for frying

Soak the peas for two to four hours. Take a large saucepan and put in the drained peas; cover with six pints water, and simmer, covered, without salt for one or two hours. Add the bacon and pig's trotter and simmer two hours more. In a separate pan soften the fresh vegetables in butter while you sieve or liquidise the pea soup, having first removed the meat to a plate. Add the softened vegetables to the puréed pea soup and cook on for an hour more, over a very low heat. Stir from time to time to prevent it from catching. Leave, covered, overnight. Next day chop the meat from the knuckle into small pieces, and add it with the sliced frankfurters to the soup, which should have set solid. Heat through, taste for seasoning, and if the pea-starch, which expands, has made it too thick, add a little water. You can adjust the amount of bacon and sausages to the number of people and their appetites. The pig's foot is thrown out, but it does a lot for the texture of the soup and adds nourishment.

☐ *This soup is very filling and can be eaten as a meal on its own. It is best if made the day before.*

For 6–8

Lettuce Soup

1 lettuce (keep the heart for sandwiches), or a few
    small lettuces from thinning the rows
1 large onion
1 large potato
½ oz butter
1½ pints delicate chicken stock (or stock cube and
    water)
½ pint milk
salt and freshly ground black pepper
1 egg yolk (optional)

Wash the lettuce and break up the leaves; chop the
onion and potato roughly. Melt the butter in a large
pan and soften the lettuce and onion in it without
browning. When they are soft add the potatoes and
the boiling stock. Simmer uncovered for 20–30
minutes until the potatoes are cooked; sieve, mouli
or liquidise for just a few seconds, moistening with
milk. Add the rest of the milk and taste for seasoning. Heat through and serve with hot, well-fried
croûtons. An egg yolk, stirred in at the last moment,
makes a much richer soup.

☐ *You can use sorrel to make this soup, or lettuce and
sorrel together.*

For 4

Pasta e Fagioli

6 oz haricot beans, previously soaked
3 medium potatoes, peeled and cubed
3 sticks celery, cut small
1 fennel root (if available) cut in strips
4 cloves garlic
salt and freshly ground pepper
4 oz short macaroni
parsley, chopped
2–3 tablespoons Parmesan, grated

Put the haricot beans in a large pan with two quarts
of water, bring to the boil and cook gently for one
hour, adding no salt. Then add the vegetables cut
up small and the whole cloves of garlic. Add salt and
pepper and simmer another 20–30 minutes until all
the vegetables are tender, turn up the heat, and
when the soup is gently boiling throw in the
macaroni.

Chop a handful of parsley and throw it with the
grated cheese into the soup as soon as the pasta is
tender. Serve immediately. If the soup seems too
thick, add a little more water. If it is too thin, you
can stir in a couple of tablespoons of mashed potato,
or if this is not available, ladle out some of the
vegetables in the soup, purée them, and return them
to the soup.

For 6–8

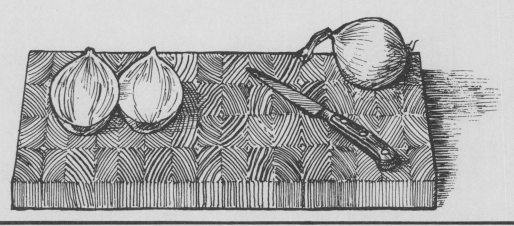

Gaspacho

1 pint tomato juice (unseasoned tinned or made
   with fresh tomatoes)
1 pint water (iced)
2–3 slices bread (crusts off)
salt, pepper (white if possible)
4 tablespoons olive oil
1 tablespoon wine vinegar
1–2 cloves garlic
For the garnish:
2 or 3 tomatoes, ½ cucumber, 1 green pepper,
   1 hardboiled egg
1 onion, croûtons

This is very easy to make if you have a liquidiser. Pound the peeled garlic in a mortar. Soak the bread in iced water. Put tomato juice, salt, pepper, garlic, bread, water and vinegar into the liquidiser and whizz till smooth. Add the oil drip by drip, and put the resulting soup-base into the refrigerator until ready to serve. (If you have no liquidiser, pound the bread with the garlic, add the oil drop by drop and then dilute slowly with the tomato juice, vinegar and water.) Peel and slice the onion and soak the slices in water while you prepare the other garnishes. Peel and chop the tomatoes, removing the seeds if you like, peel the cucumber and chop it finely. Remove the seeds from the green pepper and chop it finely. Peel and chop the egg. Add iced water to the soup if it is too thick. Just before serving drain the onion and chop it finely. Serve each item of garnish in a separate little dish on a bed of crushed ice if possible. Serve soup in bowls, each guest helps himself to garnish.

☐ *This is an iced soup, very refreshing and nourishing for summer.*

For 6

Spanish Soup

1 onion, 4 small leeks
1 small aubergine
3 small potatoes
½ pint stock
2–3 tomatoes
2 small red or green sweet peppers
4 oz French beans
2 cloves garlic
few sprigs parsley
pinch sweet paprika
olive oil, salt

Chop the peppers into one-inch squares, removing every seed. Simmer in oil for 30 minutes. Slice the onion across and quarter it. Cut the cleaned leeks into half-inch pieces. Cut the aubergine into cubes and sprinkle these with salt. Set them to drain. Start cooking the onions and leeks in a pan with 1½ pints cold water. Cube the potatoes and add them after 15 minutes with ½ pint stock. Taste for seasoning. Skin and chop the tomatoes; add them to the soup after twenty minutes with the peppers, the rinsed aubergines and the beans broken in pieces. Cook until the beans are tender, then season again if necessary. Sprinkle chopped garlic and parsley and a large pinch of paprika into each plateful of soup.

This is a very adaptable soup. If you haven't got beans, leave them out; if you have courgettes, put them in; if you have marvellous fresh cabbage, put in a few good inner leaves, cut up. In Spain it is a real stand-by and they regard it as quick to make, which may explain why lunch is never ready until three o'clock.

For 2–3

Carrot Soup

1 lb nice tasty carrots, preferably young or middle-aged
1 very small turnip (or ¼ large one)
1 onion
1 leek
1½ oz butter
1 lump sugar
salt, fresh-ground white pepper
2–3 pints chicken stock, or cube stock

Clean the vegetables and cut them into small pieces. Melt the butter in a heavy pan. Add the vegetables and sugar, stir to coat them in butter, cover the pan tightly and turn the heat very low. Allow the vegetables to soften slowly for ¾ hour to an hour. If you use a thick enough pan you can stew them in butter for ages without burning.

When they are soft, but not brown, sieve or liquidise them with the stock. Season with plenty of salt and pepper and return to the stove. Serve very hot but don't allow the soup to boil. Chopped parsley and a knob of butter or croûtons fried in butter are served with this.

☐ *This soup bears no resemblance to the dreary 'Potage Crecy' often found on hotel menus.*

For 6–8

Hot Cucumber Soup

1 small cucumber, peeled
1 medium-sized potato, peeled
4–5 spring onions
1½–2 pints good chicken stock
butter
salt and freshly ground pepper

Grate the potato and cucumber coarsely; strain off the liquid that forms and put the vegetables to sweat with the finely chopped onions in enough butter to cover the bottom of a medium saucepan. Heat the stock to simmering point and add to the vegetables. Simmer gently for 20–25 minutes. Check seasoning and serve with a knob of butter in each bowl.

☐ *Cucumber used to be eaten hot as often as cold; Eliza Acton recommends this highly, but lots of people have forgotten about it. It tastes quite different cooked, and is strangely interesting.*

For 4

Cold Cucumber Soup

1 cucumber
1 5 oz pot plain yoghurt
milk, straight out of the refrigerator
a couple of sprigs of fresh mint, chopped
salt, freshly ground pepper

In your liquidiser blend the peeled, chopped cucumber and yoghurt. Add enough milk to make up to one and a half pints. Chop the mint by hand and stir it in. Season and chill.

☐ *This is almost too simple if you have a liquidiser, but impossible if not. It is deliciously refreshing on a hot day.*

For 4

Fresh Pea Soup

2 lbs fresh peas
1 bunch spring onions
½ chicken stock cube } or 1 pint fresh chicken stock
1 pint water
1 pint creamy milk
1 tablespoon cream
few chives, chopped
salt, pepper

Shell the peas and cook them with the chopped spring onions in the stock. When tender, sieve finely or put them through a mouli or liquidiser. Add the milk and heat through. Season. Serve with a tablespoon of cream and a sprinkling of chopped chives on each bowl. This is also good cold.

For 4

Leek Soup

1 lb leeks
1 onion
1½ oz butter
1½ oz flour
2 pints chicken or veal stock
salt and pepper
dash of cream or top of the milk *or* croûtons *or* crisply
    fried bacon

Clean the leeks, leaving as much green as you can, and peel the onion. Chop both as finely as possible, which takes ages. Melt the vegetables in the butter in a large pan for about 15 minutes, stirring often, and without browning. Stir in the flour, allow it to thicken and then add the stock gradually. Season and simmer covered until the leeks are tender but still a pleasant green. Serve with croûtons, or a spoonfull of cream or little cubes of crisply fried bacon thrown sizzling into the soup bowls.

☐ *Very filling.*

For 4–6

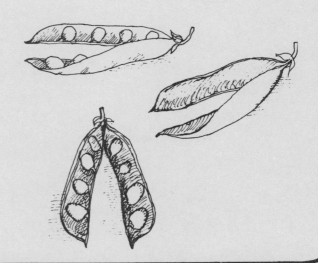

Red Bean Soup

½ lb red haricot beans (soaked overnight)
3 medium onions
¼ lb streaky bacon in a piece
2–3 pints stock
salt, pepper
butter
parsley

Cook the soaked beans with the quartered onions and bacon in a light, but not salty, stock until they are tender. Sieve, removing the bacon first, add enough stock or water to make the soup the consistency you prefer. Heat without reboiling, season with salt and pepper, and add a large knob of butter. Stir it in and serve with chopped parsley.

☐ *Delicious, and a very pretty pinky-beige. It can also be made with other beans, for instance white haricots, flageolets, kidney beans or any other dry beans.*

For 6

Clear Beetroot Soup

3 pints home-made consommé or very good clear stock (duck or beef stock are excellent for this soup)
juice of ½ lemon
2 lumps sugar
2 raw beetroots
sour cream
salt, pepper

Heat the stock. Peel the beetroots and grate them into a bowl. Pour the hot stock over them, return them to the pan together with the sugar and lemon juice and bring to the boil. Skim if necessary and simmer for 20 minutes. By this time the soup will be a beautiful clear garnet colour and the beetroot will be lightly cooked. Season and serve either with the beetroot in or strained and with a dollop of sour cream in each bowl.

For 6

Lentil Soup with Salt Pork

½ lb brown lentils
¼ lb piece salt pork or bacon
1 large onion, chopped
2–3 sticks celery, cut up into 1 inch pieces
3 cloves garlic
a handful of Italian dried mushrooms (cèpes)
salt, pepper, parsley, olive oil

Soak the lentils overnight and the salt pork if necessary (the butcher will tell you). Also soak the dried mushrooms for about an hour, keeping the water they have soaked in. Put the lentils, pork, mushrooms with their water, garlic cloves, onion and celery in a pan and cover with about 2 pints cold water. Bring slowly to the boil, skim and simmer until the lentils are tender (up to 1½ hours). Add more water if necessary and a glass of red wine if you like. Taste for seasoning and serve just as it is, with a slice of the pork in each bowl if you like it. Sprinkle each soup bowl with chopped parsley and pour in a teaspoonful of olive oil or add a knob of butter.

For 5–6

Lentil Soup with Pasta

Make the soup as described above and about 10 minutes before the end throw in 3 ounces of small soup pasta and cook on until the pasta is done. Add more boiling water if more liquid is needed. Taste for seasoning and serve with a spoonful of olive oil in each plate and grated Parmesan.

□ *An exceedingly filling and soothing winter soup.*

Crab Bisque

1 shell and legs of a large cooked crab
1 small cooked crab
1 halibut or cod's head
1 glass white wine (or less)
1 onion
2 carrots
peppercorns, salt
a few twigs of fennel
4–5 tomatoes
⅛–¼ pint cream
a small glass sherry

Remove the meat from the small crab and keep it on one side. Put the well-washed and crushed crab-shells, fish-head, white wine, onion, carrots, peppercorns, salt and fennel into two pints of water. Simmer for one hour. Add the roughly chopped tomatoes and cook a further 20 minutes. Strain, taste for salt and pepper, add sherry and reduce a little. (At this stage it might look a rather gloomy colour, in which case a little tomato purée will improve it.) Add the crab-meat from the small crab and all but a couple of spoonsfull of the cream. Serve as soon as it is thoroughly heated through, with a dollop of cream in each bowl.

□ *You eat the meat of the large crab at another meal with brown bread and butter and mayonnaise, or just quartered lemons. This soup is on the costly side, but a hundred times nicer and cheaper than tinned. You could make it for a treat, rather than every day, and the amount of crab-meat could be quite small leaving more for salad. The fish-head is included to give the soup more body as well as to help the flavour.*

For 4

Smoked Haddock Soup

1 smoked medium-size haddock (about 12 oz)
water
1 onion, chopped and peeled
1 pint milk
few tablespoons mashed potato (better made
    specially for the soup — use 2 potatoes)
½ oz butter
salt and freshly ground pepper
parsley

Skin the haddock, and set the skin aside. Put the haddock in a shallow pan and pour on enough boiling water to cover. Bring slowly to the boil, then add the chopped onion. When the haddock is just tender remove it from the pan, take the flesh off the bones and flake it. Put the bones and skin back in the pan and simmer, covered, for one hour. When the skin, bones and onion have thoroughly flavoured the stock, strain it, bring it to the boil again, and add the milk, brought to the boil in a separate pan, and the flaked fish. Slowly add enough mashed potato to give the soup a creamy consistency. At the last moment taste for salt and pepper and stir in the butter. Serve sprinkled with chopped parsley, or put another lump of butter in each bowl.

For 4

Cockle Chowder

2 quarts cockles, well washed and scrubbed
4 rashers bacon, cut small
1 oz butter
1 Spanish onion, chopped
2–3 parboiled floury potatoes, cut into cubes
¾ pint milk (or up to 1 pint)
handful chopped parsley
freshly ground pepper

Take a large pan with a lid and bring about an inch of water to the boil in it. Throw in the cockles, put on the lid and leave over a high flame. Shake the pan from time to time, or stir the cockles once or twice with a wooden spoon; after four to five minutes all the shells should be open and the cockles slightly cooked. Remove all the shells, put the cockles aside and strain the liquid through a cloth. In another pan melt one ounce of butter, let the pieces of bacon sizzle in it, add the onion and cook gently until it is transparent. Add the potatoes, ¾ pint of the strained cockle liquid, and the milk. Let this simmer very gently until the potatoes are soft but not a total mush. Add the shelled cockles, pepper and parsley; heat thoroughly but gently, and test for saltiness (it should not need any extra salt as the cockle liquid is salty, and so is the bacon).
Serve with thick, hard ships' biscuits. Lovers of *Moby Dick* might break their biscuits into the soup. Water biscuits or crackers will do.

☐ *An English seaside version of clam chowder.*

For 4

Eggs and Cheese

It is a long time since everybody living in the country had a coop of laying hens in the orchard, and foxes and broodiness were genuine threats to the family egg supply. Eggs, packed in their own beautiful fragile shells, are abundant, and farms with a quarter of a million chickens apiece keep the poor birds laying night and day. Luckily, although one may not approve of chickens being treated as egg-laying units, the massive production methods and subsidies do mean that eggs stay comparatively cheap, and therefore it is worth being lavish with them; they are such an incredibly unwasteful way of handing out first-class protein, and after all, a really perfect soufflé is just as much of a treat as a fresh salmon trout or a fillet of beef, and is very much easier to make than people suppose.

It is probably worth buying large eggs for eating and small eggs to use in cooking, for cakes, sauces, and for brushing the tops of pies and so on. Otherwise this can be wasteful, though both yolks and white can be kept in the refrigerator, covered with foil. Eggs in their shells do not have to be kept in the refrigerator. They are so beautiful and they get eaten up so quickly, it is surely more sense to keep them somewhere they can offer the cook a bit of inspiration; anyway, lots of sauces can't easily be made with a chilled egg.

One of the greatest companions for eggs is cheese. We are only concerned here with cheese for cooking, and the recipes use a tremendous amount of Parmesan and Swiss Emmenthal, or Gruyère, which is similar but with smaller and less frequent holes. These are not the cheapest cheeses there are by any means, but they are invaluable in the kitchen because they cook so well, and keep for weeks, scarcely suffering at all; however dry they get they can still be used for grating. Keep them wrapped in greaseproof paper in the larder or refrigerator. Many Italian provision shops and delicatessens sell Parmesan, but if the price really staggers you, there are cheaper, slightly stronger, versions of it: Pecorino Romano, which is called Vacchino Romano when made with cow's milk, and Caprino Romano when made with goat's milk, and Sardo which is the same cheese but made in Sardinia. It really is an extravagance to buy ready-grated

Parmesan in little pots; not only does it cost more, but it tastes terrible. If you cannot go often to an Italian supplier, invest in a really large lump of one of the grating cheeses: it is worth the pain of momentary extravagance. Wrap it in greaseproof paper and then foil and put in an airtight plastic container. It will keep for ages in the bottom of the refrigerator.

Good cooking cheeses, which can always be substituted for the imported ones if necessary, are Lancashire, Cheddar, Cheshire (or Chester as the French call it). Fresh Mozzarella, which is referred to in one or two recipes, is another Italian cheese, soft and round and white, which traditionally was made with buffaloes' milk, but now probably only of cows' milk, and which should be stored in a bowl of cold water in the refrigerator. It is dull on its own, but wonderful with a salad or cooked, when it becomes rich and succulent. If it is not available, Bel Paese is a fairly good substitute.

Scrambled Egg

or

before adding to the scrambled egg, cook one of the following in butter:

(1) sliced button mushrooms
(2) chopped chicken livers
(3) cubes of bacon
(4) cubes of cooked potato
(5) skinned diced lambs' kidneys
(6) chopped spring onions

or serve plain scrambled egg

(1) in an open, buttered and seasoned baked potato
(2) on a bed of spinach

or make a Pipérade (opposite)

It was Boulestin who raised scrambled egg from a humble breakfast dish to the sort of food you could offer your friends and guests. He was right: there is nothing more delicious than *well* scrambled egg and there are lots of variations on the plain creamy golden sort that one eats when alone in the house.

How to cook scrambled egg, if you haven't already got a perfect method. Melt a large lump of butter in a saucepan, add as many lightly beaten eggs as you need, seasoned with salt and pepper, and stir continuously with a wooden spoon over a medium to low heat until you have a pan of creamy eggs. Take it off the heat just before you think it is set as it goes on cooking, by its own heat and that of the pan, for a few seconds.

Variations on Scrambled Egg

Make scrambled egg as usual and before it sets add one of the following:

(1) cold cooked salmon, flaked
(2) cold cooked smoked haddock, flaked
(3) grated cheese or cheese cut in little squares
(4) mussels, cockles or fresh shrimps, cooked and
       shelled
(5) anchovies previously soaked in milk and drained
(6) chopped tarragon or chives or a combination
       of parsley, chives and chervil
(7) skinned chopped tomato, first grilled whole
(8) chopped ham or tongue

Brillat-Savarin's Scrambled Eggs

1 or 2 eggs per person
grated Gruyère cheese
butter
a little or no salt
pepper

Weigh the eggs. Take one third of their weight in grated cheese, and one sixth of their weight in butter. Melt the butter and add it to the beaten eggs with the cheese and a little salt and pepper. Cook gently in a saucepan stirring all the time until it resembles scrambled eggs and serve at once with sippets of fried bread.

Piperade

2 medium onions
2 cloves garlic
3 tablespoons oil
2 red peppers
4 tomatoes, skinned
4 eggs
salt and freshly ground pepper

Melt the sliced onions in the oil in a heavy pan, add the crushed cloves of garlic and cook gently, without browning, for 15 minutes. Meanwhile slice up the peppers, removing all the seeds, add them to the onions, and cook on without browning until the peppers are tender. Chop the tomatoes and add them to the stew. Add a little salt and simmer on for about 25 minutes until the mixture is moist but not wet. Now beat the eggs lightly in a bowl, season with salt and pepper and stir them into the vegetables as you would for scrambled eggs. When the eggs begin to thicken, it is cooked. Serve it in a plain earthenware dish with triangles of fried bread, or have mounds of fresh bread and butter on the table.

☐ *This was originally a dish eaten by Basque sailors; it is both rich and simple.*

For 4

To make Baked Eggs

First method — straightforward and foolproof
Heat the oven to Reg 4/350°. Butter the cocottes and season with salt and freshly ground pepper before you put the eggs in. Put a baking tin half full of water to warm up on top of the cooker. Gently lower the cocottes with their eggs into the hot water and go on gently heating until the eggs look cloudy at the bottom. Then put the whole thing in the centre of the oven for 15–20 minutes, while you gently heat some seasoned cream in a pan. See if the eggs are set, and if so take them out of the oven and put them on to plates before pouring the hot cream on them. This way you can be sure they are neither under- nor overcooked because you can see the eggs.

Second method — quicker but less foolproof
Heat the oven to Reg 4/350°. Butter the cocottes and break an egg into each. Pour on enough cream to cover each egg completely. Season with salt and freshly ground pepper, and place in the oven. After 15 minutes keep looking at the eggs and shaking them to see if they are cooked. When the white under the cream just won't shiver, but before it is solid, they are cooked.

One or two per person

To Poach an Egg

Shallow pan of boiling salted water with a tablespoon
  of vinegar or lemon juice in it
Eggs (very fresh)

First method
When the water, about two inches deep, is boiling
in the pan, turn it down to a perceptible simmer and
break an egg, sliding it into a nice still part of the
pan. With a spoon keep the white together. Let it
simmer until completely opaque. Lift out carefully
with a slotted spoon.

Second method
When the water, about three inches deep, is boiling,
whirl it round gently with a spoon or fork, and if
nervous break the egg into a cup before you put it in
the water. When the egg hits the water the strands
of egg white will neatly spin round the yolk with the
action of the water. It will sink to the bottom of the
pan but rise to the surface as it cooks. Lift it out
with a slotted spoon after three to four minutes.
Drain well.

To cook more than one egg
Use a larger pan, break them all into one bowl and
slip the whole lot into the water at once. Lift out
gently one at a time, or two by two and separate
them when you have them on a plate or dish. Drain
well.

Poached Egg Salad

1 egg per person
lettuce
1 tablespoon mayonnaise for each egg
chopped herbs — any one of the following:
  parsley, tarragon, dill, chervil, chives.

Poach the eggs very carefully till the whites are
set but the yolks still soft, drain and trim them
and leave them to cool.

Use only the best inner leaves of the lettuce,
and break them up into pieces you can get on to
a fork. Arrange a cushion of lettuce on each
person's (small) plate. Put a poached egg in the
middle of each — neither egg nor lettuce must be
wet in any way — and cover just the egg with a
thick spoonful of well-flavoured mayonnaise,
into which you have stirred the chopped fresh
herbs. Serve immediately.

☐ *This is delicious as a first course or as one of
several salads at a summer lunch.*

Oeufs en Gelée

4 eggs
½ pint jellied home made consommé (page 4) or
 one tin consommé
2 tablespoons sherry, if there is none in the
 consommé
2 slices smoked ham
tarragon or flat (Greek or German) parsley

Stir the sherry into the melted consommé.
In a separate pan poach the eggs carefully (opposite). The yolks should still be runny, otherwise the
results will be very disappointing. When they are
cooked add half a pint of cold water to the pan to
prevent them cooking any more, unless you are
ready to use them immediately, in which case lift
them carefully out of the water and drain them a
little. Trim off the rough outside edges. Lay half a
slice of ham, folded up, in the bottom of each of four
cocottes. Lay a trimmed egg carefully on to each.
Lay the tarragon leaves or parsley in a pattern on
top of each egg and pour in enough consommé to
come just over the top of each egg. Let them set in a
cool place. Some people put pâté in the bottom
instead of ham but this can be rather sickly.

☐ *Make these the day before you want to eat them.*

For 4

Oeufs Mollets aux Fines Herbes

1 (or 2) egg(s) for each person
½ oz butter per egg
3 or 4 twigs tarragon
3 or 4 sprigs parsley or, better still, chervil
bunch of chives
salt and freshly ground pepper

Bring a pan of water to a steady boil, put in the eggs,
which should be at room temperature, not straight
out of the fridge, and boil them for exactly five
and a half minutes, six for large eggs. Remove and
hold under the cold tap until they are cool enough
to handle. Tap the shell of each egg carefully all
over. Peel with great concentration or large chunks
of the white will come zipping out and the egg will
sag and crack. When the eggs are shelled they should
be soft but not so soft that they break open. Keep
them warm in a bowl of warm water.
Melt the butter but don't let it sizzle or start to
brown, Strip the tarragon leaves off the stalks and
chop the herbs together finely. Stir them into the
butter, add a little salt and pepper and pour it over
the drained eggs. Serve hot. They won't be absolutely scalding hot, they aren't meant to be.

For 2–4

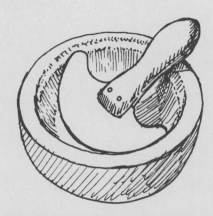

To Make an Omelette

2 or 3 eggs
salt and pepper
butter

Beat the eggs lightly in a bowl with a little salt and pepper. You can add a tablespoon of water but it is not essential to a good omelette. Melt a large hazelnut of butter in a steel omelette pan used only for its proper purpose. Swirl the butter round to coat the bottom and sides of the pan, and when it starts to brown pour in the eggs at once. Keep a wooden fork or spoon to make omelettes, as a metal one would spoil the surface of the pan. Over a medium heat stir the centre of the omelette briefly. Then, tipping the pan this way and that, lift the setting sides of the omelette to let the uncooked egg on top get to the heat. When there is no more uncooked egg give the pan a short brisk jerk to loosen the omelette, tip to start it rolling over, and help it with your fork; roll it out of the pan on to the middle of a warm plate. It should be plump and juicy and not very brown.

For 1

Omelette Arnold Bennett

1 smoked haddock on the bone (about 1 lb)
½ pint milk
½ pint water
3 oz butter
1½ oz flour
2 oz Parmesan, Emmenthal or Cheddar cheese, grated
salt and freshly ground pepper
8 eggs

Trim tail and collar bones from the haddock and poach gently in half a pint each of milk and water, until the bones come away easily. Make a thick Béchamel sauce with the flour, half the butter and the cheese, using some of the liquid in which the fish has cooked. There should be about half a pint of thickish sauce. Bone the fish and put the flaked pieces into the sauce, reserving about three tablespoons of sauce. Season with pepper and add salt if necessary. Keep it warm while you beat the eggs lightly with a little salt and pepper. Fold the fish mixture into the eggs.
Preheat the grill and a serving dish. Heat the remaining butter in a thick heavy frying pan, tipping it from side to side until it is just starting to brown. Gently pour in the mixture, using the reserved sauce to make a pattern on the top of the omelette, rather like a hot cross bun. Cook gently, allowing the uncooked egg to reach the heat by lifting the omelette carefully and tipping the pan.
When it is set underneath, but still undercooked on top, sprinkle with more cheese and put under a hot grill until the top is just a little brown here and there. Slide it on to a large heated dish, not too hot or the omelette will go on cooking, and serve at once, cut in slices like a cake. The top and bottom should be firmly set and the inside still juicy and slightly runny.

For 4 (main course), or 8 (first course)

Omelette in an Overcoat

8 eggs
½ lb mushrooms
3 oz butter
¼ pint single cream
salt and freshly ground black pepper
1 oz flour
½ pint milk
1 oz Parmesan, freshly grated
2 oz Gruyère, freshly grated

Slice the mushrooms and cook them in two ounces of the butter. Add the cream, salt and plenty of freshly ground pepper and reduce until the mixture thickens. Keep the mushrooms warm while you make a cheese sauce with the remaining butter, flour, milk, salt, pepper and cheese; a dribble of cream kept from the quarter pint could well go into this sauce, it makes it brown so beautifully. With the eight eggs, beaten lightly and seasoned, make a very large omelette into which you put the creamy mushroom filling. Fold the omelette on to a hot (but not very hot) serving plate and pour the cheese sauce all over it. Put the omelette under a hot grill for a minute or two and watch it. When it is a beautiful brown serve it immediately with a green salad.

For 4

Soufflé Cheese Omelette

8 eggs
1 oz flour
1 oz butter
½ pint milk
salt and freshly ground pepper
2 oz Emmenthal cheese, grated
2 oz Parmesan cheese, grated
top of the milk
butter for cooking the omelette

Make a thickish cheese sauce with the butter, flour, milk and grated cheese; add a little top of the milk and seasoning and beat the sauce well until it is glossy. Separate the egg yolks from the whites; beat the whites until they are fluffy. Preheat the grill and a serving dish. Beat the yolks with a little salt and pepper. Heat a tablespoon of butter in a large frying pan, swirling it over the sides and bottom to prevent the omelette from sticking. Rapidly fold the whites into the yolks and when the butter starts to brown slip the mixture into the pan. Let it cook over a moderate heat without stirring until set and golden brown underneath. Then put the pan under the grill for a minute or two. Slide the omelette on to the hot dish, folding it in half. Pour the sauce over it and put it back under the grill to brown quickly. Serve straight away. The omelette should be fluffy inside and the sauce creamy and rich. Eat with a green salad.

☐ *This is a very good main course; it isn't heavy but it is filling.*

For 4

Kidney Omelettes

2 lambs kidneys, or ¼ lb ox kidney
1 oz butter
salt, pepper
½ dessertspoon flour
dash of white or red wine ⎱ not more than ¼
a little stock or water ⎰ pint together
4 eggs
salt, pepper

Skin, core and slice the kidneys into small pieces. Sprinkle them with salt and pepper. Put half the butter into a small saucepan, and make a roux with the flour, add the wine and then the stock, and let it simmer while you briskly fry the kidneys in a small frying pan with the other half of the butter. As soon as they have changed colour from dark to pale pink, tip them with all their butter into the sauce. Taste for seasoning, and leave off the heat, but keep it warm while you make the omelettes. Just before each omelette is ready put half the kidneys in their sauce along the centre of it, and tip the whole thing onto a hot plate so that the omelette rolls neatly round its filling.

For 2

Florentine Omelette

6 eggs
¾ pint cheese sauce (page 249)
1 lb fresh spinach, or one 6 oz packet frozen spinach, chopped
1 oz Parmesan
a little cream
salt, pepper, knob of butter

Strip the stalks from the spinach, wash well and cook, covered, with a little salt but no more water until tender. Drain very well and chop finely. If you are using frozen spinach melt it with a little butter, and salt and drain it very well. Stir the spinach into a little of the sauce and keep it hot while you make the omelette. Have the grill hot for the final stage before you begin. If you can, make a single omelette with all 6 eggs in one go, otherwise make 2. Just as the omelette is set (it should be under, rather than over-cooked), spoon the spinach filling into the middle, flip it over (opposite) and into a heatproof serving dish, stir the cream into the cheese sauce, pour the sauce over the folded omelette, sprinkle with Parmesan and leave under the grill until brown and bubbling. Serve at once.

For 3

Tortilla

6 eggs
4 potatoes
2 onions
salt, fresh ground black pepper
olive oil

Peel and slice the potatoes and onions and fry them in your best frying-pan (one that doesn't stick and has a lid) in ¼ pint of olive oil. Cook them fairly slowly with the lid on, stirring often, until they are soft and cooked through but not brown, or only very slightly. Break the eggs into a large bowl and beat them with a rotary whisk until they are frothy. Season. Turn the heat up until the oil is really hot, then pour in the eggs and turn down the heat and let the tortilla cook on a moderate heat for 3–4 minutes, loosening the edges a little with a wooden fork. If it seems to be sticking slip a little butter down the inside of the pan. Put a plate over the frying pan and turn it upside down. Slide the omelette, uncooked side down, back into the pan.

The plate will have quite a bit of raw egg left on it. After two minutes put the plate on the pan again and turn it over, slide the omelette back into the pan — it will take most of the raw egg with it. Fry for 1 minute then repeat again. By this time the omelette will have re-absorbed all the raw egg. Serve the tortilla at once.

☐ *In Spain they use 1 egg for each person, but more is better. You can add bits of bacon and green pepper. Tortillas make very good picnic food, eaten cold.*

For 4

Oeufs Bénédictine

4 eggs, poached

For Hollandaise (*page* 250)
2 extra yolks
squeeze lemon juice
4 oz butter
salt and pepper
4 large tablespoons smoked haddock purée
4 rounds fried bread

Spread a layer of haddock purée on each piece of fried bread, put a poached egg on top and pour the Hollandaise sauce over. Serve straight away. This was originally made with salt cod, never with ham (though that can be nice too), as it was a Lenten dish.

For 4

Spinach Soufflé

½ oz butter
6 oz fresh spinach purée or cooked frozen spinach
4 egg yolks and 5 egg whites
2 oz butter
1½ oz flour
½ pint milk
salt and pepper
1 oz grated Gruyère
1 oz grated Parmesan

Preheat oven to Reg 6/400°. Butter a 7″ × 3″ soufflé dish and dust inside with grated Parmesan. Heat the spinach gently in a closed pan with a little butter. Do not fry. Make a Béchamel sauce (page 247) with the flour, butter, milk and seasoning. Let it cool a little and add egg yolks one by one to the sauce, beating them in with a wire whisk. Stir in the spinach purée. Beat egg whites until stiff, stirring a quarter of them and most of the cheese into the spinach mixture. Fold in remaining egg whites, turn into the soufflé dish and sprinkle with the rest of the cheese. Place in middle of oven, and turn heat down to Reg 5/375°. Bake for 25–30 minutes.

For 4

Cheese Soufflé

1½ oz butter
1 oz flour
scant ½ pint milk
3 oz cheese, grated
3 egg yolks and 4 whites
salt and cayenne pepper

Preheat the oven to Reg 7/425°. Prepare a soufflé dish five or six inches in diameter, by buttering liberally and then coating the inside with flour, shaking out any excess.
Make a Béchamel with the butter, flour and milk. Now add the cheese, stirring all the time. Season with salt and cayenne pepper, remove from the heat and beat in the egg yolks one at a time. This mixture should be left off the heat, but somewhere quite warm, while you beat the egg whites to a firm snow. Add one tablespoon of whites to the sauce and stir it in, then fold in the remaining egg whites, add more salt and cayenne pepper if necessary, and turn lightly into the soufflé dish. Put in the oven, turn down the heat to Reg 6/400° and bake 20–25 minutes. Serve straight away while it is brown and puffy and light. Soufflés are definitely better a bit sloppy inside than dry and overcooked. They are nowhere near as sensitive as people think and it is really quite difficult to make a failure. The most frequent disaster is that no one is ready and waiting when the soufflé is just right and it either collapses while it hangs about, or gets overcooked in the oven. There is only one answer and that is to have everyone at the table, forks in hand.

For 4

Little Tomato Soufflés

6 really large tomatoes
1 oz flour
1 oz butter
2 tablespoons cream
1 tablespoon Parmesan, grated
4 eggs plus one white
salt, freshly ground pepper

Preheat the oven to Reg 7/425°. Cut the tomatoes in half and scoop out the insides. Simmer the juice and pulp for a few minutes in a small pan. Sieve and use this purée, seasoned with a little salt and pepper, to make a stiffish sauce with the butter, flour, cream and grated Parmesan. When the sauce has cooled a little, stir in four egg yolks, one at a time, beating each one in well. Beat the five egg whites to a soft light foam. Beat two tablespoons of this into the tomato mixture, and then add the rest, folding it in carefully. Dry the insides of the tomato halves, season and fill them to the top with the mixture. Put into the hot oven. After five minutes turn the heat down to Reg 6/400°. The little soufflés take 15–20 minutes to cook and should be light brown on top. They make a very nice summer lunch dish.

For 6

Smoked Haddock Soufflé

1 small smoked haddock on the bone — approx.
    ¾ lb
½ pint milk
½ pint water
knob of butter
1½ oz flour
2 oz butter
4 eggs plus 1 egg white
1 oz Parmesan, freshly grated
1 oz Gruyère, freshly grated
salt and freshly ground pepper

Preheat oven to Reg 6/400°. Cook the haddock in the milk and water with a knob of butter for ten minutes. Do not let it catch on the bottom of the pan; it is a good idea to cook it skin side up. When it is cooked, strain off the liquid and keep half a pint. Flake the haddock, removing the skin and bones, and chop finely with a knife or flake very small. Make a thick sauce with the flour, butter and half a pint of the haddock liquid, and beat in the grated cheese, keeping a tablespoon or so of Parmesan on one side. Add the haddock, and remove from the heat. Beat in the egg yolks one by one and season the sauce with salt if necessary, and plenty of pepper. Butter a three pint soufflé dish and dust the inside with grated cheese. If you use a large dish you don't have to fiddle with paper collars etc.
Beat the egg whites stiffly. Stir a quarter into the haddock mixture, fold in the rest with a palette knife, turn into the soufflé dish, levelling out the top, and put straight into the oven.
Turn the heat down to Reg 5/375° and bake 25–30 minutes until very brown and puffy. Eat it the instant it is out of the oven, with a green salad. It makes a perfect lunch.

☐ *Smoked haddock combines exceptionally well with eggs, and this is one of the best soufflés of all.*

For 3–4

Cheese and Ale

3–4 oz Gloucester or Cheshire cheese
1–2 teaspoons freshly made mustard
salt and cayenne pepper
a few tablespoons of brown ale
2 slices brown bread

Slice the cheese into thin slices and put them in a low oven in a small dish to melt like chocolate — overheating makes cheese tough and rubbery — Reg 2/300° for about 5 mins. Then spread with the mustard, sprinkle with salt and cayenne, pour on enough brown ale to cover. Mix and keep it warm while you make two pieces of brown toast and put them onto hot plates.

Now pour the ale and cheese mixture over the toast and serve straight away with a glass of ale.

For 2

Alsace Tartlets

For pastry
6 oz flour
3 oz butter
salt, iced water

For filling
6 eggs
salt, pepper
nutmeg
1 tablespoon fresh double cream
3 tablespoons Gruyère cheese, grated
1 tablespoon Parmesan, grated

Make the pastry well in advance. Preheat the oven to Reg 6/400°. Line 20 jam tart shapes with pastry rolled very thin. Beat the eggs with salt, pepper, nutmeg, cream and grated Gruyère or other cheese. Fill the pastry cases with this mixture but not too full as they puff up quite a bit. Sprinkle the tops with grated Parmesan and cook like jam tarts for 15 minutes until they are a good golden colour. Serve hot.

☐ *Eat these as an hors d'œuvre or at a party. They can be made in advance and reheated.*

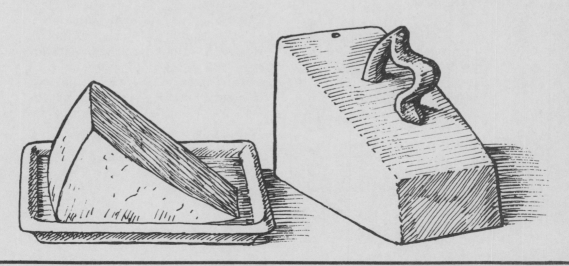

Eggs in Baked Potatoes

6 eggs
6 large, perfect potatoes
butter
top of the milk or thin cream
salt and freshly ground pepper
freshly grated Parmesan cheese

Bake the potatoes in the oven, Reg 2½/315°, for 2 hours, cool a little and through a hole in the top scoop out enough of the insides to make room for an egg. Put in a knob of butter, salt and pepper. Break an egg into each, add a little cream and Parmesan and bake in a hot oven, Reg 6/400°, for about 15 minutes or until the eggs are set.

☐ *Very good for children's lunch.*

For 6

Oeufs à la Tripe

6 hard-boiled eggs
½ pint onion sauce (page 253)

Slice the eggs into thick rounds and cover with hot onion sauce. Serve hot.

☐ *This is a good first course.*

For 4

Eggs in their Dish

2 eggs
1 small onion, chopped
1 tomato, peeled and chopped
salt and freshly ground pepper
oil, butter or bacon fat for frying
additional if liked
1 or 2 rashers of bacon, cut small, *or*
1 sliced cooked potato, *or*
pieces of salami, *or*
pieces of red or green pepper

Use a very small frying pan or enamel gratin dish that you can eat from. Fry the onion (and green pepper if wanted) gently in a teaspoon of fat or oil, until it is transparent but not coloured. (Put the bacon, potato or salami in with the onion.) Peel and chop the tomato. Add it to the onion, season with salt and pepper. Wait until the tomato is beginning to soften but not until it disintegrates. Gently break one or two eggs onto the bed of onion etc. Cook gently. When the bottom is set dot the top with a little butter and finish under a medium grill. The eggs are half poached, half fried and you eat them straight from the dish.

☐ *A very quick lunch if you are by yourself.*

For 1

Egg Croquettes

1 ½ oz butter
1 ½ oz flour
½ pint milk, previously infused with a sliced onion,
    6 peppercorns and a bayleaf
4 hard-boiled eggs
flour
1 beaten egg
dried breadcrumbs
salt, freshly ground pepper, and a pinch of nutmeg
oil for deep frying
bacon (optional)

Make a stiff Béchamel with the butter, flour and flavoured milk. Peel the hard-boiled eggs and sieve the yolks into the sauce. Add the whites, coarsely chopped, season well and add a good pinch of nutmeg. Run a china plate under the cold tap for a few seconds, then spread the Béchamel on it and leave it covered in a cool place overnight or for several hours. It should set firmly enough to roll into small cork shapes (about 12 rolls 2 ins. long). Roll these in flour, dip in beaten egg and then coat with breadcrumbs. Deep fry in oil, drain on kitchen paper, and serve very hot either on their own or with tomato sauce (page 253).

You can put chopped bacon, lightly fried, into the mixture with the chopped, hard-boiled egg.

☐ *These ideally should be made a day ahead as the mixture becomes easier to handle after standing several hours.*

For 4

Eggs in a Nest

1 ½ lbs potatoes
milk, nutmeg, butter
salt, freshly ground pepper } for mashed potatoes
cheese, grated
8 eggs
butter

Peel and cut the potatoes in pieces. Boil them until tender in salted water. Sieve or mash, using plenty of *hot* milk and butter. When they are light and fluffy, season with salt, pepper and a pinch of nutmeg. Add two tablespoons of grated cheese if the children like it. Butter a shallow oven dish of glass or china, put in the mashed potatoes and make eight depressions with the back of a spoon. Gently break an egg into each hollow and sprinkle with a little more grated cheese and some small pieces of butter. Season with a little salt and pepper. Bake at Reg 4/350°, until the eggs are set (10–20 minutes), or bake gently under the grill. Serve at once. The yolks should be runny and the whites firm.

☐ *Very good for children's lunch and for using up mashed potatoes.*

For 4

Oeufs à la Soubise

6 hard-boiled eggs
1 lb onions, poached in milk until tender, seasoned
    and sieved
½ pint creamy, well-flavoured Béchamel (page 247)

Make a mound of onion purée on a hot dish. Place the eggs on top and cover with Béchamel. Serve hot.

For 4

Fisherman's Toast

4 slices slightly stale white bread, crusts removed
2 eggs, beaten with salt
milk
dripping, butter or bacon fat

Soak the slices of bread in milk, then dip them in the beaten egg. Melt the fat in a large frying-pan and fry the bread slices until golden both sides. Very good for breakfast or supper. A sweet version uses sugar instead of salt; fry in butter or oil and serve sprinkled with sugar, when it is known as *pain perdu.*

☐ *Makes two eggs do for four people.*

For 4 children

Croque Monsieur

2 slices bread
1 slice ham, with not too much fat
1 thin slice Gruyère, with not too many holes
½ oz butter
½ tablespoon oil

Cut the crusts off the bread and thinly butter one side of each slice. Make a sandwich with the slice of ham and slice of Gruyère and press firmly shut. Heat a frying pan with the butter and a dash of oil, and when hot fry the sandwich. Both sides (turn carefully) should be pale gold and the cheese starting to melt; eat at once. It is the French version of Mozzarella in Carrozza (page 36).

For 1

Egg Curry with Tomatoes
from Harvey Day's
'Curries of India'

6 eggs, 2 oz butter
2 onions, chopped fine
2 cloves garlic, chopped fine
2 green or red chillies (optional)
½ teaspoon ground coriander
½ teaspoon ground cumin
½ teaspoon (or less) ground chilli
¼ teaspoon ground turmeric
3–4 large tomatoes, skinned and chopped
½ oz tamarind (or juice of half a lemon)
salt

Cook this curry in a fireproof dish that you can take to the table. Fry onions, garlic and chillies, de-seeded and cut in strips, in the butter, until lightly browned. Add spices and stir for a minute; add tomatoes and ⅓ pint warm water. Cook slowly for ten minutes. Stir the tamarind into ¼ pint water, soak for five minutes and strain the resulting juice into the tomato sauce, or add lemon juice. Add salt to taste and return to the boil. Gently break the eggs into the sauce. Serve when they are set, after about five minutes. Eat with lots of bread or rice.

☐ *A red-hot chilli and tomato sauce in which you poach the number of eggs you need.*

For 3

Mozzarella in Carrozza

2 eggs
8 slices home-made type white bread (preferably
  slightly stale)
2 Mozzarella cheeses (or use ¾ lb Bel Paese)
salt and pepper
olive oil

Beat the eggs on a plate with a little salt and pepper.
Soak the bread, cut in three-inch rounds, in the egg
on one side only for about ten minutes. Shake off
the surplus egg.
Cut the Mozzarella into rounds a quarter of an inch
thick. Make thick sandwiches with the cheese and
the soaked bread, eggy side out, and fasten with
toothpicks. Deep fry in olive oil or fry carefully and
not too fast in shallow oil, turning once with great
care. Take out the toothpicks and drain the sandwiches before eating them.
The cheese melts completely inside a crisp brown
crust and when you bite it goes into long strings. In
Italy they are eaten with ham inside and also dipped
in breadcrumbs before they are fried. The simple
thing that can go wrong is that the cheese doesn't
melt but this only happens if the bread is too thick.

☐ *By varying the thickness of the bread you can
make a hefty lunch, or a fairly light start to a meal.*

For 4

Onion, Potato and Anchovy Gratin

2 onions
1 clove garlic, chopped
butter
1 tablespoon olive oil
3 eggs
½ pint milk
1 lb potatoes
10 anchovy fillets
a little cream
salt, if necessary, and freshly ground pepper
cheese (optional)

Make this like the gratin of potatoes and ham
(page 139), but instead of ham and cheese, add the
anchovies and cream to the potato mixture before
you turn it into the gratin dish. Bake as before and
finish under the grill. Go easy on the salt because
of the saltiness of the anchovies.
You can add cheese to this if you like, using the
same quantity as is used in the gratin of ham.

For 4

Fromage des Oeufs

12 eggs
salt
1 pint mayonnaise
a few anchovies

Break the eggs into a round flat dish that has been copiously buttered (and lined with buttered grease-proof paper if you want to be extra careful). Be very sure the yolks don't break; although it doesn't spoil the flavour it is not so pretty.
Sprinkle a little salt over the eggs and bake in a bain marie in a slowish oven Reg $3\frac{1}{2}$–4/350°, for 35–40 minutes. Allow to cool, turn out, remove the paper and decorate the top with anchovies in a lattice if you like it to be smart.
Serve the mayonnaise separately.

☐ *This is an alternative way of making egg mayon-naise; the eggs come out in a nice shape like a Brie and you cut it like one. This accounts for the name, as there is actually no cheese in it.*

For 6–8

Cream Cheese Mousse

1 pint consommé , or 2 tins consommé
8 oz plain cream cheese
2 hard-boiled eggs
salt and freshly ground pepper

Slice the hard-boiled eggs and lay them in a white soufflé dish. Mix half the consommé, melted, with the cream cheese until it is a smooth cream. Season, pour it into the dish carefully without disturbing the eggs, and chill until firm. Melt the remaining consommé, but it must be cool when you pour it over the cheese mixture, Chill again. It is ready to eat, a pale, creamy mousse with a deep amber layer of consqmmé on top.

☐ *A very good summer lunch dish with a green salad. It is cool, fresh and pale and it doesn't take much of an appetite to eat.*
Make the day before.

For 6

37

Quiche

1 large onion, finely sliced
1 oz butter
1 teaspoon oil
3 small eggs
½ pint milk
1–2 oz cheese, grated
12 anchovy fillets
salt, if needed, and freshly ground pepper
9 oz flan pastry

In the following recipe the filling can be almost anything you like. Instead of onions and anchovies you can put ham or bacon with more cheese; chopped leeks softened in butter, with cheese; cooked crab or shrimps; mushrooms, previously sweated in butter; fresh asparagus with a little cheese; cooked potatoes cut in cubes with ham and chives; a great big panful of softened sliced onions; smoked haddock with a little cheese; or just a really fresh bunch of mixed herbs, finely chopped. Make a flan case. Keep the oven at Reg 5/375°. Soften the onion in the oil and butter in a small frying pan, without browning. Beat together the eggs, milk and cheese. Put the drained, tender onions in the flan case, lay the anchovies on top and pour on the egg mixture. Bake ten minutes at Reg 5/375°, then another 15–20 at Reg 4/350°. When it is nicely browned and puffed up it is ready. It is better sloppy-ish than overcooked, and pre-cooking the flan case makes sure that the pastry won't be raw. It can be eaten hot or cold, or even tepid, which seems a good temperature for the custard.

For 4 (main course) or 6 (starter)

Making Flan cases

This is for savoury flans or sweet flans such as apple that don't need a very rich, short, sweet pastry. Have some dried beans or spaghetti shells that you always use for flans. Keep them in a specific place and then the whole performance becomes miraculously easy. Throw them out every so often and start with fresh ones, as they develop a strong smell of burned flour which could transmit itself to the flan.

Method:

(1) Preheat the oven to Reg 5/375°.

(2) Butter a 7–8 inch flan tin with a loose bottom.

(3) Roll out the pastry to ⅛″ to ¼″ thickness.

(4) Line the flan tin with pastry lifted into place on the rolling pin. Trim the edges with a generous hand as the pastry does shrink.

(5) Prick the bottom all over with a fork.

(6) Line the flan case with a round piece of greaseproof paper.

(7) Spill in the beans.

(8) Put it into the oven for 15 minutes.

(9) Take it out of the oven, remove the beans and paper.

(10) Cook it a further ten minutes until the bottom is no longer soggy. It is now ready to be filled with a quiche mixture, apples or whatever you like and cooked in the normal way.

Plain Pie or Flan Pastry

6 oz plain flour
1 ½ oz slightly salted butter
1 ½ oz cooking fat
½ teaspoon salt, cold water

Sieve the flour and salt into a bowl. Chop the butter and cooking fat into it with a knife and then rub it in, lifting your hands several inches above the bowl with each movement, so that the fat is cooled by the air as it falls into the bowl; this may sound far-fetched but it really helps keep the pastry cool and therefore light. When it looks like fine breadcrumbs, carefully add water as you mix the pastry with your other hand until you have a light firm dough. Knead it together lightly, to distribute the moisture evenly. Stand it in a cool place, wrapped or covered, for at least an hour, before rolling out.

PASTA

PANCAKES, GNOCCHI
DUMPLINGS & FRITTERS

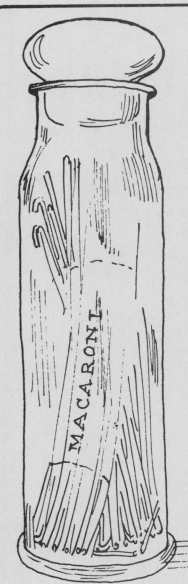

Pasta, Pancakes, Gnocchi, Dumplings and Fritters

Packets of spaghetti in their traditional deep blue paper with red and yellow labels are always an encouraging sight in the larder; as long as they are there, preferably lying alongside a large tin of tomatoes and a can of olive oil, you will never be short of a meal. But the truth is that these packets won't keep for years and, especially in the case of noodles, it is better to eat them within a few months of purchasing or you may find yourself serving a bowl of nicely shredded cardboard. Always choose pasta made in Italy — they do know how to do it there — and always cook it with care, it is so boring once it has gone completely soft. The instructions for cooking pasta (page 48) apply to every kind there is from fettucine, tagliatelli and linguine, which are all types of noodles, to macaroni and cannelloni, which are the larger kinds of pasta. Some of the shapes, such as *conchiglie* which are shells and *ruote*, which are wheels, are pretty to have about, but need lots of sauce to make a good dish. Pasta with a sauce, preferably with a heavy aroma of fresh herbs, is a perfect lunch followed by a green salad, cheese and fruit. And if you serve it in the summer on a terrace or under a tree, it can produce a state of euphoria.

Gnocchi are more delicate than pasta and tend to be eaten with less abandon because they cannot be bought but must be freshly made, which seems to give them a touch of luxury although they are a simple form of food. Gnocchi are a wonderful vehicle for sauces and some, such as the green ones, need nothing more than extra butter and Parmesan. They are made with humble ingredients, semolina, potatoes and flour, and so are a very inexpensive meal, but they are rather a fiddle to make.

Pancakes, stuffed with a velvety filling, are a delicious vehicle for the despised left-over; chicken, spinach, smoked haddock, mushrooms, ham, chicken livers, scallops, can each make a good stuffing for a pancake. Bind them in a smooth, not stodgy, well-flavoured sauce, and make the pancakes as thin as possible, light and crisp. As with any other dish that uses left-overs, there is a vital rule to follow: don't be tempted to use more than one in each stuffing. However much you long to get rid of little dishes of sweetcorn and peas sitting neglected in the refrigerator, they will probably bring your pancake down to the mish-mash level.

Dumplings and fritters are often forgotten because they are so plain, and plain cooking is not fashionable. Both are useful and not too taxing ways of extending the possibilities and filling power of ordinary foods, and a stew with light little dumplings swimming in it looks as though somebody really cared about it. Fritters can be quite delicious, especially if made with a very light batter that doesn't hold too much oil (page 56), but it is always vital to drain them really well on kitchen paper. Several vegetables make good fritters; aubergines, courgettes, salsify and sorrel or spinach, dipped a leaf at a time into the egg-white batter, are all excellent. So are mussels, and slices of cheese, not to mention the worthy spam or corned beef fritters, both of which children still admire tremendously.

Rice is an essential for the storecupboard, first as the basis for many quick and worthwhile dishes, and secondly as a pure and natural filler. Get to know the three main types – long-grain for pilaus, curries and stuffed vegetables, oval Italian or Spanish (which is white or yellow) for risottos and round for puddings – do not try to use pudding rice for anything else. Cook rice carefully, plenty of rinsing beforehand to wash off the extra starch makes it almost foolproof. For most purposes 2 ounces of rice per head is the right amount.

Cooking Pasta

The difference between pasta cooked well — light, slightly *al dente*, each thread or shape separate — and pasta cooked badly — heavy, glutinous and clinging — is drastic. It's very hard to make a packet of spaghetti that has been hanging about for months taste good, and it *should* always be bought at a shop that sells plenty of it so it is more likely to be fresh. Points to remember if you want to produce a perfectionist dish of pasta:

(1) A teaspoon of butter or oil in the water while the pasta is cooking prevents it from sticking to the pan.

(2) Three ounces of dried pasta is enough for one person.

(3) Ideally you need two gallons of water to cook one pound of pasta, though less will do.

(4) Use one and a half tablespoons of salt to every gallon of water.

(5) Stir the water round before you put the pasta in, and again as soon as the pasta is in, and during the cooking to make sure it doesn't stick together.

(6) Don't overcook the pasta. It should be *al dente*, with a slight resistance when you bite it, so after ten minutes test it every now and then by biting a piece.

(7) When cooked and drained, tip it at once into a large heated dish and stir a little olive oil or butter into it.

(8) Serve it as soon as possible to eat it at its best. If it *must* wait a little while, pour boiling water over it, drain, add butter or oil and keep it warm over a pan of hot water, or in a low oven, covered with a cloth.

(9) Serve most sauces separately and have freshly grated Parmesan and more butter on the table, plus copious amounts of rough red wine. People also like plenty of freshly ground pepper and large chunks of bread.

Freshly-made pasta — if you are lucky enough to get it — is cooked in the same way but for less time; start testing it after eight minutes.

Home-Made Pasta

½ lb plain flour
2 small eggs, beaten
2–4 tablespoons olive oil (if using large eggs cut down on the oil)

Make a dough with the flour, eggs and oil. Add more flour if it seems sticky. Knead well and if you have time leave in a cold place for at least 1 hour, covered. Roll the pasta out as thinly as possible *really paper thin* (it swells in cooking). If you haven't got a long Italian rolling-pin made specially for pasta-making, divide the dough into two before you begin. Transfer the sheets of what is now 'Pasta' to clean tea-towels and allow to dry for 1 hour (you can leave them flat or hang them over the back of a chair). Fold the sheets lightly and cut wide strips for lasagne or narrow strips for tagliatelle, squares for cannelloni, and so on. If you want to keep these before using them sprinkle lavishly with fine ground semolina (not flour as it makes them stick together).

To cook pasta bring a large pan of salted water to the boil and cook the strips of pasta for 10–12 minutes. This basic pasta is also used for Chinese dumplings and soup noodles (won ton for example). You can also use it for home-made ravioli.

☐ *Laborious to make but a great improvement on packeted pasta.*

For 4

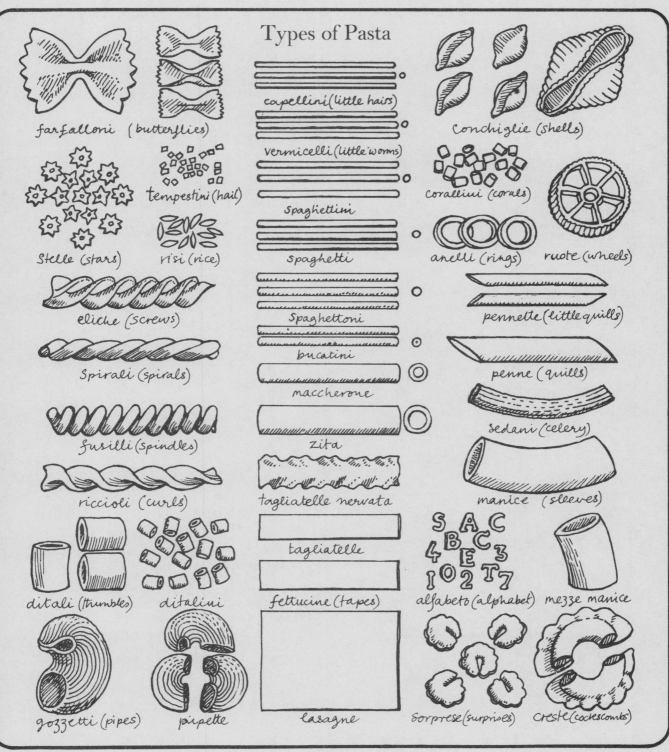

Types of Pasta

farfalloni (butterflies)

Stelle (stars)

risi (rice)

tempestini (hail)

eliche (screws)

Spirali (spirals)

fusilli (spindles)

riccioli (curls)

ditali (thimbles)

ditalini

gozzetti (pipes)

pipette

capellini (little hairs)

vermicelli (little worms)

spaghettini

spaghetti

Spaghettoni

bucatini

maccherone

zita

tagliatelle nervata

tagliatelle

fettucine (tapes)

lasagne

conchiglie (shells)

corallini (corals)

anelli (rings)

ruote (wheels)

pennette (little quills)

penne (quills)

sedani (celery)

manice (sleeves)

alfabeto (alphabet)

mezze manice

sorprese (surprises)

creste (cockscombs)

43

Ravioli

Roll out ¾ lb pasta (see Home-Made Pasta, overleaf) as thinly as you can. Make two sheets of equal size — don't let them get dry, cover them with a cloth if you have to fiddle with the filling. When it is ready, put teaspoons of the filling in rows about 1½ inches apart on one sheet of pasta. Moisten the pasta between the fillings and lay the other sheet on top. Press between the blobs of filling with your finger tips to seal the little pockets. Run a pastry-cutter between the rows so that you make little squares. Do not lay them on top of each other as they will stick together.

Drop them into plenty of boiling salted water into which you have put a teaspoon of oil, which should prevent them sticking to each other or to the pan. Boil them for 15–25 minutes depending on how thin your pasta is and serve, well drained, with melted butter and grated Parmesan or with cheese or tomato sauce (pages 249, and 253).

Cheese Filling for Ravioli

4 oz ricotta cheese
4 oz cooked drained spinach (frozen will do)
1 oz Parmesan, grated
1 egg yolk
salt, pepper, nutmeg

Beat the egg yolk with ricotta, Parmesan and seasoning, including the nutmeg. Drain the spinach well and chop it finely or sieve it. Mix it into the cheese.

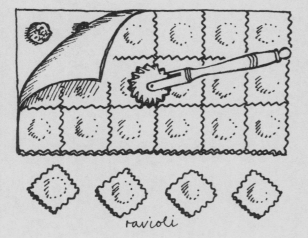

ravioli

Spinach and Brains Filling

2 oz finely minced pork
2 oz cooked brains
4 oz cooked spinach
1 oz Parmesan, grated
1 egg yolk
salt, pepper, nutmeg

Fry the pork in a little butter to cook but not to brown it. Mix it with the rest of the ingredients, having previously beaten the egg yolks and mashed the brains.

Meat Filling for Ravioli

3 tablespoons olive oil
1 onion, chopped
1 carrot, chopped
1 stick celery, chopped
¾ lb freshly minced beef
salt, pepper, nutmeg
3 tablespoons tomato purée
dash of water
2 egg yolks
handful fresh breadcrumbs
2 oz Parmesan

Fry the onion, carrot and celery in the olive oil, until beginning to soften. Add the meat and stir it about until it is browned. Season with salt and pepper and moisten with the tomato purée, dissolved in a little water — just enough to bind it without making it wet. Cover the pan, turn down the heat and simmer for 1 hour. Allow to cool and then put this meat sauce through the finest blade of the mincer, so that you have a thick fine-grained sauce. Add the egg-yolks, breadcrumbs and Parmesan and check for seasoning. It should be a soft but firm paste. If it is too soft add more breadcrumbs.

Makes about 1 lb of filling.

Filling for Cannelloni

½ lb minced pork
½ lb minced veal
1 onion
thyme, oregano
2 cloves garlic
1 8 oz tin Italian tomatoes or 4 tomatoes
¼ pint red wine
salt
1 tablespoon olive oil
2–3 tablespoons cream

Cannelloni can be made of 4-inch squares of your own pasta cooked, rolled around the filling and then covered with a thin layer of very cheesey Béchamel, sprinkled with more grated cheese and a pinch of ground mace or nutmeg. Bake in a hottish oven, Reg 6/400° for ½ hour or until brown and bubbling. Alternatively you can either buy cannelloni, but these are often broken in the boxes, or make them by cooking bought lasagne, rolling it round the stuffing and proceeding as above. Yet a third method is to use small thin pancakes (page 185) and roll them round the filling with the join facing downwards.

For 6

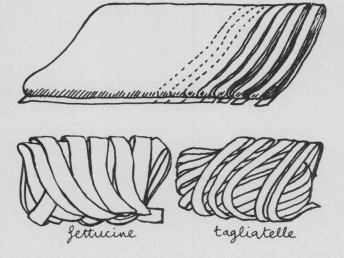

fettucine   tagliatelle

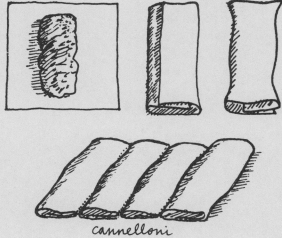

cannelloni

Spaghetti Carbonara

¼ lb spaghetti or other pasta
3 rashers bacon or slices ham
1 egg
salt and freshly ground pepper
Parmesan, freshly grated

While the pasta is cooking in plenty of boiling water, cut the bacon or ham into thin strips or small squares. Put the rinds or pieces of ham fat into the pan on a low heat and when the fat starts to run take them out and add the bacon or ham strips. Let them cook until the bacon is crisp, or the ham sizzling hot; keep hot. Beat the egg, and season with salt and pepper, unless you know the bacon to be very salty, when you must be very careful with the salt.
When the pasta is ready (15–20 minutes), drain and tip it into a very hot serving dish, then quickly add the beaten egg to the hot pasta and stir it about. Add the bacon or ham and the fat it cooked in. The egg is lightly cooked by the heat of the pasta, but if this seems daunting you can lightly (but very lightly) scramble the egg with the bacon in the pan before pouring it on to the pasta. Sprinkle with cheese, serve more cheese with it at the table. Eat it at once.

☐ *This is useful if you have no tomatoes or other sauce.*

For 2

Spaghetti with Chicken Liver Sauce

12 oz spaghetti
3 tablespoons olive oil
1 onion, chopped
2 cloves garlic
1½ lbs tomatoes
parsley, thyme and marjoram, fresh or dried
salt and freshly ground pepper
small glass red wine
¾ lb chicken livers
1 tablespoon butter
Parmesan, freshly grated, if liked

Heat the olive oil in a large shallow saucepan. Chop the onion and garlic and sweat them for 15 minutes in the oil without browning. Skin the tomatoes, chop roughly and add them with the wine, salt, pepper and plenty of chopped herbs, and simmer uncovered for about an hour until you have a thickish sauce. Cook the spaghetti. While it is boiling chop the chicken livers into pieces the size of a hazelnut and sauté in butter for a few minutes until they are brown on the outside. Add them with their juice to the tomato sauce and serve straight away with the spaghetti, with or without grated cheese.

For 4

Spaghetti Bolognese

12 oz spaghetti
3 tablespoons olive oil
1 onion, chopped
¾ lb freshly minced beef, pork, or veal and pork
5 tomatoes, skinned and chopped
1 clove garlic
1 tablespoon tomato purée, diluted with a little water
salt and freshly ground pepper
sprig thyme
small bunch parsley
large pinch basil
Parmesan, freshly grated

Heat the oil in a saucepan, peel and chop the onion and sweat in the oil for five minutes without browning. Turn up the heat and, when the oil is very hot, add the meat and fry fiercely to brown it, stirring all the time to keep it crumbly. Peel the tomatoes, chop them coarsely and add to the meat. Chop the clove of garlic finely and add with the diluted tomato purée, salt, freshly ground black pepper and roughly chopped herbs. Cook gently, uncovered, for ¾–1 hour, stirring from time to time. The sauce will condense considerably and should seem bathed in oil and tomato. Serve on pasta (this page), with grated Parmesan as usual, or use in lasagne or cannelloni.

For 4

Noodles with Cockles

¾ lb spaghetti or 1 lb noodles
3 cloves garlic
1 onion, chopped
3 tablespoons olive oil
1 lb tomatoes, skinned, de-seeded and chopped
3–4 sprigs parsley, coarsely chopped
salt and freshly ground pepper
2–3 pints fresh cockles, well washed (pickled ones are horrible)

Chop the garlic and onions and soften in the oil for 15–20 minutes. Add the tomatoes, parsley, salt and pepper and cook a further five minutes. (The tomatoes should be very lightly cooked for this dish.) Meanwhile cook the noodles or spaghetti in plenty of boiling salted water. Shake the well washed cockles in a thick pan over a low heat until they are open, and then remove from their shells. Add them to the sauce at the last minute and heat through. No cheese with this dish unless you are fanatic about it, but you can add more chopped parsley and a dab of butter as you serve it.

For 4

Noodles with Crispy Bacon

1 lb packet egg noodles
4--5 rashers bacon, rinds removed
½ pint cream
2 egg yolks
salt and freshly ground pepper
garlic
Parmesan, freshly grated
chives, chopped

Cook the noodles in boiling salted water until they are tender but with a bite. Meanwhile fry the bacon briskly in a dab of butter until it is crisp and brown but not burned. Beat the egg yolks, chives and cream together, add the drained bacon, broken into bits, season if necessary and heat gently in a double boiler until thick enough to coat the back of your spoon. You can add a little crushed garlic if you like. When you have drained the noodles, stir in the bacon mixture, coating the noodles thoroughly, and serve with grated Parmesan, and more chopped chives if you like.

☐ *This is an anglicised version of spaghetti carbonara.*

For 4–5

Noodles with Cream and Fresh Herbs

1 lb egg noodles, fresh if possible
¼ pint cream
parsley
chives
rosemary
2 cloves garlic
4 oz butter
salt and freshly ground pepper
Parmesan, freshly grated

Warm the cream. Cook the noodles in boiling salted water until just tender but with a bite. Drain thoroughly. Chop the herbs together coarsely. Stir into the noodles the heated cream, half the butter, the pounded garlic and chopped herbs, and season with salt and plenty of ground pepper. Put a tablespoon of grated Parmesan on top of each plateful of noodles and a good knob of butter on top of that. A plate of these looks particularly good: creamy white with green herbs and a yellow pool of butter in the centre.
As in all spaghetti recipes this sauce can be used on any kind of pasta, but is best on the thinner, more delicate kinds: spaghetti, tagliatelle, linguine etc.

For 6, or 4 as a main dish

Lasagne

½ lb lasagne
2 onions
2 cloves garlic
olive oil
¾ lb minced pork
¾ lb minced veal
1 lb tomatoes
salt and freshly ground pepper
thyme
stock if necessary

for the sauce:
3 oz butter
3 oz flour
1 ½ pints milk
2 oz Parmesan, grated
salt and pepper
bayleaf
grating of nutmeg
butter
cheese for sprinkling on the top

Heat the olive oil in a saucepan and fry the chopped onions and garlic. Add the meat and fry until it is browned, stirring all the time. Skin the tomatoes, chop them roughly and add to the meat with the thyme, salt and pepper. Let the tomatoes soften. If they do not make enough liquid to cook the sauce in, gradually add a little stock, but always a bit less than you think is necessary. Cook the sauce gently, stirring occasionally, for as long as you like, ¾ hour should be enough. Meanwhile cook the lasagne, a few at a time, in a huge pan of boiling well-salted water for 11 minutes, moving them around from time to time to prevent them sticking together. Scoop them out and drain on a cloth.
At the same time make 1½ pints Béchamel sauce flavoured with Parmesan, salt, pepper, a bayleaf and plenty of nutmeg.
Preheat the oven to Reg 3½/340°. When everything is ready remove the bayleaf from the sauce. Put a layer of meat in a buttered gratin dish, add a layer of Béchamel, then a layer of slightly overlapping pieces of lasagne. Add more meat, more Béchamel, more lasagne and finish with a layer of meat covered with Béchamel. Sprinkle the top with cheese, dot with butter and bake for ¾ hour.

☐ *This is not worth making for less than six, but is well worth doing for more.*

For 6

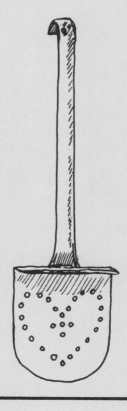

Macaroni in Pasticciere

1 lb tomatoes, fresh or tinned
2 onions
3 cloves garlic
¾ lb minced beef (finely minced)
small glass of red wine
1 tablespoon tomato purée
thyme, rosemary
¼–½ pint stock
salt, pepper
olive oil (2 tablespoons)
¾ lb macaroni

Skin the tomatoes and chop them. Peel, slice and chop the onions and garlic. Fry the onions and garlic in olive oil until soft and then add the beef and fry until nicely brown over brisk heat. Add the wine and let it bubble. Add the tomatoes, herbs, salt, pepper, purée and ¼ pint stock. Cook gently for 1 hour. Add more stock if necessary.

SAUCE

2 oz butter
3 oz flour
2 oz grated Parmesan
1 pint of milk (infused with bay leaf, sliced onion and salt)

Make sauce by melting butter, stirring in flour, adding strained milk gradually, then the grated Parmesan. It should be rather stiff.

Drop the macaroni into salted water. Allow to cook until just tender. Drain, mix with the meat sauce in a large bowl. Butter an oven dish and put in the macaroni mixture, level it out and then put the cheese sauce on top. Bake in the oven Reg 3/325° for ½ hour.

☐ *It is a rather quicker and easier dish to make than Lasagne. Children love it.*

For 8–10

Gnocchi with Semolina

½ pint milk
½ pint water
1 onion
bayleaf
5 tablespoons semolina
salt and freshly ground pepper
½ oz butter
3 oz Parmesan, grated
tomato sauce (page 253)

Infuse the milk and water with the sliced onion, bayleaf and salt, simmering very gently for five minutes. Strain and return to the pan. Bring back to the boil and add the semolina, beating with a wooden spoon until smooth. Cook for ten minutes over a moderate heat, stirring often to prevent lumps. Remove from the heat and add 2 oz grated Parmesan, the butter and freshly ground black pepper. Beat thoroughly, then spread the mixture evenly in a flat oiled dish. Cool, and you will find it has set enough to cut in one-inch squares or rounds. Arrange the gnocchi overlapping on a buttered gratin dish, sprinkle with the remaining Parmesan, dot with butter and put under a hot grill. When brown serve with tomato sauce and more cheese.

☐ *Of all gnocchi these are probably the easiest to make at home. They are quite light and have a marvellous flavour.*

For 4

Green Gnocchi

1 lb spinach, washed and chopped
¾ lb Ricotta cheese or cottage cheese, sieved
2 egg yolks
4 tablespoons Parmesan, grated
½ teaspoon salt
1–2 oz flour
melted butter for serving

Cook the spinach (if using fresh spinach) in a little salted water for five minutes. If using frozen spinach allow it to thaw completely. In both cases drain very well so that the spinach is dry. You can purée the spinach at this point for a finer texture. Mix thoroughly with the Ricotta, egg yolks, half the Parmesan and the salt. Shape into little balls the size of a large marble, rolling them lightly in flour. You can prepare them in advance to this point — they will keep for several hours in a cool place. Then drop them one by one into a large pan of simmering salted water, where they will rise to the surface. After four minutes' gentle simmering, remove them carefully with a perforated spoon. Put in a hot serving dish and serve sprinkled with melted butter and the rest of the Parmesan. They are feathery light, pale green melting globes, a marvellous light lunch or start to a dinner-party.

For 4

Norfolk Dumplings

8 oz self-raising flour
1 teaspoon salt
water

Sift the flour and salt into a bowl and mix with water to make a dough. Shape the dough into balls the size of a walnut. A good way of doing this is in the floured palm of your hand. Put in a steamer and steam exactly 20 minutes. Do not remove the lid during cooking time or the dumplings will spoil, and remember that dumplings are like soufflés: they will not wait. Called fillers these are served with gravy or butter or brown sugar. Called swimmers they are served with jam or syrup. You can steam these dumplings by sitting them on the top of a dryish stew for 20 minutes, keeping the pot closed. They are very good, too, with chopped herbs in them, parsley or marjoram.

For 4 or more

Basic Savoury Pancakes (1)

4 oz plain flour
1 egg
½ pint milk
salt

Beat the egg thoroughly into the milk. Season the flour and stir in the milk and egg mixture gradually, to make a smooth lump-free batter.

Beat for several minutes with a wooden spoon with the bowl of the spoon turned over, so that the air in the hollow of the spoon gets into the batter, or beat with a balloon whisk or an electric beater. Allow to stand for two hours before using.

☐ *This mixture makes 6-8 pancakes; make it two hours before it is needed.*

Savoury Pancakes (2)

Use the same recipe as before but add two teaspoons of melted butter to the mixture, after you have combined the other ingredients. This makes the pancakes just slightly richer, and they can be put under the grill without drying up.

Fish Pancakes

8 large pancakes
1 oz butter
1 oz flour
½ pint milk, or fish stock if you have it
½ lb cold cooked fish such as cod or haddock (fresh or smoked), salmon etc.
2 oz Parmesan, freshly grated
salt and freshly ground pepper
thin cream, or top of the milk

Make the pancakes and keep them hot. Make a sauce with the butter, flour and milk, or milk and fish stock. Add the cheese, salt and pepper. Use half the sauce to bind the fish, which must be skinned, boned and flaked. Check the seasoning. Put a line of the fish mixture down the edge of each pancake, roll them up and lay them in a flameproof dish. Pour on the rest of the sauce, with a little cream or top of the milk if available, and grill gently until warmed through and lightly browned.

For 4

Spinach Pancakes

These are made like fish pancakes (this page) but with spinach, cooked, drained and chopped, instead of the fish, added to the sauce. You can use frozen spinach but add some grated cheese to the sauce for flavour.

Layered Pancakes

8 pancakes

Use two kinds of filling. Choose from spinach, chicken, fish, or diced hard-boiled egg and bacon. Alternate the layers, stacking the pancakes up, one on top of another, in a deep dish with the fillings in between. Cover with a final layer of sauce, cheese is the best for this, and put in a moderate oven to heat through. It is best to use hot sauces and pancakes to cut down the time in the oven as much as possible. Serve cut in slices like a cake.

For 4

Chicken Pancakes

12 large pancakes
4 oz button mushrooms
1 oz flour
1 oz butter
½ pint chicken stock, or failing this, milk
salt and freshly ground pepper
½–¾ lb cooked left-over chicken, chopped or pulled
  into manageable pieces
parsley, chopped
Emmenthal cheese, freshly grated, or ½ pint cheese
  sauce
butter

Make the pancakes and keep hot. Peel the mushrooms and simmer the peel in the chicken stock. Strain the stock and add the sliced mushrooms, simmer a few minutes more.
Make a white roux of the flour and butter and add the stock and mushrooms gradually. Season and let the sauce cook slowly for ten minutes. Add the chicken pieces together with any jelly that has set in their dish. Stir in the chopped parsley; season again if necessary. Put a line of the filling into each pancake, and fold in or roll up with the ends open. Lay the pancakes side by side in a gratin dish, and either sprinkle with cheese and melted butter and cook under a slow grill for 15–20 minutes or until hot through, or pour the cheese sauce over and then brown — this prevents them from drying up.

For 6

Pizza

¾ pint well-seasoned tomato sauce made with
    tinned or fresh tomatoes
1 or 2 Mozzarella cheeses or ¼–½ lb Bel Paese
anchovy fillets
black olives, stoned
oregano, basil or marjoram
olive oil
1 lb pizza dough (opposite)

Preheat oven to Reg 6/400°. When the dough has risen and been kneaded, shape it into flat rounds or oblongs the size of the pizza you want to make, and lay them in greased tins. Spread liberally with the tomato sauce and lay slices of cheese, anchovy fillets and black olives on top. Sprinkle with oregano, basil or marjoram and a generous amount of olive oil, about 1 dessertspoon for each small pizza. Don't take the filling right to the edges, although it is tempting, because the crust makes a sort of bank to keep the filling in while it cooks. Leave 20 minutes to rise again. Bake at Reg 6/400° for 15 minutes, then at Reg 5/375° for a further 15–20 minutes. This is a Neapolitan pizza. There are lots of other fillings you can put in a basic pizza, but perhaps the simple olive and anchovy is really the best of all.

3 large or 6 small

Other variations

American Hot: slices of red pepper sautéed in oil, slices of hot Italian sausage and strips of fresh or bottled chillies on top of the usual tomato and cheese.

Mushroom: mushrooms sliced and lightly sautéed in oil or butter, instead of anchovies and olives.

American Sweet: slices of red pepper sautéed in oil and slices of ordinary salami or sausage, marjoram and the usual tomato and cheese.

Onion: the Neapolitan pizza with lightly fried onion rings strewn on with the anchovies etc.

Aglio e Olio: simply garlic, olive oil and fresh chopped marjoram — no cheese, no tomatoes.

Alla Romana: without tomatoes or anchovies but with sliced Mozzarella, Parmesan and fresh basil.

Mussels: with tomato sauce, oregano, garlic, parsley and little shelled mussels (or clams).

The pizza can also be covered with another piece of dough before baking if full of extra juicy filling, although this can make it stodgy.

Pizza Dough

1 lb flour
1 oz yeast (or ½ oz freshly bought dried yeast)
1½ teaspoons salt
¼—½ pint water
3 tablespoons olive oil

Dissolve the salt in ½ pint warm water (blood heat or less). Put the flour in a bowl, make a well in the centre and pour in the yeast, dissolved in about two tablespoons of the warm water. Mix with one hand, gradually adding more water with the other. When you have a stringy mass give it a few good turns and nudges, and when it is the right consistency — elastic, springy and not wet — put it in a lump in a large bowl, cover with a floured cloth and a lid and leave it to rise for an hour or so, until it has about doubled in size. Take it out, knead it well, then add the oil, working in a small quantity at a time with your hands. When it has absorbed about three tablespoons and is a good pliable, smooth consistency again, make it into three or four nice flat rounds and leave them to prove for 20 minutes. Then put on the sauce, cheese etc. Alternatively put the sauce and cheese on before proving. In the *Pizza Express* they don't prove before baking, so if you are in a hurry you can leave out this step, but the pizza may not be so light.

□ *You can also buy dough from bakers who bake their own bread.*

For 4 pizzas

Spinach Fritters

½ lb spinach leaves (fresh *not* frozen)
½ onion or 4—5 spring onions, chopped
4 oz flour (plain or wholemeal)
2 eggs
salt
1 teaspoon oil
Just under ¼ pint milk and water mixed
oil for frying (or lard)

Make a thick creamy batter by stirring the eggs into the flour and salt, then gradually adding the milk and oil, keeping the batter lump-free by beating hard with a wooden spoon.

Wash the spinach, shake dry in a cloth like lettuce, then chop it finely and stir it into the batter with the finely chopped onion. Allow to stand half an hour or more to allow the spinach and batter to marry together.

Heat oil to a depth of ¼ inch in a heavy frying pan. Drop the mixture, a spoonful at a time, into the hot oil and fry until a good golden brown, turning once. Serve these fritters, golden and green, crisp outside and soft within, as an accompaniment to roast chicken or on their own with grated Parmesan.

□ *Children who wouldn't otherwise eat spinach love these. It is also good made with Swiss Chard.*

For 4

Simple Fritter Batter

4 oz flour
1 egg
salt
1 tablespoon oil
¼ pint milk, or less

Sieve the flour with a pinch of salt into a bowl, and make a well in the centre. Separate the egg and keep the white aside. Mix the yolk carefully with the flour, blending well with a wooden spoon. Add the oil and then the milk, a little at a time, drawing in the flour gradually. When you have a thick, smooth, creamy batter stop adding milk and beat the mixture well. Allow it to stand as long as possible in a cool place; about two hours is ideal. Just before you need it, beat the white of the egg stiffly and fold it into the batter.
This is for fritters to be fried in deep oil. If using it for sweet things you can add a spoonful of liqueur to replace some of the milk.

☐ *This is good for sweet fritters, or fairly solid things like corned-beef fritters.*

Enough for fritters for 4–6 people

Delicate Fritter Batter

4 oz flour
3 tablespoons melted butter
¼ pint lukewarm water
salt
1 egg white

About two hours before it is needed, start the batter. In a bowl mix the flour, a pinch of salt and the melted butter, then add water gradually until you have a thickish creamy mixture. Let it stand in a cool place. At the last moment beat the egg white to soft peaks and fold it into the batter mixture.

☐ *Very good for savoury fritters, vegetables etc.*

Enough for fritters for 4–6 people

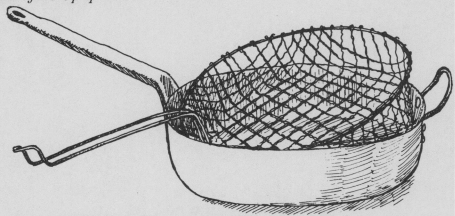

Chinese way of Cooking Plain Boiled Rice

2 oz rice per person
salt, water

Persian Rice

3 oz rice per person
2 oz butter
1 tablespoon salt

Wash the rice by running the cold tap over it until the water runs clear (this can be done in a tilted basin or pan, or sieve).

Using a saucepan with a perfectly fitting lid, put the rice in, with water to cover it by about $\frac{3}{4}$ inch, and add salt. Boil fast until the rice has absorbed all the water, and little holes appear on the surface of the rice (this should take 10–15 minutes).

Put the pan on an asbestos mat and turn the heat right down. Cover as firmly as you can with a lid, and leave, barely cooking, for 10 minutes. When you take the lid off, the rice should be beautifully separate and fluffy and not sticking at all to the pan. A lot depends on how well you washed it at first.

Pour a kettle of boiling water over the rice in a sieve. Separate the grains and soak for three or four hours in cold water. Wash thoroughly and put in a large pan with copious amounts of cold water and a tablespoon of salt. Boil for exactly eight minutes, until the rice is almost, but not quite, tender. Wash again under the cold tap and drain.

Put one ounce of melted butter in a flameproof casserole and put in the drained rice. Pour over another ounce of melted butter, cover with a cloth and then with the casserole lid. Put over a very low flame for 15–20 minutes. Each grain is separate, perfectly cooked and delicious. At the bottom of the pan is a golden crust which is much sought after by the Persians.

This is a complicated way of rice-cooking, but very good. You can leave out some of the soaking, if you don't have time.

☐ *Use Basmati or best Patna rice. These are the best quality, long-grain rices and more likely to cook to perfection than nameless packets or semi-prepared brands.*

For 4–6

Pilau Rice

½ lb patna rice, 2 oz butter
1 onion peeled and sliced into rings
½ teaspoon turmeric or 1 packet saffron (large pinch)
6 cloves, 6 cardamoms
1–2″ cinnamon stick
1 teaspoon coriander seeds
½ teaspoon caraway seeds
1 teaspoon cumin seeds
2 teaspoons pistachio nuts browned in butter
1–2 oz blanched almonds browned in butter
2–4 oz raisins browned in butter

Soak the well-washed rice in water for 1–2 hours or longer, even overnight. Drain it well and shake it as dry as possible in a cloth. Soak the saffron in a tablespoon of water.

Fry the onion in the butter in a heavy sauté pan with a lid. Add all the spices except the saffron. Then add the rice and stir it until the grains are well-coated with butter. Then add salt, soaked saffron and enough cold water to cover. Stir and cover. Cook, adding more water when necessary, until the rice is tender and dry. Finish by adding the fried almonds, raisins and the pistachio nuts.

☐ *This is a marvellous accompaniment to curry, especially curried meat dishes.*

For 4

Risi Bisi (Risotto with Peas)

2 shallots or small onions chopped
1 oz butter
2–3 rashers, green bacon or 2 slices ham, cut small
1 lb of peas
1½ pints chicken stock
6 oz rice (Italian or long grained)
Parmesan cheese grated
salt and pepper

Melt the butter in a saucepan or earthenware dish. Soften the chopped onion in it without browning. Add the ham or bacon, and when they are cooked add the peas, stir them until they are coated with the butter and then add ⅓ of the heated stock. When it comes to the boil add the rice, and as it absorbs the stock add more liquid and continue to do this until the rice is cooked and the mixture of a creamy consistency. Season if necessary, depending on the strength of the stock, and stir in half the grated Parmesan cheese. Serve it with more grated Parmesan.

☐ *If you like you can stir in a few spoons of cream and allow it to heat through, just before serving. This form of risotto is supposed to be served 'rippling' which means it is much moister and creamier than usual. Italian rice absorbs more liquid than long grain rice, and takes a little longer to cook.*

For 4

FISH

Fish

Fishmongers seem to be a vanishing race, and if you live inland and can find a fish that has been for a swim in the last week, you are lucky. If you do have an excellent fishmonger, or live near the sea and know that the catch has just come in, fish is one of the greatest treats. But it is an absolute must to have fish that is fresh; you can tell by the smell, and by the general glossiness of its condition. Really fresh fish looks fresh and not at all dingy, and if it is a herring it will be floppy and slippery, if a mackerel stiff and a radiant blue or green. You should always ask the man behind the counter what he recommends. If he wants you to come back he is unlikely to suggest something doubtful.

Shellfish have sadly become more and more expensive, but fresh cockles and mussels really are worth buying – or looking for by the seaside. *Always* eat them cooked as the source is unlikely to be pure. It is no longer so easy to catch your own shrimps, but the small brown British ones, if you can get them, are worth having; although they are fiddly to shell, they have a really good flavour and are lovely for tea with brown bread and butter. Fish from the freezer is second best, for although it is spanking fresh when it goes into the freezing plant, most of it comes out in such unpromising looking doorsteps that it makes dreary material for any recipe.

If you have the choice between deep-sea and inshore fish, the deep-sea fish are possibly better quality, because they have richer grounds. But they may not have been netted quite so recently, as deep-sea boats stay out for relatively long periods. If you eat a lot of smoked fish you may have wondered about the difference between smoked haddock on the bone, smoked haddock fillet, golden cutlets and golden fillets. The chief difference is that cutlets and fillets are dyed bright yellow before they are smoked, otherwise they get a white line across them where they hang on the line in the smokehouse, whereas the much more genuine-looking whole split haddock on the bone is strung on a stick through the collarbone and so has no white line. Golden cutlets are not usually particularly good quality and are correspondingly cheaper – they are usually haddock, but if cod is cheaper that week then they may be cod. They are

probably cured and smoked in Scotland which means they
are likely to be strong and salty; London smoked haddock
are the best in the world if you can get them. Golden fillet
may be haddock, whiting or possibly cod.

Although almost all fish is rather expensive now – skate,
haddock, cod, turbot, and shellfish are getting more
expensive all the time – there are still cheap kinds to be
found. Apparently the reason nobody likes coley (also
called saithe or coal-fish) is because of the dingy grey
colour, but.it goes almost white when you cook it.
Billingsgate merchants regard it highly enough to make
into a fish pie, which is most children's favourite way of
eating fish anyway. Red-fish, also known as Norway
haddock, soldier and bergyld or sometimes misleadingly
called bream fillets, is quite a good, little-known fish.
Dabs and witch-soles, especially deep-sea ones, are tasty
little fish and so are small lemon soles; fry them in crisp
breadcrumbs to improve their texture. Small haddocks
can be cheap and so can delicious, firm but bony conger
eel.

Herrings, sprats and sometimes mackerel are still good
cheap fish though not so plentiful as they were once. Try
poaching mackerel instead of baking, frying or grilling
them. Both smoked and tinned fish keep their nutritional
qualities, and tinned tunnyfish, sardines and anchovies are
useful standbys. Another useful preserved fish is salt cod,
which makes a base for some excellent dishes which we
give in this book. It is not an easy taste to acquire,
somewhere in the region of tripe as far as oddness of
flavour and texture goes, but if you like interesting peasant
food it can become a great favourite, especially made into a
brandade. Don't be put off by the smell,.and allow plenty
of time for preparing it.

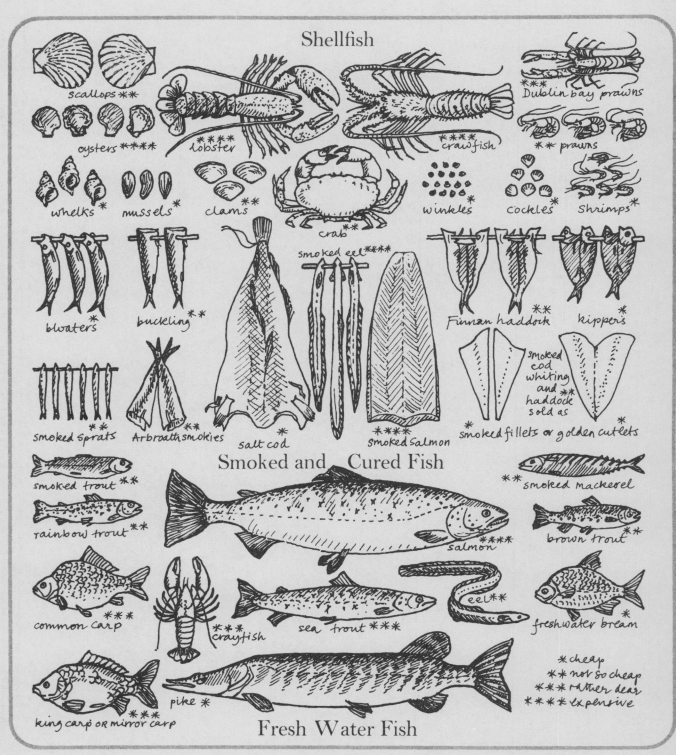

Shellfish

scallops *** oysters ****

lobster *** crawfish **** Dublin bay prawns *** prawns **

whelks * mussels * clams ** crab winkles cockles shrimps *

bloaters * buckling ** smoked eel **** Finnan haddock ** kippers *

smoked sprats ** Arbroath smokies salt cod * smoked salmon **** smoked cod whiting and haddock sold as smoked fillets or golden cutlets *

Smoked and Cured Fish

smoked trout *** smoked mackerel **

rainbow trout ** salmon **** brown trout

common carp *** craytish *** sea trout *** eel ** freshwater bream

king carp or mirror carp *** pike *

*cheap
** not so cheap
*** rather dear
**** expensive

Fresh Water Fish

62

Salt Water Fish

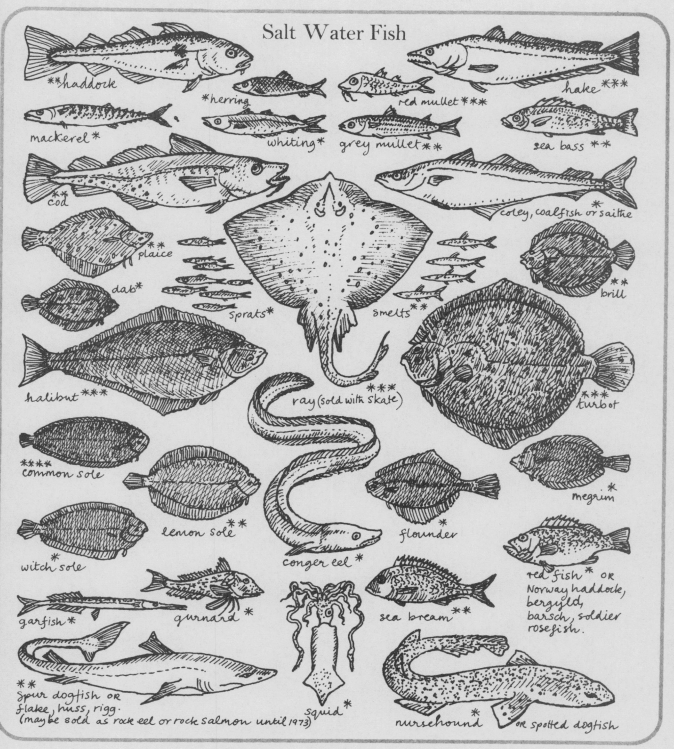

haddock, herring, red mullet, hake

mackerel, whiting, grey mullet, sea bass

cod, coley, coalfish or saithe

plaice, sprats, smelts, brill

dab

halibut, ray (sold with skate), turbot

common sole, lemon sole, flounder, megrim

witch sole, conger eel, red fish or Norway haddock, bergyldt, barsch, soldier rosefish.

garfish, gurnard, sea bream

spur dogfish or flake, huss, rigg. (may be sold as rock eel or rock salmon until 1973), squid, nursehound or spotted dogfish

Fresh Cod with Aïoli

2–3 lbs centre cut of cod (must be fresh)
12 egg-sized potatoes, preferably new, washed but
    not peeled
6 hard-boiled eggs, 1 lb cleaned carrots
6 courgettes   ⎫ if in season, but fish,
1 lb French beans   ⎬ carrots, potatoes and eggs
6 small green artichokes ⎭ form a very good dish
                       together
aïoli (page 246) *or* melted butter
court-bouillon:
2 quarts water, ½ pint cider vinegar
1 sliced onion, 1 stick celery, 1 bayleaf, 12 peppercorns

Boil the ingredients for the court-bouillon together
for 25 minutes and allow to cool to blood heat. Add
two teaspoons of salt. Cook the cod in this by simmering for ten minutes to a pound. Boil or steam the
potatoes and other vegetables separately, until just
done (avoid overdoing them).

Serve everything on a large dish, each kind of
vegetable and the eggs in separate groups, the fish
in the centre. Serve with plenty of stinging strong
aïoli (or melted butter for those who don't like
garlic).

☐ *An English version of salt cod with aïoli, it makes
a marvellous weekend lunch, and is very good for a
large family.*

For 4–6

Cod with Cheese Sauce

1 cod cutlet per person
1 pint court-bouillon (this page)
½ pint cheese sauce (page 249)
butter
2 tablespoons cheese, grated

Poach the cod steaks gently in the court-bouillon
for 15–20 minutes, while you make the cheese sauce.
Put half the well-seasoned sauce in the bottom of a
gratin dish, then the drained, poached fish. Pour
the rest of the sauce over the top, dot with butter,
sprinkle with grated cheese and bake in a moderate
oven until browned, or put under a gentle grill.

For 2

Cod Mayonnaise with Capers

1 whole fresh cod weighing about 6 lbs, or 3½ lbs
   centre cut of cod
court-bouillon (page 64)
½ pint mayonnaise (page 251) made with the caper
   vinegar
capers

Buy the whole fresh cod on the bone, remove the
head and cook this in the court-bouillon in a huge
pan or fish kettle for 20 minutes. Allow the court-
bouillon to cool to blood-heat, take out the cod's
head and put in the rest of the fish. Poach it gently
with the lid on for 10 minutes per lb. When just
cooked, but not falling to pieces, take out the fish
and drain it. Remove the skin and flake the flesh
from the bones.
Make the mayonnaise with a little caper vinegar
and a little wine or cider vinegar, and thin it down
with wine vinegar until it is the consistency of
thick cream, *or* use cream or water; add a handful
of capers. Pile the cod flakes on a dish, pour the
mayonnaise over and chill. Dot the mayonnaise
with a few more capers.

For 8–10

Cod Portugaise

4 cod cutlets
3 tablespoons lemon juice
4 tablespoons olive oil
12 peppercorns
salt
1 bayleaf
1 clove garlic, crushed
½ pint pizzaiola sauce (page 252)
parsley

Make a marinade from the lemon juice, olive oil,
peppercorns, salt, bayleaf and crushed clove of
garlic. Marinate the fish in this for not less than
half an hour, turning once. Drain the cutlets,
put them in a buttered oven dish and bake, covered,
for half an hour at Reg 4/350°. Heat the pizzaiola
sauce, pour some over each piece of fish and return
to the oven for ten minutes. Serve sprinkled with
freshly chopped parsley.

For 4

To Prepare Salt Cod

Choose 2 lbs of cod (middle cut if possible) and ask the shop to cut it into pieces about 3 or 4 inches across. Put these in a bowl a day or 2 days before you want to eat it, and stand the bowl overnight under a dribbling tap so that the water is slowly but constantly changing. When the cod is very soft it is ready. Drain and rinse, put in a pan of cold water, bring it slowly to the boil and as it reaches boiling point remove it from the heat and let it stand 10 minutes. It is now cooked and ready to use in a Brandade for example, or any of the salt cod recipes which follow.

Salt Cod with Tomatoes

1 lb cooked salt cod, skinned and boned
1 medium onion, peeled and sliced
¾ lb tomatoes, peeled and chopped
2 cloves garlic, chopped
4 oz black olives, stoned if possible
olive oil, salt, pepper

Flake the fish. Put it in an oiled shallow oven-proof dish. In another pan, cook the onion till soft in oil, add the tomatoes and garlic and cook until almost a purée. Season and pour over the fish and heat it through in the oven, or under the grill. Dot with black olives and serve with good fresh crusty bread.

☐ *More for grown-ups than for children, this is a very good lunch or supper dish, the black olives are the making of it, so don't be tempted to leave them out.*

For 4

Brandade de Morue

2 lbs prepared salt cod
1–2 cloves garlic
scant ¼ pint milk
scant ¼ pint olive oil
2 tablespoons mashed potato
2 eggs
a handful of chopped parsley
4 slices white bread and oil to fry it in

Skin the cod, which will be very gelatinous indeed, remove the bones and chop it with a large knife. Pound the garlic in a pestle and mortar, add the cod a little at a time, and as each lot is pounded to a rough fibrous paste transfer it to a wide bottomed pan.

Gently warm the milk and oil separately — they should be just over blood heat. On an asbestos mat on a *very* low flame add the milk and oil alternately to the cod. Keep the cod on one side of the pan, pour the liquids onto the other side a teaspoon at a time and draw them gradually into the mixture, mixing well with your wooden spoon. Add the mashed potato, stir it in then add the eggs and cook on, stirring as you would for scrambled eggs, until you have a purée the consistency of very creamy mashed potato. Meanwhile, cut the bread into triangular sippets and fry them. At the last minute stir the parsley into the cod and serve with the fried bread.

For 6–8

Devilled Herrings

1 herring for each person
1 teaspoon Dijon mustard for each herring
dried breadcrumbs
olive oil
salt

Fillet the herrings and (if you can bear it) skin them so each one makes 2 skinless pieces. Spread mustard over one side, sprinkle with breadcrumbs and salt and then sprinkle with olive oil. Turn fillets over and do the same to the other side. Grill for about 4–5 minutes on each side and serve very hot, with mashed potato.

Soft Herring Roes

½ lb soft roes
1 beaten egg
fine dried white breadcrumbs
oil for frying (or butter)
salt

You need large whole roes for this.

Separate the roes and dry them a little. Beat the egg and dip the roes into it. Roll in breadcrumbs and deep fry until nicely browned. Sprinkle with salt and serve with tomato sauce (page 184) or simply roll them in seasoned flour and fry in 1–2 oz of foaming butter. Eat them on toast.

For 2

Filleted Herrings in Oatmeal

2 good herrings
handful porridge oats
salt and freshly ground pepper
lard
1 lemon *or* fresh tomato sauce

Mix the oats with salt and pepper on a board or plate and pat them onto the opened, filleted fish. Fry in lard, top first so they end up skin side down. They take about 2½ minutes each side, depending on the size of the fish. Serve with lemon wedges or with fresh tomato sauce.

For 2

Stuffed Herrings

4 herrings
4 oz fresh breadcrumbs
1 oz butter, well softened
chopped parsley, savory or tarragon
lemon rind, grated
egg to bind
salt and freshly ground pepper

Mix all except the herrings together and season well. Open the herrings, remove the backbones, put the stuffing inside, press together lightly and bake in a moderately low oven, Reg 3/325°, for half an hour.

☐ *A lot of people object to eating herrings because of all the spiky little bones that seem to get in every mouthful. It is very easy to take the bones out and you are left with a very good fish.*

For 4

Pickled Herrings

12 fresh herrings
2 pints water
4 oz coarse or block salt
1½–2 pints distilled vinegar
1–2 tablespoons pickling spice
1 onion, sliced lengthwise
2 bay leaves
2 chillis
allspice, cloves, coriander, peppercorns, etc.

Cut the heads and tails off the herrings, and clean out the insides. Remove backbones (see diagram). Dissolve the salt in the water and soak the herring fillets in this brine for about 2 hours. During the soaking put the pickling spice into the vinegar, bring it slowly to the boil and leave it to cool. Drain the brine from the fish, and roll up the fillets, skin side out, wide end first, and secure with tooth picks. Slip a sliver of onion inside each roll. After you have rolled them, place in a suitable jar and strain the vinegar over them (it should cover them), add the bay leaves, chillis and spices, put a lid on.

Leave 10–14 days before eating. In a cool place they will keep for a month and more. Eat with sour cream, raw onion rings, brown bread and chopped apple.

☐ *A good standby for summer lunches.*

Makes 24 fillets

How to Fillet a Round Fish

Use a rather inflexible, not too pointed, sharp knife. Note: herring and mackerel are sold un-gutted, so pull out their gut as you cut off the head. Also if you wish to stuff them, be careful not to cut along the stomach after stage 2.

1. Cut off the head to include collar bone and front fin.

2. Turn the fish on its side, insert the knife along the centre of the back, keeping the blade flat above the bones.

3. Keep your left hand flat on the fish while you detach the fillet from the bones with the knife. Don't cut through the stomach if you wish to stuff the fish (herring, sprats, mackerel).

4. If you are dividing the fish in two and not stuffing it, remove the first fillet completely, turn the fish over, and starting at the tail bring the knife towards you, along the fish rather than across it. Very slightly turn it up as you come to the central spine then flatten it again the other side.
(The fishmonger keeps his hand flat on the fish while doing this, but until you get good at it you might prefer to lift the fillet up as you go, so that you can see what you are doing.)

5. Remove second fillet, trim off fins and 'lug'. Use the head and bones for stock.

6. If you are stuffing the fish remove the back-bone, starting at the tail as shown.

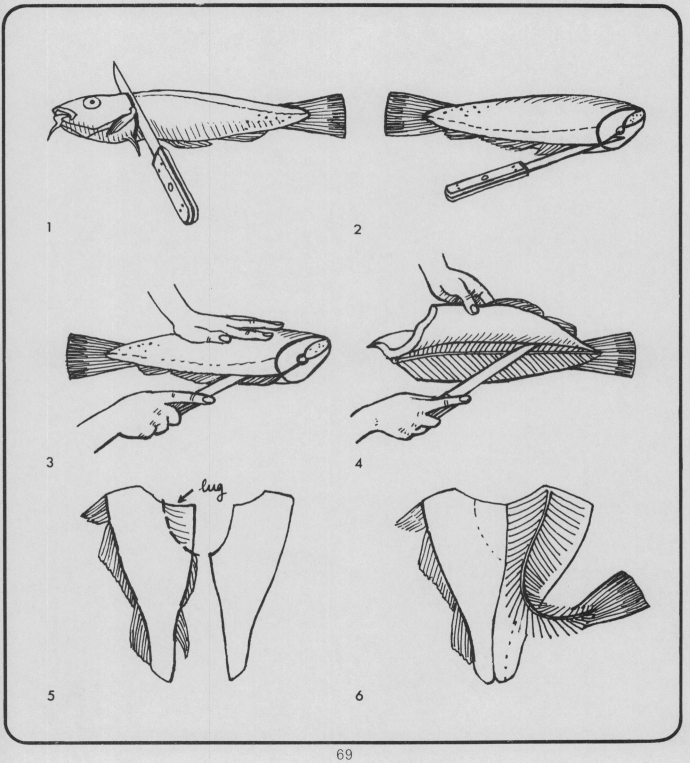

1

2

3

4

5   lug

6

69

Stuffed Sprats

1½ lbs fresh sprats
3 oz breadcrumbs
1 large onion, peeled and finely chopped
fresh or dried marjoram and chopped parsley
1 egg
salt, pepper
flour, fat or oil for frying

Choose large sprats as they have to be filleted,
and small ones are very fiddly. Chop off the heads,
split the fish and remove the tails and bones
(see page 53). Mix the onion, breadcrumbs,
marjoram, beaten egg, parsley and seasoning,
adding a little milk if necessary, but the
mixture must not be too wet. Lay the sprats
out flat in matching pairs. Put a little stuffing
between each pair of fish, as if making a sandwich, skin side out. Flour them on both sides and
fry until golden on both sides. Serve with lemon
wedges. They stay together very well.

☐ *You can also do this with filleted fresh sardines,
small whiting, or herring.*

For 4

Breton Mackerel

4 mackerel

Court-bouillon
4 pints water
salt
¼ pint vinegar
a bunch of parsley
3 bay leaves
1 onion
1 carrot
6 peppercorns

Boil the ingredients for the court bouillon
together for 10 minutes. Let it cool, add the
cleaned mackerel. Poach them gently for 15–20
minutes. Remove them from the liquid and skin
them carefully. When cold remove the fillets from
the bones. Arrange on a dish and pour over them
a Breton Sauce (page 248).

☐ *These poached mackerel would also be delicious
with a Salsa Verde (page 252).*

For 4

Marinated Mackerel with Marjoram

6 mackerel
3 bayleaves
glass white wine or cider
$\frac{1}{4}$–$\frac{1}{2}$ pint cider vinegar or wine vinegar
$\frac{1}{4}$–$\frac{1}{2}$ pint water
sprigs of marjoram, or failing this oregano or parsley
12 peppercorns
salt

Get the fishmonger to fillet the mackerel, or do it yourself (see page 69). Cut the fillets in two lengthwise. Roll the fillets up from the tail end and put in a fireproof dish all facing the same way and with all the silver to one side and the dark blue to the other. Pour over the wine and vinegar. Add enough water to cover. Put in the marjoram and peppercorns and a little salt and cook in a very slow oven, Reg 2/300°, for one hour. Allow to cool, when they will set in a nicely-flavoured jelly.

☐ *You can also do this with herrings.*

For 6

Mackerel Stuffed with Gooseberries

1 mackerel per person
1 or 2 oz gooseberries per mackerel
salt and freshly ground pepper
sugar

Simmer the gooseberries in a little water, mashing while they cook, until you have a purée. Season generously with salt, pepper and sugar.
Fillet the fish (see page 69) leaving them joined along the belly. Open them flat and spread the purée on one side. Press the fish together again, lay in a buttered dish and cover with greased paper, or wrap them individually in foil parcels. Bake in a moderate oven, Reg 4/350°, for 30 minutes or longer. depending on the size of the fish.

Kipper Salad

2 good uncooked kippers — these must be fresh,
   undyed, old-fashioned kippers, not frozen or
   wrapped
oil
1 lemon
1 small onion, sliced thinly into rings
1 large cold cooked potato, peeled and diced
1 green pepper (optional), seeded and diced
salt, freshly ground pepper and a pinch of paprika
parsley, chopped

Skin and bone the uncooked kippers; this is quite
easy if they are fresh and juicy. Cut them into small
squares, and cover with oil and the juice of half the
lemon while you prepare the other ingredients. Put
a dressing of oil and lemon, salt and pepper on the
potatoes. Mix the onion and green pepper with the
kipper. Serve the kipper salad sprinkled with
parsley and the potato salad sprinkled with paprika,
side by side.

For 2

Tarama (Smoked Cod's Roe)

½ lb smoked cod's roe
1 slice stale white bread
milk
½ cup olive oil
a crushed clove of garlic
juice of half a lemon
pepper

Scrape all the roe carefully away from the skin
and put it in a bowl. Squeeze the bread in milk,
then mash it into the cod's roe with a wooden
spoon, together with the finely-crushed clove of
garlic, a little lemon juice and fresh-ground black
pepper. When it has amalgamated add the oil
little by little, beating it in with your spoon until
the roe begins to shine. Then give it a last
pounding, and pack it into a pot. Serve it with
slices of hot toast and butter.

For 6

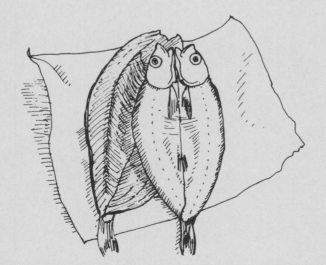

Smoked Haddock Salad

1 large smoked haddock on the bone
1 pt mixed milk and water
1 bay leaf
⅓ pt mayonnaise
3–4 hard-boiled eggs
black olives
a few prawns to decorate if possible
5 oz rice

Poach the haddock in the milk and water with a
bay leaf until you can take the fish from the
bones (about 5–10 minutes). Reserve the liquid
(discarding the bay leaf) and put aside the flaked
fish. Cook the rice until just done (do not overcook). Make the mayonnaise and dilute it with
some of the liquid from the fish until you have
just over half a pint of creamy sauce. Mix this
with the fish and rice. Add some chopped hard-
boiled egg. Fork it into a pyramid and if you
want to be grand add some prawns and black
olives for decoration. Serve with green salad.

☐ *This is a sort of kedgeree, but for hot weather.
You could mix curry powder into the mayonnaise
for a change. Very delicious.*

For 4

Tunny Fish Salad

6 oz dried haricots, soaked and cooked
8 oz tin tunny fish
3–4 tablespoons olive oil
1 large tablespoon wine vinegar
½ clove garlic, crushed
a few onion rings
chopped parsley
salt, plenty of pepper
optional
a handful of black olives
1 hard-boiled egg

Mix the cooked drained haricots with the tunny
fish broken into chunks. Make a vinaigrette with
the oil, vinegar, garlic, salt and pepper. Mix it
into the salad. Strew the top with onion rings
and chopped parsley. If your onions are too
strong in flavour, soak the rings in milk for half
an hour before adding them to the salad. You
can add black olives or sliced hard-boiled eggs.

For 4

Fish Mousse

1 lb smoked haddock on the bone
2 eggs
½ pint milk, and ½ pint water
1 small onion
1 small carrot
1 bay leaf
½ oz butter, ½ oz flour
½ oz gelatine
¼ pint cream
a handful of parsley
salt, pepper

Hard-boil one of the eggs. Poach the haddock until tender in the milk and water (about 10–15 minutes). Save the liquid. Flake the fish and put the skin and bones back into the pan with the onion, carrot and bay leaf. Simmer, covered, for about 20 minutes. Make a roux with the butter and flour and slowly add about ¾ pint of the fish liquid, to make a Béchamel, add more milk if necessary and taste for seasoning. Separate the raw egg and stir the yolk into the sauce. Add the fish and some parsley and pound or liquidise. Add the cream (if it is thick enough, whip it first). Dissolve the gelatine in about 3–4 tablespoons of water over gentle heat, and add it to the fish mixture. Set aside to cool, and as it begins to set whip the egg white very stiff and fold it in to the mixture. Slice the hard-boiled egg and lay it in a pattern at the bottom of a wetted soufflé dish. Pour over the mousse mixture and leave it to set. Turn it out just before eating and serve with salad.

☐ *Good weekend food.*

For 8

Hake or Haddock Patties

1½ lbs baby hakes (filleted) or fresh haddock fillet
1 large slice bread (a doorstep, crusts removed, soaked in ¼ cup water)
1 onion, grated
1 egg, beaten
pepper, salt
½ teaspoon sugar
Flour, oil

Skin the fish and cut it into small pieces, then, using a large board, and long sharp knife, chop it finely for 5 minutes. When it is soft and fine add the egg, grated onion, salt, pepper and sugar, and the soaked bread crumbled finely. Continue to chop for another few minutes so that it is of a well-mixed soft consistency adding water if necessary. Shape into flat round patties (a tablespoon is helpful for this) and flour them. Fry them gently in shallow oil until golden brown both sides. Serve with chips, and tomato sauce

☐ *These make a change from fishcakes made with potato.*

For 4 (makes 12 patties)

Creamed Smoked Haddock

1 lb smoked haddock on the bone
½ pint milk
1 oz butter
¾ oz flour
2 tablespoons Parmesan, grated (optional)
plenty of freshly ground pepper
salt if necessary

Poach the haddock in the milk until it comes easily off the bone — about ten minutes, taking care not to let it burn at the bottom, and then strain the milk into a jug. Remove the skin and bones, and shred the fish as finely as possible with a knife and fork, or sieve through the coarse disc of the mouli, or liquidise for a few seconds.

Make a sauce with the butter, flour and the milk in which the fish was cooked. Add the cheese, pepper and the fish. Taste for salt.
Serve the purée on golden fried bread cut in triangles.

☐ *Good for a first course or for supper with a poached egg on top.*

For 2

Fish Pie

¾ lb smoked haddock
¾ lb fresh haddock
1 ½ lbs potatoes, boiled and mashed with plenty of butter and milk
½ oz butter
1 ½ oz flour
¾ pint milk
½ pint water
1 teaspoon white wine- or cider-vinegar
salt and freshly ground pepper
3 hard-boiled eggs
parsley, chopped

Preheat the oven to Reg 5/375°. Poach the fish in the milk and water for 15 minutes, or until the skin and bones come away easily, basting with the liquid a couple of times. Make a sauce with the butter, flour and enough of the fish liquid to give it the consistency of double cream. Add the vinegar, seasoning, flaked fish, sliced eggs and parsley to the sauce. Arrange the mixture in a pie dish and cover with mashed potato. Dot with butter and bake at Reg 5/375°, for half an hour or until brown. This pie is very much liked by children; if it is for adults you can add chopped scallops sautéed in butter, for the brief glorious couple of months they are in season, but it is excellent anyway.

For 6

How to Fillet a Flat Fish

Use a **sharp**-bladed inflexible knife.

1. Cut the head off. Note the position of the hand **and the** direction of the cut, which leaves all the fish **and takes** away only the bony head.

2. Turn the fish over to the white side, insert the knife **as** shown. The knife is above the bone.

3. Slide the knife outwards and towards the tail taking **care** to leave the fins behind.

4. Work across the other side of the spine, using short **cutting** strokes, until the first fillet is freed.

5. Turn the fish over again, and score through the edge of the skin, starting at the tail end and leaving the fins attached to the bones.

6. Insert the blade at the tail end and cut the second fillet from the bone, working over the spine and across to the other side, again being careful to leave the fins attached to the bones.

7. You now have 2 fine fillets. Leave the skin on.

N.B. Sole have very little flesh along the spine, so it is easier to make 4 fillets, dividing each side along the spine. It is necessary to skin sole.

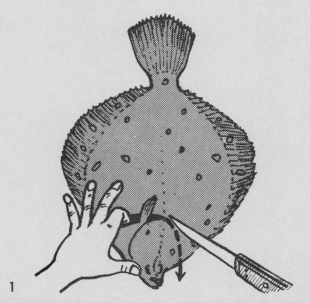

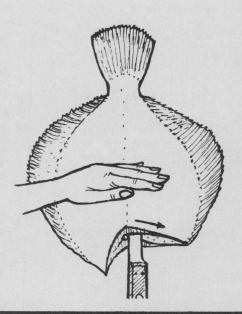

1

2

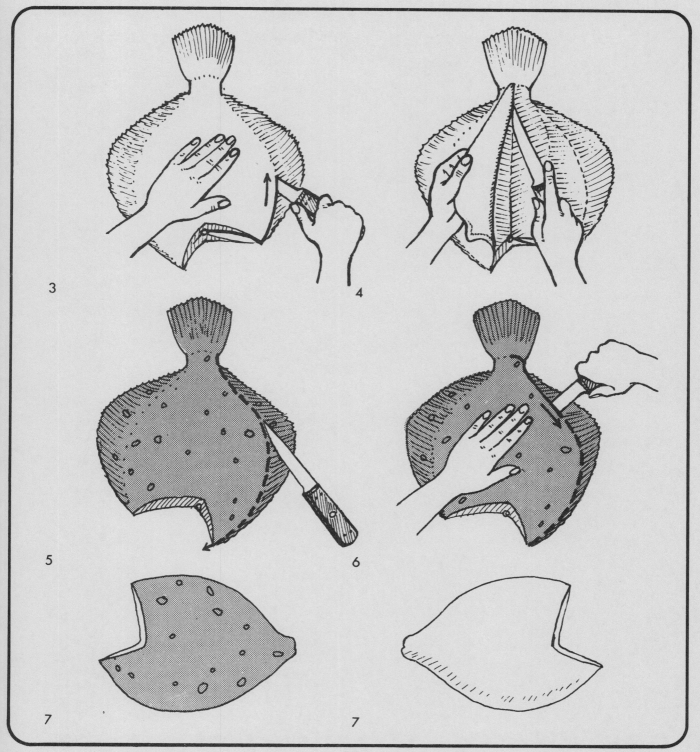

3

4

5

6

7

7

Fish and Chips at Home

1 thick piece of fish per person
1 potato per person
1 egg, milk
3 tablespoons flour
½ teaspoon salt
2 tablespoons breadcrumbs
flour, salt
lemon juice, lemon slices
parsley
corn oil for frying

First make the batter. Mix the flour, salt and breadcrumbs. Beat the egg, add a little milk, stir into the flour mixture, beat well, let it stand half an hour. It should be thick.
Skin the fish season it with salt and pepper and lemon juice, dip fish into the flour, then into the batter and fry it to a nice golden colour when the fat is smoking blue (don't use a basket, the batter will stick to it). Keep fish warm on a dish with kitchen paper.

Peel the potatoes, cut into chips, wash them very well and dry them before frying, with a basket, in another lot of hot fat.

Keep them warm, and sprinkle with salt, like the fish. Serve with lemon wedges and parsley.

□ *You should choose fillets of cod, coley, haddock, plaice or* hake.

Deep-fried Sprats

1 lb sprats
deep-frying oil (use a whole bottle, strain it after each time you use it and keep it for fish)
seasoned flour
1 lemon

Wash the sprats and pat them dry in a piece of kitchen paper. Flip each one in a heap of seasoned flour, shaking off the surplus before dropping them one by one into hot oil, with a blue haze (*not* smoke) rising; when pale gold they are done. Drain off the oil as you take them out and keep the fish hot on a paper-lined dish in a low oven.
Remove the paper, and serve them, complete with heads and tails, with lemon wedges. If you haven't had sprats before they will be a great discovery; they are simply delicious fried like this. If you are finicky about bones you can split the sprats before flouring and remove the backbones, leaving heads and tails on; they will fry a fraction faster.

For 4

Kedgeree

1½ lbs smoked haddock on the bone
½ pint milk
½ pint water
12 oz rice
2 oz flour
1½ oz butter
2 tablespoons cheese, grated, or ½ teaspoon curry
   powder
3 hard-boiled eggs

Poach the haddock gently in milk and water until
the flesh comes off the bones easily (after about ten
minutes). Keep aside the liquid in which it is cooked.
Wash the rice and boil in plenty of salted water for
12 minutes; drain and wash it well. Make a sauce
with the flour, butter and haddock liquid. If you
like a slight curry flavour, cook the powder in the
butter for a few moments before adding the flour.
If you prefer cheese, leave out the curry and add the
cheese to the sauce. It should be fairly thick, but
the rice will absorb some of it, so if you like sloshy
kedgeree, make the sauce thinner by adding more
milk.
Add the flaked fish, chopped hard-boiled eggs and
cooked, drained rice. Put the mixture in the top of a
double saucepan and steam for 20–30 minutes.
Serve with a lump of butter on each helping.

For 4–6

Fish Soup (Bouillabaisse)

2 lbs mixed fish. Choose from haddock ; whiting ;
   mullet, red or grey ; brill ; gurnet ; bream ; and
   shellfish as available — mussels ; prawns ;
   scallops etc.
2 onions, 3 cloves garlic, 1 bayleaf
large sprigs thyme, parsley, and fennel (use bulb
   fennel or seeds if no fresh)
2 tomatoes, 1 strip orange peel
large pinch saffron, salt and pepper
4 tablespoons olive oil, dash of white wine
Parmesan, grated, rouille (page 252)
4 slices of French bread dried slowly in the oven

Cut the cleaned fish, scraped to remove the scales,
in two-inch pieces. Make a stock with the bones,
trimmings and heads while you crush the garlic,
and peel and chop the onions and tomatoes.
Put the vegetables in a pan with the garlic, herbs,
orange peel, seasoning, saffron and oil. Cook for
five minutes without browning. Put the coarser
varieties of fish in with the vegetables and strain the
boiling stock over them. They should be covered,
so add water if necessary and a dash of white wine.
Boil fast for five minutes, add the more delicate fish
and boil on for another five to ten minutes. Add the
shellfish five minutes before the end. Remove from
the stove and serve with the toasted bread and a
good stinging rouille (page 252) and grated Parmesan
cheese.

For 4

Matelote Normande

2–3 lbs fish — hake, haddock or whiting (whole
  fish if possible)
2–3 quarts mussels
2 sticks celery
3–4 onions
4 oz butter
chopped parsley
juice of ½ lemon
2–3 teaspoons flour
salt, pepper

Keep the fish whole. Clean the fish but leave the
skin on and, in the case of a whole fish, the head
and tail. Clean the mussels. Chop the celery and
the onions separately. Melt 1 oz of the butter in a
large saucepan. Soften the celery, add a glass of
water and bring to the boil. Throw in the mussels.
When they are open remove them from the
liquid and keep it on one side.

Meanwhile soften the onions in another ounce of
butter for 20–30 minutes, with some chopped
parsley.

Leaving the celery out, put the onions and the
strained mussel liquid into a fireproof dish or pan,
which will just hold the fish. Lay the fish in it,
stomach up, and add water if necessary, to come
halfway up its sides. Taste for salt — the mussel
liquid may provide enough — add pepper and
cook gently, basting frequently, until the fish is
just done. Two minutes before serving, add the
remaining butter into which you have worked the
flour and more chopped parsley. Add the lemon
juice, and the mussels from their shells. Allow to
come to the boil and cook until thickened. This
should be done quickly. The fish is served in its
soup straight from the dish it is cooked in and
sprinkled perhaps with more parsley. You can
add a few shrimps with the mussels if you like.

☐ *This is a main course and could be served simply
with bread and a green salad.*

For 6

Moules Marinières

1 or 2 quarts mussels, depending on how greedy
  you are
2 oz butter
1 medium onion, finely chopped
1 clove garlic (if liked)
small glass white wine
handful of fresh parsley, finely chopped
freshly ground pepper

Scrape, scrub and thoroughly clean the mussels
under running cold water. Throw away any which
float, or are open or damaged. Melt the butter and
fry the onion gently in a capacious saucepan with a
well-fitting lid; add garlic as and if you like. When
the onion is transparent, after about 15 minutes,
grind in some pepper and pour in a small glass of
white wine; let it bubble a minute. Now add the
mussels and slam on the lid, turning up the heat as
high as it will go. Shake the pan once or twice, and
after about four or five minutes, look. It is ready if
all the shells are wide open. Ladle the mussels, as
they are, into a hot china tureen. Strain the now
considerable amount of liquid over them carefully,
because in spite of your cleaning it may still be
gritty. Sprinkle chopped green parsley over the
shiny black-blue shells and serve, providing another
dish for empty shells. It should need no salt if the
mussels are fresh and have recently been living in
the sea.
If you find your own mussels do make sure they
aren't living near a drain. Soak them for a couple of
hours in fresh water, or their liquid will be much too
salty to drink in the soup.

☐ *This is very simple.*

For 2

Grilled Mussels

1 quart mussels
1–2 oz salted butter
3 cloves garlic, finely chopped
handful fresh parsley, finely chopped

Wash the mussels in cold water to clean off the worst of the mud. Cut off the beards, stray limpets (best banged with the back of a knife) and spots of mud. Wash again in clear cold water. Bring about an inch of water to the boil in a large pan. Throw in the mussels and cook, covered, over a high heat, shaking the pan a couple of times, until they are all opened. It only takes a few minutes. Meanwhile chop the parsley and garlic finely and mash them into the butter with a fork. When the drained opened mussels are cool enough to handle, remove the empty half of each shell and put a hazelnut of garlic butter on each mussel. Put them in a grill pan under a moderate grill until the butter is bubbling hot; serve with plenty of bread to mop up the juice. About 12 mussels each is plenty. They are rather like juicy snails.

For 2

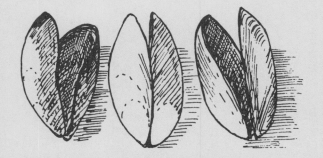

Cockle and Mussel Risotto

2 quarts cockles and mussels (1 quart of each)
2 tablespoons olive oil
1 medium onion, chopped
8 oz Italian rice
½ glass white wine
1 large pinch saffron
1 red pimento, chopped

As you are going to use the liquid from the shell-fish to cook the rice, it is very important to wash them thoroughly. Since they are full of salty water, do not add any more salt to the water in which you cook them.

Take a large pan with a lid. Bring to the boil sufficient water to come half way up the cockles and mussels. Throw them in, put on the lid and shake the pan once or twice. After five minutes they should all be opened; strain off the liquid and remove most of the shells. Keep the shellfish warm in their liquid while you cook the rice.

Heat the olive oil in a wide shallow pan and cook the chopped onion in it for about 10 minutes without browning; add the rice and stir it round until it becomes transparent.

Dissolve the saffron in the wine, if using powder, or soak the strands in it, and add to the rice. Stir until the rice has absorbed most of the wine. Taste the shellfish liquid and if it is too salt dilute it with fresh water. Pour about half a pint on to the rice, stir it about and add the chopped red pimento. Cover the pan and let the rice simmer, adding more liquid as necessary. When the rice is tender, stir in the shelled cockles and mussels, heat through and pile into a heated dish. Decorate the top in a haphazard way with the cockles and mussels left in their shells.

☐ *This can be made with either cockles or mussels or with both.*

For 4

To Prepare and Dress a Crab

Bang the underneath of the back end of the cooked crab on the side of a table, holding the crab by the shell. The body and legs should come away and you can detach this piece. If the crab is watery when you open it up, this does not mean anything is wrong with it.

First scoop out all the soft creamy parts from the inside of the shell. The fresher the crab, the moister and more succulent this part will be. Pile it on a plate. Now from the inside of the body part, in a sort of V, scoop out the brown meat and slush, having first removed the finger-like gills which lie on either side of the V. They are not — and do not even look — edible. Put the brown meat with the creamy meat. Now pull the claws off the body and put them on one side. With a sharp knife make a V-shaped cut, right through the bony body, with the point of the V at the back end so that it falls in three pieces (see diagram). With a skewer, empty all the cavities you have revealed by your cuts, and pile the meat on a separate plate. Crack the claws with a hammer or nutcrackers and pick all the meat out, again with the help of a skewer. Add to the other white meat. Add some dried, browned breadcrumbs and a little salt and pepper to the brown meat, and mash it with a fork. It gives a good texture and makes it go further. Flake all the white meat. Put the two kinds of meat in separate piles on the same dish, and serve either with mayonnaise, or simply with lemon juice or even vinegar, and brown bread and butter.

A crab five inches across the shell will serve two people with ease. It is very filling and incredibly cheap compared with most other shellfish, and it's certainly just as good. Some people put chopped hard-boiled egg white in the white meat to make it go further.

It is worth dressing your own crab because it soon dries up and loses its flavour once it has been done. It is perhaps a bit cheaper too, as you know exactly what proportion of crab to breadcrumbs you are getting, the sort of information no fishmonger would think of revealing!

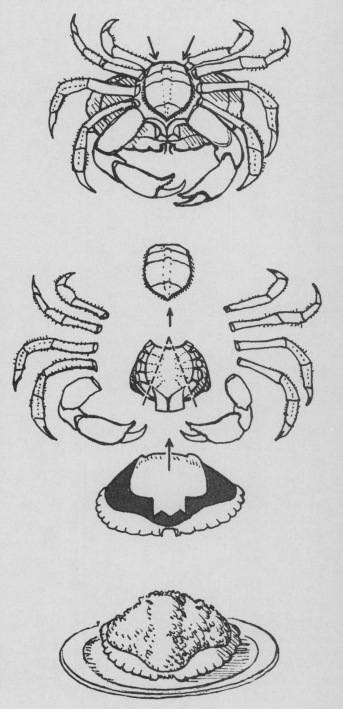

Hot Crab

8 oz crabmeat (the meat from a 1 lb crab)
½ pint thickish Béchamel sauce made from 1 oz
    flour, 1 oz butter and ½ pint milk
¼ teaspoon made mustard
1 tablespoon chopped parsley
1 tablespoon lemon juice or white wine
1 tablespoon cream
salt and freshly ground pepper

Flake the crabmeat, add to the Béchamel with the
mustard, parsley, lemon juice or wine, cream and
seasoning. Use the hot mixture to fill little pastry
shells or serve it on triangles of bread, fried golden
brown in a mixture of oil and butter.

☐ *This is only good with really fresh crab.*

For 2

Winkles and Cockles

Gather the winkles from a part of the beach that is
known to be clean and pure. Try to take some clean
sea water home, to cook them in. Wash them well
under a running tap, scrambling them round with
your hand, to remove all the mud and sand.

Put a pan of well-salted water or sea water, deep
enough to cover the winkles, on to boil. When the
water comes to the boil throw them in and turn the
heat up. When it returns to a full boil, let them
cook for one or two minutes, then drain and run
under the cold tap to cool.

Eat them with a pin or toothpick, removing their
little black lids before you dexterously hook them
out. Some people put vinegar on, but it is not an
improvement. They are very good for tea with
bread and butter.

Wash cockles well, as for winkles. Bring some *well-
salted* water to the boil. Throw in the cockles, turn
the heat to moderate and watch carefully. As soon
as they open take them out. Very good with drinks
taken out of their shells, and with a squeeze of
lemon and a sprinkling of parsley.

Fried Cockles

2 quarts fresh cockles
2 lemons
masses of freshly ground black pepper
a little salt
olive oil for frying

Wash and dry the cockles very thoroughly.
Heat two or three tablespoons of oil in a large
frying pan. Drop the cockles in, stir them round
until they open, then smother them in freshly
ground pepper and the juice of two lemons. Hardly
any salt is needed. Eat straight away.

☐ *In Spain these are served with drinks.*

For 6–8

Squid Risotto

2 lbs squid
1 small onion, sliced
1 clove garlic, sliced
olive oil
1 wineglass red wine
1 glass warm water
1 small tin tomato purée
salt and freshly ground pepper
10 oz Italian rice

Peel the skin from the body of the squid, pull off
the head and with it come the entrails. Take out the
bone from the body and cut the tentacles from the
head; throw away head, bone and innards. Slice the
body into thin rings, chop up the tentacles, and
wash well to get rid of any sand.
Fry the onion and garlic in oil in a sauté pan with a
lid; add the pieces of well-washed squid. Let it
stiffen and become less transparent; add the wine,
let it simmer for five minutes and add salt, pepper
and the tomato purée, plus a glass of warm water.
Cover the pan, turn the heat right down and simmer
for one hour. Add the rice, well washed under
running water, stir from time to time and cook until
tender, 20–30 minutes, adding more warm water if
it becomes dry. Correct the seasoning and serve.

For 4

Buckling Pâté

2 smoked buckling, or 1 smoked mackerel
2 slices white bread, crusts removed
milk
1 clove garlic
2–3 oz butter, softened
juice of ½ lemon
salt and freshly ground pepper

Remove the skin and all the visible bones from the
fish. Soak the bread in milk and squeeze dry. Pound
the garlic in a pestle and mortar, add the bread and
the fish. Pound thoroughly, removing any little
bones you may have missed before. Add the butter
and lemon juice, plenty of pepper and some salt if
necessary. Pound again, pack the mixture into little
pots, and chill. Serve with hot toast and butter.
This keeps several days in the refrigerator. It is
surprisingly rich and a little goes a long way, but it
is quite delicious and very easy to make. If you have
a liquidiser you can make it even more rapidly.

For 4

Bloater or Kipper Pâté

1 bloater, or 1 kipper
2–3 oz softened butter
lemon juice
salt and freshly ground pepper
pinch cayenne or nutmeg

Pour boiling water over the fish and let it stand for
ten minutes. Remove the flesh from the bones and
pound, mince or liquidise, adding butter, lemon
juice and seasoning. Mix to a fine paste, and remove
any whiskery bones left sticking out. Pack into little
pots and fork the top. Chill until needed; it keeps
several days in the refrigerator.

PÂTÉS

TERRINES, PIES & BRAWNS

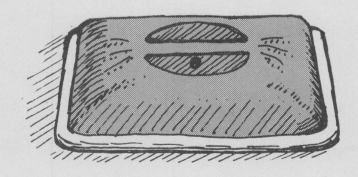

Pâtés, Terrines, Pies and Brawns

Pâtés, terrines and pies are all quite considerable tests of
cooking ability, because although mincing up the meat and
putting the thing together is all quite straightforward, it is the
blend of flavours that demands judgement, and the appearance
that makes it appetising or not. But even an ugly-looking
home-made pâté is a very useful thing to have around, and it
should keep for a week in the refrigerator. Ideally the finished
pâté should be nicely browned outside, still pink inside (salt
pork included in the mixture helps) and enclosed in a good
clear layer of jelly or some crisp brown pastry. When you are
very practised you can marble each slice with cubes of pork
back fat, fillets of the meat you are using, and perhaps pistachio
nuts or pieces of ham or tongue layered through the mixture in
carefully placed lines, so that each slice gets its share.

The meat is flavoured with a balanced selection of thyme, garlic,
juniper berries, bay, mace, lemon-peel, peppercorns, salt, white
wine and brandy. Once you have experimented with these you
will know what you like using most, and will be unlikely to end
up with what is too frequently offered, even in France, a boring
sort of meat-loaf.

It is a great triumph if you can get your butcher to mince the
meat for you every time, but if not, an electric automatic chopper
is a great help in making pâté and potted meat, as it really chops
the meat instead of squeezing and grinding it. Otherwise it is
the mincer and plenty of energy, and apart from this the only
equipment necessary is a terrine or bowl that will go in the oven.
Potted meats are best made and potted in small quantities, so
small, straight-sided, round white cocotte dishes are useful for
this. Potted meat and fish have very rightly had a revival
recently — they used to be one of the staple British breakfast
foods — and are a very useful way of storing cold ham, tongue,
smoked fish or almost any sort of game until you can face eating
it again. Don't serve potted meat too chilled, as the butter it
contains makes it rather solid and difficult to spread. It is a great
treat for tea on hot buttered toast, or even as a first course to a
meal.

The recipes in this section include one for pork pie, which is tremendously fiddly to do, so don't be surprised if the first one you make looks a bit strange; it gets better with practice, and it is a lovely thing to be able to produce at a picnic. Of course you can perfectly well buy cold pies, but that is about the limit of charcuterie in this country. You can't always buy interesting pâtés and rillettes or brawns, or things set in jelly or specially good salads made with calves' heads, so you just have to make them if you want them. Luckily they nearly all use the cheaper pieces of meat and are inexpensive provided you don't count the cost of your time.

Chicken Liver Pâté

½ lb chicken livers, frozen or fresh
1 small shallot, chopped very finely
1 oz butter
2 sage leaves, chopped very finely, or ½ teaspoon
   thyme leaves
1 small clove garlic, mashed
salt and freshly ground black pepper
dash of port, sherry or brandy, or a little white wine

Sort through the chicken livers, washing and drying
thoroughly if in doubt, removing strings and yellow
areas. Chop into small pieces and sprinkle with salt
and pepper while you fry the shallot in a small
saucepan in the butter, without browning. Add the
seasoned chicken livers, herbs and garlic, and
increase the heat a little, stirring constantly with a
wooden spoon or wooden fork (an old salad server is
useful for this dish). The livers will crumble as you
do this. Keep mashing and add the wine, brandy or
other alcohol. When all the livers have become
pinkish brown (after about five minutes), remove
from the heat and continue mashing until the whole
thing is smooth. Put into a little soufflé dish, or
individual cocotte dishes and serve well chilled.
This pâté improves with keeping, but if it is to be
kept for several days, pour melted butter on top.

For 4

Pig's Liver Pâté

12 oz pig's liver
4 oz salt (preferably) or fresh belly of pork
1 onion
1 clove garlic
salt, freshly ground pepper, pinch mixed spice
small glass white wine
small glass water
1 pig's foot, split in half
rosemary, bayleaf, thyme and parsley, tied together
   with a thread
bacon fat

Mince the pig's liver and pork with half the onion.
Crush the garlic and add it to the meat with the
mixed spice, a generous amount of pepper, and salt
only if you are using fresh pork. Put the liver
mixture into a large terrine or other mould and press
down evenly. Pour in the water and wine which
should cover the meat by half an inch. Slice up the
carrot and remaining onion, and lay them on top of
the pâté with the herbs and pig's trotter. Cover the
dish with foil and bake in a bain-marie at Reg 2/300°
for three hours. Remove the trotter, herbs and
vegetables. When cold pour melted bacon fat over
the top to seal it. Eat cold the following day when
the jelly will be set.

☐ *A very spicy pâté with a good jelly round it.*

Makes 1 lb pâté, for 8–12 people

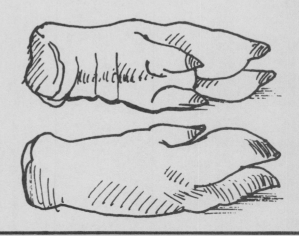

Hare Pâté

The back legs of a hare (or 1½ lbs boned hare
   meat)
the liver of the hare
6 oz salt pork
1–2 cloves garlic
glass of wine
a little stock, salt, pepper, pinch of mixed spice
thyme, bay leaf
4–5 rashers of thin streaky bacon
a marinade as for the one in game pie

Marinade the hare and liver for 24 hours (see the
marinade in game pie, opposite). Take out the
legs and simmer them in a little stock or water
for 20 minutes. This is not to cook them, but
just to make the meat easier to bone, chop and
mince. Slice the best meat into neat fillets and
chop or mince the rest, with the pork. Stiffen
(sauté briefly) the liver in a little pork fat or
butter, and mince that too. Add the crushed
garlic, wine, salt, pepper, spice and thyme to all
the meat, and if it needs a little more moisture
add some stock or some of the marinade.
Preheat the oven to Reg 2/300°. Fill a pâté dish
with the mixture and press it well down. Cover it
neatly with bacon rashers and put a bay leaf on
top. Cover with silver foil. Put the pâté in a bain
marie and cook for 2 hours. Take the foil off for
the last ½ hour to brown the top. Press and cool.
Eat when set next day.

Potted Tongue or Ham

8 oz cooked tongue or ham
8 oz butter (cheapest unsalted), clarified
½ level teaspoon mace
freshly ground pepper
salt if necessary

Chop up the meat and put in the liquidiser, with
5 oz melted clarified butter, the mace and pepper.
Make a fine purée (if you don't have a liquidiser you
can do this by pounding it in a pestle and mortar),
taste for salt. Pack it into a pot, pressing well down
to eliminate air. Chill for half an hour and when firm
smooth the top and cover with melted, clarified
butter; what is left will just about do the trick. The
potted meat is a beautiful pink and should be
put in a neutral coloured pot, white, cream or beige,
to look its best, with the yellow butter in a layer
over the top.

Makes 1 lb, for 8–12

A Raised Pork Pie weighing 2 lbs.

1 lb lean end of belly of pork, or blade (about three
    parts lean to one part fat)
salt and freshly ground pepper
water, dried sage
½ pint stock made with 1 pig's trotter and the trim-
    mings from the pork
for the pastry:
12 oz plain flour, pinch salt, 4 oz lard
¼ pint water, 1 egg yolk (for glaze)

Trim the meat, mince half of it as finely as you can
and chop the other half into pea-sized pieces; it
takes a long time. Season well, add sage to your
liking and moisten with half a wine glass of water.
Preheat the oven to Reg 8/450°

To make the pie-crust

Sift the flour with the salt and put to keep warm
in a large bowl. Melt the lard, cut in pieces, in the
water in a small saucepan, and then bring to the
boil; as it boils pour it on to the flour. Mix rapidly
with a wooden spoon until it is smooth. Reserve a
quarter of the pastry for the lid, keeping it warm.
Flatten out the rest as soon as it is cool enough to
handle. When it is about quarter to half an inch
thick, mould it into a pie shape on the bottom of a
large greased jam or storage-jar. Lift it, jar and all,
on to a greased baking tin, wait until the crust is
cool, and gently ease the jar away. It may collapse a
bit, but never mind. You should have a case about
five inches in diameter and two or three inches high.

Fill the case with the meat, pressing it down well;
roll out a lid from the last piece of pastry, and damp
the edges with water before sealing it on very carefully. Press the edges together with your fingers and
decorate them by indenting with the back of a knife
at half-inch intervals or by forking. You can
decorate the pie with pastry trimmings cut into
leaves and flowers. Tie a band of oiled greaseproof
paper round the pie. Paint the top with egg yolk,
and make a round hole in the middle for the steam
to escape and to pour the juice through.

Bake in the centre of a hot oven for half an hour
and then turn the heat down to Reg 5/375° and
cook for another hour. Remove the pie and allow it
to cool a little. Strain the pig's foot stock and reduce
to about ⅓ pint. Season with salt, take it off the
heat and pour it on to half a teaspoon of gelatine in a
jug to make sure it sets. Stir and allow to cool a
little. Fill the pie with this liquid, using a small
funnel. Let it set and keep the pie overnight if
possible. Eat it cold.

For 6–8 people

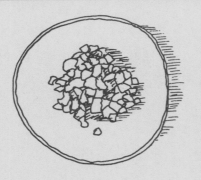

Cornish Pasties

10 oz steak, well trimmed and cut up very small
1 small potato, peeled and cut up small
1 onion, peeled and chopped finely
parsley, chopped finely
salt and freshly ground pepper
3 tablespoons gravy, stock or water
¾ lb shortcrust pastry made from 8 oz plain flour,
   3½ oz fat, pinch salt and water to bind
1 egg, beaten, or milk, to glaze pastry

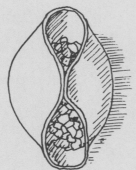

Preheat oven to Reg 7/425°. Mix the steak, potato, onion, parsley, salt and pepper, and moisten with the liquid. Roll out the pastry and cut out six circles with the help of a saucer. Put a dollop of the mixture on the centre of each, brush round the edges with beaten egg or milk, and fold the pastry up pinching the edges together in a pretty serpentine pattern. Place on a greased tin, brush with more beaten egg or milk, prick the tops with a fork to let out the steam and bake in the top of the oven for 10–15 minutes to cook the pastry; then turn the oven down to Reg 2/300°, and depending on the quality and tenderness of the steak, bake for a further ½–1 hour. To reheat, put for 15 minutes in a low oven.

6 smallish pasties

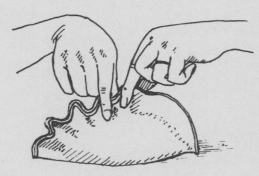

Brawn

half a pig's head, singed, with the teeth removed,
   split in three pieces by the butcher
2 onions, 4 carrots
2 turnips, 2 leeks
2 sticks celery
bouquet garni
4 or 5 peppercorns, salt
bunch of fresh parsley
1 lemon
2 hard-boiled eggs, sliced
½ bottle of dry white wine or cider

Clean the pig's head with a damp cloth and put it in
a pan with the cleaned chopped vegetables, herbs,
peppercorns and a little salt. Cover with water and
white wine or cider and simmer for three hours, until
it is falling apart. Strain off the liquid, skim off the
fat and return the liquid to the pan. Add lemon
juice and a piece of lemon peel and reduce by half.
Taste for seasoning — add a drop more lemon juice
if too bland. Meanwhile discard the vegetables,
remove the fat and bones from the meat and skin
the tongue. Put all the lean meat and tongue on a
board and chop it fairly finely. Chop the parsley and
mix into the liquid. Put a layer of hard-boiled eggs
in the bottom of a basin, put in some of the meat,
pour in the liquid. Add the rest of the meat. Put a
weighted plate on top of the brawn and leave it to
set in the refrigerator for several hours or overnight.
Serve with a green salad or as an hors d'oeuvre.

☐ *Suitable also for calf's head.*

For 6–8

Rabbit in Jelly

1½ lbs rabbit cut in pieces
1 large onion, sliced
1 pig's foot, split
1 bunch parsley
1 lemon
small glass white wine if available
salt and 6 peppercorns

Put the rabbit pieces in a large pan with the sliced
onion, pig's foot, a few sprigs of the parsley, a strip
of lemon peel, wine, a little salt and the peppercorns. Just cover with cold water, bring to the boil,
skim, and simmer very slowly, covered, for about 1½
hours, until the meat comes off the bones easily.
Strain and return the liquid to the pan with the
pig's trotter. Put in a fresh piece of lemon peel and
simmer, uncovered, until the liquid is reduced to one
pint. Skim, and flavour with lemon juice and more
salt if necessary. Strain the liquid, skim again and
add a good handful of chopped parsley. Put the
rabbit meat pulled from the bones and the pink
inside pieces of the pig's foot (scarcely visible little
scraps of delicious meat) into a square or oblong
earthenware dish. Pour the liquid over the meat and
chill. It will keep three or four days in the refrigerator.
For a very firm jelly dissolve a leaf of gelatine,
or half an ounce of powdered gelatine, in the
liquid, before you add the parsley. Instead of the
parsley you can put half a cucumber, cut into small
cubes, into the dish with the meat, but as the
cucumber is watery the jelly will not stay firm quite
as long.

☐ *Ideal for a cold lunch on a hot summer day.*

For 4–6

Galantine of Breast of Veal

3 lbs breast of veal, boned (keep the bones)
6 oz minced pork, or sausage meat
6 oz ham or tongue, or 3 oz of each
1 small onion, finely chopped, softened in butter
1 small glass white wine
salt, pepper, parsley, thyme
1 oz butter
½ pint stock
2 onions, chopped
2 carrots, chopped
bouquet garni
for prettiness : truffles or pistachio nuts (optional)

Using the veal bones and whatever else you like, make a stock while you prepare the stuffing. Cut the ham or tongue into small pieces, but don't mince. Mix into the minced pork or sausage meat, season well, add herbs, wine, softened onions and truffles or pistachio nuts. Spread the mixture on the boned veal and roll it up. Tie it up with easily seen thread, leaving long ends. Melt the butter in a flameproof casserole, brown the rolled veal all over, remove it and put in the chopped onions, carrots and bouquet garni. Let them sweat for several minutes, then add stock to cover the vegetables, replace the meat, bring the liquid to the boil, cover and continue cooking in the oven at Reg 2/300° for two hours, basting occasionally. When it is ready remove the meat and leave it to cool. Untie it and spoon a little of the cooking liquid over the meat, just before it sets, to give it a shine. You may have to do this basting several times.

☐ *Serve the veal cold in neat slices with salads. This stuffing can also be used to stuff a boned duck or chicken (pages 158–9).*

For at least 10

Boning a Breast (Lamb or Veal)

(1) Breasts are sold sometimes complete, or as shown by the dotted line, halved. The following diagrams deal with the half that has the bones in, left and right sides.

(2) With a sharp knife (A), cut back the flap made by the diaphragm, until 3–4 thin white bones are visible.

(3) With the point of the knife (B), lift out the first 2 or 3 bones, which will be easy. Leave the more firmly attached ones till later.

(4) Cut along the joints between the ribs and the breast bone, marked by knife (C), along the dotted line. Remove each rib as shown by knife (D).

(5) Make another cut along the breast bone as shown by knife (E). Remove the remaining flexible ribs and any other bones.

(6) Spread the stuffing, using recipe on this or on page 245.

(7) Roll and tie.

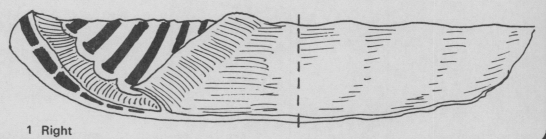

1   Right

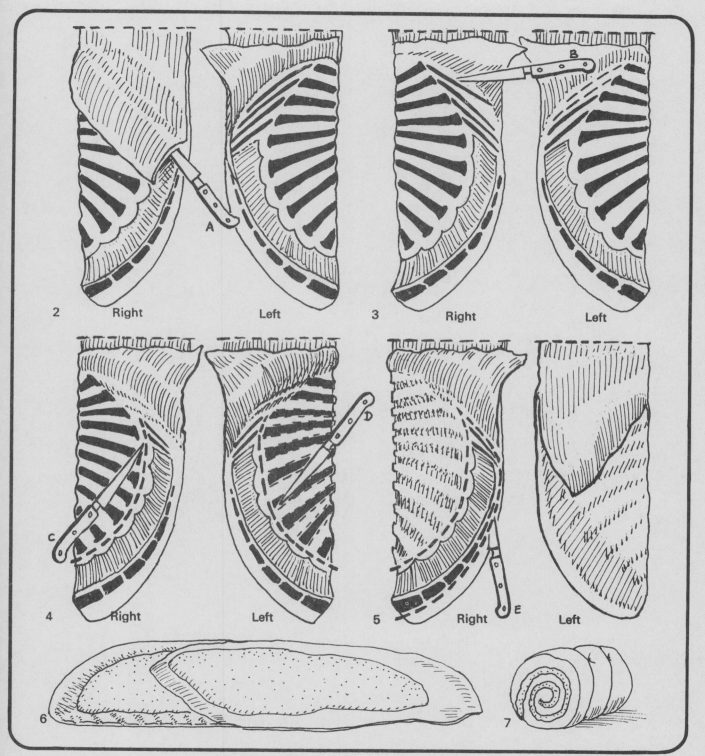

2   Right   Left   3   Right   Left

4   Right   Left   5   Right   Left

6

7

95

Faggots

1 large onion, peeled and chopped
1 clove garlic
1 lb pigs' liver
½ lb fresh belly of pork
2 oz pure pork fat
sage or thyme, and parsley if you like
salt, pepper, scrape of nutmeg
1 large egg
4 oz breadcrumbs (fresh, not dry)
pigs' caul (see page 130)
good stock or left-over gravy

Mince together the onion, garlic, liver, pork and fat. Season it with the herbs, nutmeg and a little salt and pepper. Lightly grease a large pan and cook the mixture *very slowly* for about ½ hour, turning it often so that none of it burns. Tip the pan and pour the mixture of fat and gravy that runs from it into a bowl. Add the beaten egg and breadcrumbs to the meat. Mix to a fairly firm mixture that you can form into balls about the size of a small apple. Wrap each ball in a piece of caul fat, and place them closely together in a gratin dish or baking tin. Heat the oven to Reg 3/325°. Mix the stock or left-over gravy together with their own gravy and pour it into the tin to come halfway up the faggots. Bake them for about 40 minutes, until they are nice and brown on top. Serve them with peas or pease pudding (page 189) and mashed potatoes. Leftovers will reheat well, but will need more gravy.

If you cannot obtain caul fat, roll the balls of mixture in flour and bake as described above, without adding the gravy, which is served separately.

For 4–6

Rillettes of Pork

2 lbs belly of pork (skin removed)
¼ lb flare fat (sold in a strip for larding by the butcher)
salt, pepper
grating of nutmeg

Cube the fat and pork into 1½″ pieces. Put them into a heavy pan with a little water. Cover and cook in a very low oven for 4 hours (Reg 1/275°). Strain off and reserve the liquid and pull the meat to pieces with 2 forks, or better still, when cooled, with your fingers, removing any bones there may be. This is a lengthy job but there is no better way. You are aiming at fine soft threads of meat in a creamy spicy body. Season well and return the liquid to the meat. Reheat until it bubbles, then put it, if possible, into stoneware jars or nice china or earthenware dishes. Cover with melted lard, about ½″ deep and put paper covers over that. Rillettes will keep for months in a cool place.

☐ *Eat as a snack with wholemeal bread. Good for Christmas presents. You can add pieces of rabbit or pigeon at the beginning, if you like, but it should be mainly pork.*

MEAT

Meat

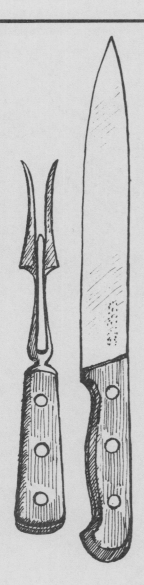

Always be extra nice and good-tempered in the butcher's shop; it really is worth being good friends with the man who sells you your meat. He is the person to steer you clear of bargain cuts that are a maze of bones and gristle, he will show you both sides of a piece of stewing steak before wrapping it up. He will advise you which piece of the animal would be most suitable, if you tell him what you want the meat for. He is also more likely to be prepared to do tedious work in the way of boning, mincing and cutting a joint just so, if he is your friend and sees that you care, and if you make a point of going into the shop when it is not particularly busy.

When choosing meat there are several things to bear in mind. Most carcasses have been frozen or chilled but reach the shop soon after slaughter, and in this short time the freezing, which is done fast and at a very low temperature, does not affect the juiciness of the meat. But what you do not want to carry home in your shopping bag is something that has been sitting in cold storage for weeks; nothing dries meat up so thoroughly, and the fat becomes granular.

New Zealand lamb has of course been frozen, but it is increasingly good as transport gets faster, and is particularly worth buying from October to Christmas, when their lambs are slaughtered and at their best. English lamb, which is slaughtered between three and five months old, is in season from May or even earlier in the year, to September/October; it is expensive but absolutely the best there is.

Avoid any butcher who has everything in the shop already hacked into tiny pieces; these pieces get drier and stringier with every hour they sit around. Better to make for the shop that has whole carcasses hanging up, even if it means waiting a bit longer for the piece you want. Beware also of any chops, steak or liver pre-packed in a cardboard tray; it may be convenient to carry home, but it will have extracted every last drop of juice from the meat by the time it gets there. Since the true art of butchery seems to be on the wane, it is as well to be equipped with the knowledge of a few boning methods, and the equipment with which to do it. A cleaver may make an unsuitable wedding present, but it is useful if you have forgotten to ask the butcher to cut up the bones and find they won't go in the pan; the flat sides can be used for beating steaks, pork fillet etc. A boning knife, having an extremely tough, narrow blade, can be slipped easily round complicated bones to pare away all the meat. A good sharpener and a set of straight-sided, sharp-pointed French knives, a carving knife and fork, plus some metal skewers for securing boned meat are the only other vital pieces of equipment, but a ham knife is useful if you are in the habit of buying large hams or pieces of gammon. Keep your knives razor sharp (a carbon steel is very good for this) and have them re-ground if possible about once a year. Little tungsten-steel wheel knife-sharpeners are not recommended because they leave a thin fragile edge that bends over as soon as you use any pressure. Table-sharpeners and electric knife-sharpeners are fine, provided you use them with care. When using a steel, keep the blade of the knife rather flat against it or you will be bending the edge backwards and forwards with every stroke, and weakening it.

Some offal, for example fry and chitterlings, is hard to buy and disappearing fast, especially in the South of England, where it is also almost impossible to buy mutton.

Stews, daubes and casseroles almost always make use of the cheaper cuts of meat, which are best bought in a piece and cut up at home, when every morsel of sinew and gristle can be carefully trimmed away; these stringy bits never really become tender and make an otherwise good stew seem less of a treat. Shin, oxtail, ox-tongue and salt-beef, especially brisket, are often disappointingly tough and the reason is almost always the same — undercooking; they must be simmered very gently for up to four hours or even longer, and plenty of time must be allowed for this. Since most daubes and casseroles reheat well, it is a very good idea to cook them the day before, so hungry people won't be kept waiting about for the oxtail to get tender. It also gives you a chance to remove all the fat from the top, before reheating. This fat, clarified, can sometimes be used for dripping.

Beef

1 Leg ** (for stews)
2 Top Rump *** (or Thick Flank, for pot-roasting)
3 Round
3a Topside *** (buttock steak from here for pot-roasting)
3c Aitchbone ** (usually included with topside or silverside)
4 Rump **** (grilling steak)
5 Fillet ***** (sometimes sold as one piece)
5a Rump Fillet *****
5b Chateaubriand *****
5c Tournedos *****
5d Filet Mignon *****
7 Wing Rib ****
8 Skirt * (for stews)
9 Kidney * (and beef suet)
10 Flank * (sold boned for stews and pies and salted for boiling, also for sausages)
11 Forerib *** (or Chine, also sold boned and rolled and as entrecote steaks ****)
12 Middle Rib ** (or Back Rib, for braising and pot-roasting)
12a Top Rib **
12b Flat Ribs ** (or oven-busters, for slow braising)
13 Brisket * (also sold boned and rolled and salted for boiling. Sometimes includes lower ends of clod, chuck, and flat ribs.)
14 Shin * (for beef tea and stock)
15 Chuck ** (sold boned, for stewing, braising or pot-roasting)
15a Top Legs ** (or Leg-of-Mutton cut)
15b Flat Ribs **
16 Neck * (or Sticking, for stewing)
17 Clod * (for stewing)
17b Part of Clod sometimes sold with brisket

1
3A
2
3C
8
9
5A
5B
6
5C
7
5D
HINDQUARTER
FOREQUARTER
10
11
13
12B
12A
12
15
15A
15B
17B
16
14
17

Beef

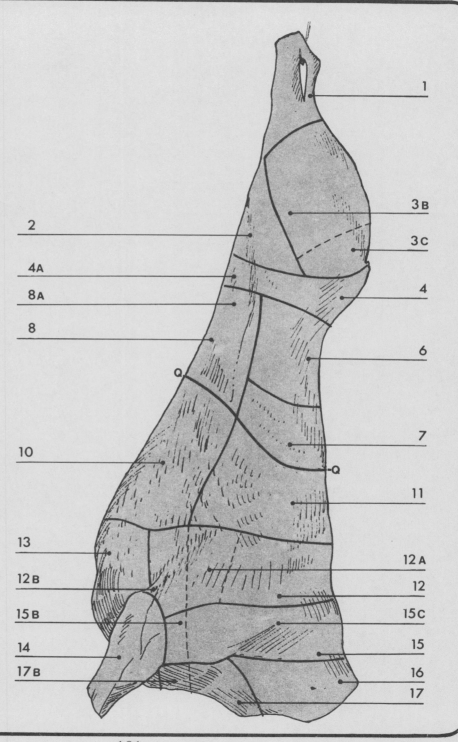

Q Quartering Line
1 Leg *
2 Top Rump *** (or Thick Flank)
3 Round
3b Silverside *** (sold salted for boiling : also for braising and pot-roasting)
3c Aitchbone ** (cheap because high proportion of bone)
4 Rump **** (grilling steak)
4a Layer of fat (Cod Fat) good for dripping
6 Sirloin **** (including Porter-house steaks for roasting, also sold boned and rolled)
7 Wing Rib **** (also sold boned and rolled for roasting and as T-bone and entrecote steaks)
8 Skirt * (or goose)
8a Cod Fat (see **4a**)
10 Flank **
11 Fore Rib ***
12 Middle Rib ** (or Back Rib)
12a Top Rib **
12b Flat Ribs ** (sometimes sold with brisket)
13 Brisket *
14 Shin *
15 Chuck **
15a Top Legs ** (or Leg-of-Mutton cut)
15b Flat Ribs ** (sometimes sold with brisket)
15c Blade **
16 Neck * (or Sticking)
17 Clod *
17b part of Clod sometimes sold with brisket.

Prices
* cheap : stew, mince
** middling : stew, braise
*** expensive : pot-roast
**** very expensive ⎱ roast, grill
***** astronomical ⎰

Note that cheap cuts come mainly from the forequarters and bellies, expensive cuts mainly from the hindquarters. Some butchers buy only hindquarters for this reason.

Also sold cheaply : Ox cheek (brawn), heart, tongue, tail, kidney, liver (rather strong-tasting), tripe, feet (or cowheels, very gelatinous—for brawn)

Pork

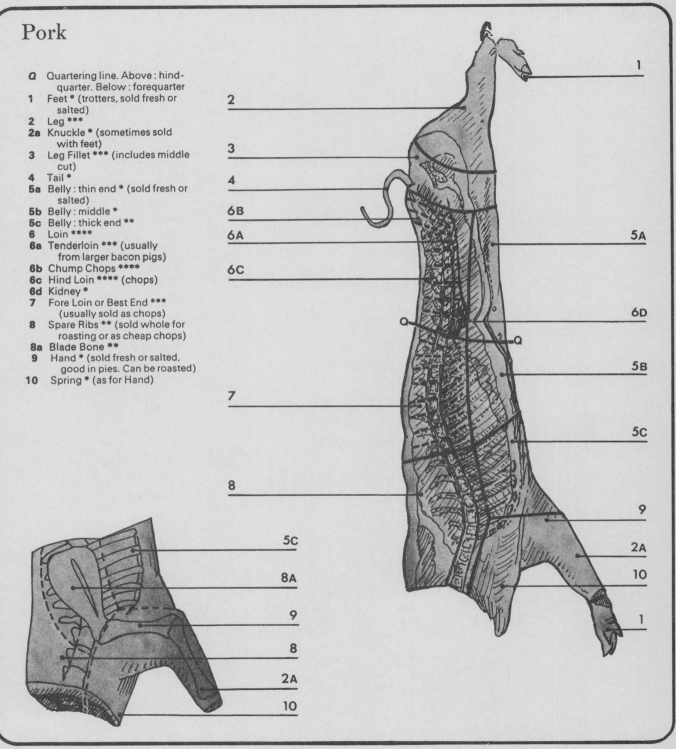

Q Quartering line. Above : hind-quarter. Below : forequarter
1 Feet * (trotters, sold fresh or salted)
2 Leg ***
2a Knuckle * (sometimes sold with feet)
3 Leg Fillet *** (includes middle cut)
4 Tail *
5a Belly : thin end * (sold fresh or salted)
5b Belly : middle *
5c Belly : thick end **
6 Loin ****
6a Tenderloin *** (usually from larger bacon pigs)
6b Chump Chops ****
6c Hind Loin **** (chops)
6d Kidney *
7 Fore Loin or Best End *** (usually sold as chops)
8 Spare Ribs ** (sold whole for roasting or as cheap chops)
8a Blade Bone **
9 Hand * (sold fresh or salted, good in pies. Can be roasted)
10 Spring * (as for Hand)

Pork

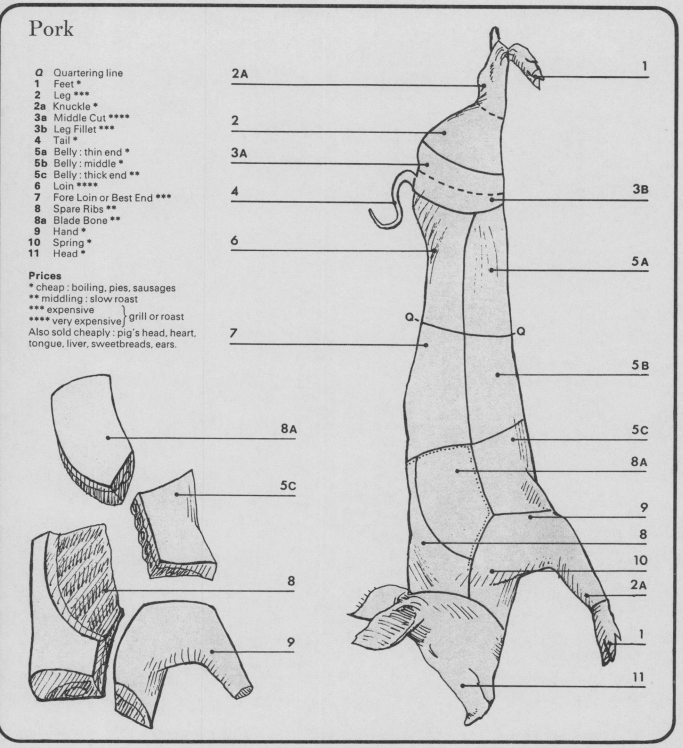

Q   Quartering line
1   Feet *
2   Leg ***
2a   Knuckle *
3a   Middle Cut ****
3b   Leg Fillet ***
4   Tail *
5a   Belly : thin end *
5b   Belly : middle *
5c   Belly : thick end **
6   Loin ****
7   Fore Loin or Best End ***
8   Spare Ribs **
8a   Blade Bone **
9   Hand *
10   Spring *
11   Head *

Prices
* cheap : boiling, pies, sausages
** middling : slow roast
*** expensive ⎫
**** very expensive ⎭ grill or roast
Also sold cheaply : pig's head, heart,
tongue, liver, sweetbreads, ears.

Veal

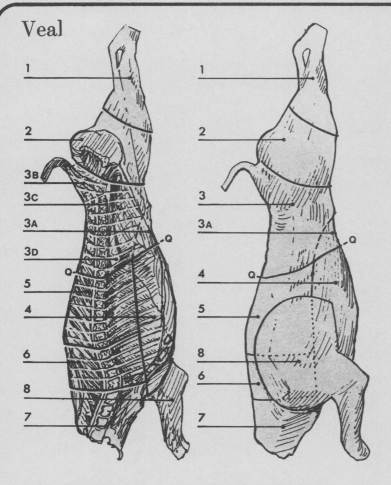

Q Quartering line
1 Knuckle ** (Osso Buco)
2 Leg Fillet **** (Escalopes)
3 Loin ***
3a Loin Flap (sometimes sold with loin or with breast)
3b Chump Chops ***
3c Loin Chops ***
3d Kidney ***
4 Breast * (can be boned, stuffed and rolled)
5 Best End of Neck ** (sold as cutlets or carré)
6 Middle neck * (cutlets)
7 Scrag *
8 Part of Shoulder

Also sold, but expensive : liver, kidneys

Q Quartering line
1 Knuckle **
2 Leg Fillet ****
3 Loin ** (sold with kidneys)
3a Loin Flap
4 Breast *
5 Best End of Neck **
6 Middle Neck *
7 Scrag *
8 Shoulder ** (can be boned, stuffed and rolled)

Prices
* cheap : pies, ragouts and stews
** middling : blanquettes, roasts
*** expensive } grill, roast, fry
**** very expensive } (escalopes)

Also sold cheaply : calves' head, tongue, brains, feet, sweetbreads, heart, tripe

Lamb

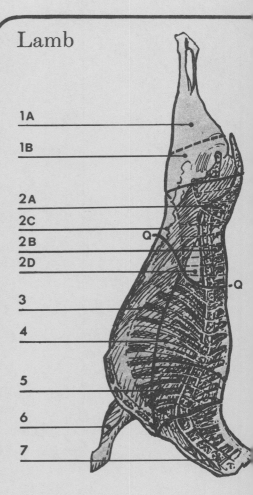

Q Quartering line
1 Leg ***
1a Half Leg, shank end ***
1b Half Leg, fillet end ***
2a Chump Chops ***
2b Loin chops ** (sold with kidneys)
2c Loin Flap (sold with loin or breast)
2d Kidney **
3 Breast *
4 Best End of Neck ** (also sold as cutlets ***)
5 Middle Neck ** (also sold as cutlets and carré)
6 Part of shoulder
7 Neck * (Scrag)

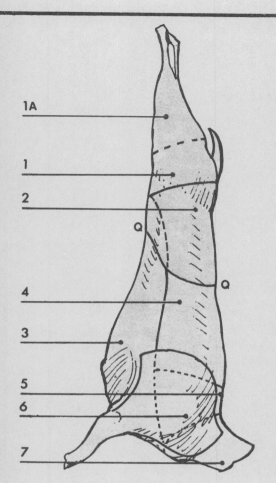

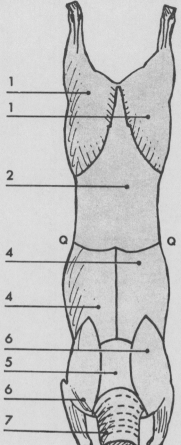

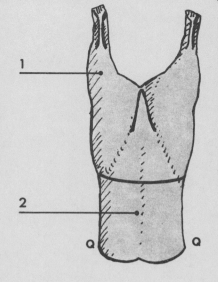

Q

Q Quartering line
1 Leg ***
1a Half Leg, shank end ***
1b Half Leg, fillet end ***
2 Loin *** (includes kidneys)
3 Breast * (can be boned, stuffed and rolled for roasting, also for soups and stews)
4 Best End of Neck **
5 Middle Neck **
6 Shoulder ** (can be boned, stuffed, rolled, or roasted whole)
7 Neck * (Scrag)

Q Quartering line
1 Legs *** (cut like this when a Saddle is required)
2 Saddle **** (includes kidneys and chump chops)
4 Best End of Neck **
5 Middle Neck **
6 Shoulders **
7 Neck * (Scrag. When combined with Best End and Middle Neck is a Target)

Q Quartering line
1 Haunch ****
2 Loin *** (Haunch and Loin together are a Baron of Lamb or Mutton)

Prices
* cheapest : stew and braise
** middling : braise and slow roast
*** expensive
**** very expensive } grill and roast

Also sold : Head, heart, tongues, brains, liver, tails, feet, and sweetbreads

Carving

All our information on carving comes from **Mr Fred Knock** of Simpson's-in-the-Strand, who has been carving there for over fifty years. His demonstrations were revelations of just how much good carving matters. A skilful carver can get nine lavish servings of beautiful slices from a joint that a bad carver will hack up into enough tough chunks for four. He can give everyone their fair share of the best, with more fat or less, outside or tender pink underdone middle, according to what they like.

BASIC RULES FOR FINE CARVING

1. Have good knives; you will need two, which you should keep specially for carving and which are not to be used for cutting up dogs' meat or sharpening pencils; first a small poultry knife with a 6″ blade, which is used for cutting through joints and removing bones; second a carving knife with a 9″ blade for slicing. For sharpening them you will need a good long magnetic steel, and for holding the meat steady have a small carving fork with curved prongs and a shield to protect your hand if the knife slips. A board with spikes is a good idea as it stops the meat sliding about.

2. Keep your knives sharp and always either wrap them up in a soft cloth before putting them away or keep them on a magnetic knife rack.

3. Allow the meat to set after it is cooked. Let it stand in a warm place for 20 to 30 minutes for a small joint or bird, longer for large joints. This makes the texture firm and means that you can cut thinner slices. The perfect way to keep it warm is over hot water — special plates used to exist — with a loosely fitting cover. A tight cover causes the skin to lose its crispness. But if you just put it on a very hot dish on the table and leave it there until everybody has washed their hands and sat down it will lose almost no heat until it is carved. You can also leave it to stand in the cooling oven.

4. Put the meat in the correct position for carving — shown in the diagrams in this section. Professional carvers always keep the best-looking uncarved side toward the diners, so that they are appetised by the view of plump juicy meat rather than shown a row of bones.

6. Cut several slices before you begin to share out the meat, so that each person gets some of the best.

7. Stand boned and rolled joints on end and carve horizontally, otherwise you will blunt your knife on the dish.

8. Use very little pressure on the knife — if it is really sharp it should slice through the meat as you draw it backwards and forwards towards you, using the full length of the blade.

9. Hold the knife with your forefinger along the back of the blade, it gives you more control.

10. Take your time at first, you will speed up with practice.

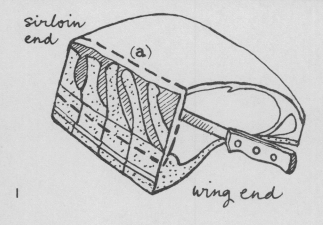

sirloin end (a) *wing end*

1

How to carve a Wing Rib or Sirloin of Beef on the Bone

Use a sharp long-bladed knife and have ready your carving fork and a spoon for the juices.

1. Having got your butcher to chine the joint — which means sawing through the backbone about two thirds of the way down, but leaving it attached during cooking to keep the meat succulent and give it flavour — cut these chined bones away (a).

2. If there is a lot of fat trim it away at (b) and (c). Trim away gristle at (c). Run the knife carefully between the meat and the bone, keeping it completely flat against the bone, so you do not waste the meat.

3. Start carving at the wing (thick) end (d), cutting at right angles to the spine but at a slight angle, otherwise you are left with an upright piece too wobbly to slice (e).

4. Finish by carving the wedge you are left with (e) gradually flattening it out.

☐ *This joint is half sirloin, half wing rib. It is rather expensive, but very good for a large party. Cooking it on the bone greatly improves the juiciness and flavour.*

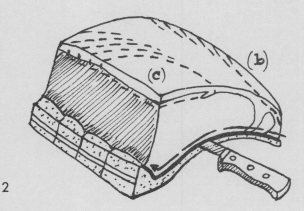

(b) (c) 2

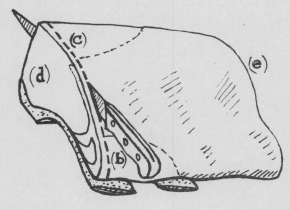

(d) (c) (e) (b) 3

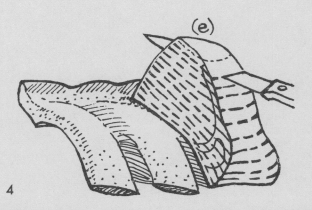

(e) 4

Flat Rib of Beef with Runner Beans

4 lbs middle, top or flat ribs (not wing or forerib)
2 lbs of runner beans (or bobby beans)
1 onion
1 tablespoon tomato purée
salt, pepper
nutmeg

Ask the butcher to leave the bones in the beef and slice off the surplus fat which you will need. Tie the joint round with string. Preheat the oven to Reg 3/325°. Cut the fat into small pieces, put it in a frying pan and render it down, with a lid on, over a low heat, while you slice the beans and chop the onion finely. Brown the meat all over in the melted fat. As soon as the meat is browned put it in a covered casserole in the oven and start cooking, while you continue with the vegetables. Fry the onions until golden in the same fat as the beef. Bring some salted water to the boil and blanch the beans. Let them boil 2–3 minutes and drain, keeping $\frac{1}{4}$ pint of their liquid. Turn the beans into the pan with the onions and fry them gently until they have absorbed some of the fat. Stir the purée into the water which you have kept from the beans, and add it to the beans and onions. Season well with salt, pepper and nutmeg. Take the casserole out of the oven, put the meat on a plate. Pour the contents of the frying pan into the casserole and put the meat back on top of the vegetables, on its side. Cover again and cook (still at Reg 3/325°) for $2\frac{1}{2}$–3 hours. Turn the meat over half way through. At the end it should have a roasted appearance and be tender, with a lot of gravy and some delicious beans. To serve, cut the bones off the joint first, then carve in neat horizontal slices. Remove the surplus fat from the gravy and strain into a jug, serve with the meat and beans.

For 6

Carbonnade Flamande

$1\frac{3}{4}$ lbs chuck steak
dripping
2 large onions, finely sliced
$\frac{1}{2}$ pint Guinness or brown ale
salt and freshly ground pepper
bayleaf, sprig of thyme, pinch nutmeg

Cut the trimmed beef into large cubes. Heat the dripping in a flame-proof casserole, and brown the meat really well all over, so that it has quite a crust on the outside. Remove the pieces to a dish and add the finely sliced onions to the dripping, adding more if necessary. Fry several minutes until the onions are nicely browned. Remove them and put them with the beef while you pour in three-quarters of the beer; let it froth up, scraping the bottom of the pan with a wooden spoon until you have loosened all the sediment. Return the beef and onions, add salt, pepper, herbs and nutmeg and simmer covered on top of the cooker, or in a slow oven, Reg 2/300°, for $2\frac{1}{2}$–3 hours, adding a little water if the gravy gets too thick.

Five minutes before serving add the rest of the beer, taste for seasoning and simmer five minutes more. Serve with boiled potatoes and drink beer with it. A salad of lettuce eaten off the same plate afterwards benefits from the juices of the carbonnade.

For 4–5

Aitchbone of Beef

This is a very large joint, consisting of rump, topside, silverside and brisket. While the quality of the meat on this cut is not as fine as best rump, fillet or sirloin, it does cost far less than half as much per pound, and is very well worth buying for large family dinners or informal parties. It can be eaten hot or cold.

A small aitchbone weighing ten pounds will feed at least ten people; when trimmed it will weigh about eight pounds. Keep the bones and trimmings removed by the butcher to make stock.

Preheat oven to Reg 7/425°. Rub the aitchbone with oil and garlic if liked. Put into the very hot oven, reducing the heat to Reg 4/350° after 20 minutes. Cook $2\frac{1}{4}$ hours, basting from time to time. There is a large amount of dripping from this joint for roast potatoes, and very good juices for gravy; because it is such a large joint it is juicier.

Serves 10–15 according to size

Boiled Beef and Carrots

4–5 lbs salt beef (brisket or silverside) tied firmly
 with string
$1\frac{1}{2}$–2 lbs large carrots, scraped and halved
3–4 Spanish onions, peeled
3–4 turnips, peeled
bouquet garni
a few peppercorns
dumplings (optional)

Always check with the butcher to see if the beef needs soaking, and if so soak overnight. Put it in a large saucepan with any bones that the butcher may have included, barely cover with cold water and bring it slowly to the boil. Skim thoroughly and add half the vegetables and the herbs and peppercorns. Cover and simmer very gently for $2\frac{1}{2}$–3 hours, longer if the meat is particularly tough. Taste the liquid occasionally, and if it is too salt add more water.

Cook the potatoes and fresh vegetables in with it for the last 25–30 minutes and, if you like, add dumplings too.

Serve the beef with the freshly cooked vegetables, dumplings and some of the broth in which it cooked. Keep the rest of the broth for soup.

For 8

A very simple Beef Stew

3 lbs stewing beef, leg or chuck
4 oz flour
salt and freshly ground pepper
1 pint best beef stock, or use plain water
oil and dripping to brown the meat
24 button onions
24 slender carrots
½ lb button mushrooms (optional)

Trim any gristle or fat from the meat and cut it into cubes. Season the flour generously and roll the meat in it. Melt one tablespoon of dripping and one of oil in a flameproof casserole, large enough for all the meat and vegetables, and brown the meat very thoroughly. If any flour remains, brown it, too, in a little more fat. Heat the stock or water and pour on to the meat. If you like lots of gravy add a further ½ pint. When it is all gently simmering, cover and transfer to a very low oven, Reg 1/275°. After one hour put the little onions and carrots, carefully cleaned and scraped, on top of the meat. Half an hour later add the mushrooms. Depending on the quality of the meat, two hours should be enough to cook this stew, but longer won't hurt.

□ *This stew tastes really rich, especially if proper beef stock is used; it is hard to believe there is no wine or garlic in it. The gravy should be smooth and velvety and a good colour.*

Beef Olives

1 lb topside or rump steak, sliced thin
3 oz breadcrumbs
1 dessertspoon parsley, chopped
1 oz suet, finely chopped
2 anchovies, chopped
1 teaspoon lemon juice
1 egg
salt and freshly ground pepper
1 oz dripping
1 oz flour
1 pint fresh stock or water

Beat the slices of beef to flatten them. Cut them into pieces about $3 \times 1\frac{1}{2}$ inches. Make a stuffing with the breadcrumbs, parsley, suet, anchovies, lemon juice, beaten egg, salt and pepper. Lay a little of this on each strip of beef, roll up and tie with a piece of string or thread. Heat the dripping in a frying pan and brown the beef rolls all over. Remove and drain on kitchen paper, while you sprinkle the flour into the pan, brown it, then add hot water or stock gradually, stirring to avoid lumps. Bring to the boil, season, return the meat and simmer uncovered for one hour, turning the rolls occasionally. When tender remove the string or thread from the olives and put them with the gravy into a hot dish.

For 4

Beef Goulash

2 lbs stewing beef, leg or chuck
2 lbs onions
1 lb tomatoes, skinned and quartered
2 dessertspoons paprika
8 peppercorns
salt
dripping

Trim the beef carefully and cut into cubes. Peel and quarter the onions, or cut into eights if very large. Fry them in two tablespoons of dripping in a flameproof casserole, put them aside and brown the beef, adding more dripping if necessary. Return the onions, sprinkle with paprika and stir in well. Add the tomatoes, peppercorns and salt to taste. Cover and put in a low oven, Reg 2/325°, for two hours or until tender.

This is very good reheated the following day. The juice from the tomatoes and from the meat and onions, which is extracted with the help of the paprika, provides an astounding amount of delicious thick gravy.

Serve with plain boiled potatoes, on to which you can sprinkle some dill seeds if liked.

For 4

Chilli Con Carne

2 lbs beef, skirt or chuck
1 lb red kidney beans
2 large onions, chopped
olive oil
2 teaspoons ground turmeric
1 tablespoon ground coriander
1–2 teaspoons ground chilli, according to how hot
   you like it
1 teaspoon fresh green chilli, chopped (optional)
2 cloves garlic, crushed
1 lb fresh tomatoes, peeled and chopped
salt and freshly ground pepper

Soak the beans overnight. Fry the chopped onions in olive oil in a flameproof casserole, turn up the heat and add the meat either cut in one-inch cubes, or minced if you like. Fry fairly fast for five to ten minutes, scraping the sediment from the bottom of the casserole. Add the spices, garlic and chilli and continue to fry, stirring, for several minutes. Then add the peeled chopped tomatoes, salt and pepper and simmer, covered, until the meat is tender, about two hours if it is cubed, less if it is minced. Meanwhile the beans should be put in a large pan of cold water and brought slowly to the boil; add salt after one hour. They take $1\frac{1}{2}$–2 hours to cook and can be combined with the meat half an hour before serving, or served separately. A dish of plain white rice is a good foil to the dark beans and hot beef stew.

For 6–8

Oxtail Stew

2 small or 1 very large oxtail, jointed
dripping, or butter and oil for browning
seasoned flour
4 oz salt pork or bacon, cut in cubes
glass red wine (optional)
2–3 large onions, peeled and stuck with cloves
2 cloves garlic, bouquet garni
2 tablespoons or 1 small tin tomato purée
1 pint beef stock, water or bouillon
1 lb carrots, 1 turnip, 1 lb leeks
4–5 sticks celery, seasoning

Start early in the morning by soaking the pieces of oxtail in cold salt water, for 2–4 hours. Remove and dry them well. Prepare the vegetables, cutting up everything but the leeks. Preheat the oven to Reg 2/300°. Roll the pieces of meat in four or five tablespoons of well-seasoned flour until they are thoroughly coated. Heat the dripping or butter and oil in a large flameproof casserole and toss the bacon or pork cubes in it until the fat starts to run. Remove them, and brown the oxtail pieces very well all over. Pour in the wine and let it bubble up, then add the pork, onions, garlic, herbs, half the carrots, the turnip and the warmed water or stock mixed with the tomato purée. Bring slowly to the boil and put the casserole, covered, into the oven. Cook at Reg 2/300° for one hour, then at Reg 1½/290° for a further 2–3 hours.

Three quarters of an hour before serving skim the fat off the top of the stew, check the seasoning and add the remaining vegetables. Continue cooking until they are tender. Skim again before serving with potatoes and/or dumplings.

☐ *This is not a traditional English oxtail stew and has a richer flavour.*

For 4–6

Corned Beef Hash

8 oz tin of corned beef, cut into chunks
1 lb potatoes, peeled, boiled and cut in cubes
3–4 onions, sliced and fried golden in lard
lard or dripping
salt, freshly ground pepper, and a dash of Worcester
  sauce

Mix all the ingredients together with a fork, in a large bowl. Heat a couple of tablespoons of lard or dripping in the biggest frying pan you have. Tip the hash into the hot fat and flatten it gently. Cook for about five minutes, shaking the pan from time to time. When a crust has formed over the bottom of the hash put a large flat plate over the frying pan and turn the whole thing over. Put another tablespoon of lard or dripping in the now empty frying pan. Slide the hash back into the pan with the crust now on top. Cook another five minutes, until there is a rustling crust on the bottom. Serve in big slices; it should be lovely and moist inside. It will keep warm in a low oven for a while without going soggy.

For 4

Beef Stew with Cloves

2 lbs stewing beef or veal
3–4 onions, peeled and sliced
2 cloves garlic, sliced
6 cloves
2 teaspoons cumin
2–3 tomatoes, peeled and sliced
a glass of red wine
salt, ground pepper
chopped parsley
olive oil

Cut the beef into large pieces, each weighing about 3 oz. Fry these pieces in oil until they are brown, remove them to a dish and fry the sliced onions, adding a little more oil if necessary. Return the meat, add the garlic, cloves and cumin. Stir well and cook fast for a minute or two. Add the tomatoes and red wine, salt, parsley and pepper. Bring to the boil and stew gently for 3 hours or until the meat is tender. If you prefer you can cook it in the oven at Reg 1½–2/275°–300°.

☐ *The very strong cumin taste makes this interesting.*

For 4–6

Beef and Tomato Stew

4 onions
2 oz pork fat or lard
2 lbs stewing steak in a piece
2 tablespoons tomato purée
2 fresh tomatoes, skinned and chopped
1 bouquet of marjoram, thyme, bay leaf and parsley
1 small glass water
salt, freshly ground pepper.

Chop the onions finely. Put them in a flameproof casserole with the pork fat and cook slowly for 5 minutes, stirring until they are beginning to soften. Meanwhile cut the stewing steak into large pieces, ½″ thick and 2″ square. Lay these over the onions, cover the casserole and cook gently for 10 minutes, until the meat has lost its redness. Mix the purée with a little water and add this, together with the chopped tomatoes, to the stew. Sprinkle with salt and pepper and lay the bouquet on top. Cover and cook gently on the top of the stove for 2½ hours, or until the meat is tender. (This can also be cooked in the oven at Reg 3/325° for 2–3 hours.) Serve with noodles or rice.

For 4

Spiced Brisket

3 lbs piece of lean rolled brisket
salt, pepper
6–10 cloves
a bouquet of herbs
1 carrot
1 onion
water

Rub the surface of the meat with salt and pepper and stick in the cloves. Check that the meat is tied firmly and put it in a saucepan with the bouquet, onion and carrot, and a little more salt. Cover with cold water, bring gently to the boil and allow to simmer quietly until completely tender (2–3 hours).

Remove from pan and drain well. Use some of the liquid for gravy and keep the rest for stock. Serve with potatoes or bread.

☐ *This is only worth doing with a large piece, as a small piece tends to get dry.*

For 6

Bollito Misto

1 small tongue, medium salted (soaked overnight)
2 lb piece topside, or silverside
1 lb belly of pork, salted or fresh (soaked if salt)
1 small 1½–2 lb chicken
2 large onions in skins (roast in the oven until slightly soft)
1–2 leeks, 2 sticks celery
3 large carrots, 1 lb new potatoes
1 lb baby turnips, 2 lbs new carrots
peppercorns, bay leaf, parsley
Parmesan, grated

Put the tongue, beef and pork belly in a casserole or large saucepan with the large onions in their skins, leeks, celery, large carrots, peppercorns, bay leaf and parsley. Cover with plenty of water, bring slowly to the boil, and turn down to simmering point. Skim *really well*, several times, this is important as the broth must be clear. Let it simmer until the tongue is almost tender (about 2½ hours) then add the chicken, and simmer on until everything is cooked (from 1–2 hours more).

Meanwhile cook — we think separately but do whichever you prefer — the new carrots, potatoes, and baby turnips. Serve the plain broth first with Parmesan, having put the meat (the tongue ready skinned) on a big dish to keep hot — it must be very hot. Now serve the meat, all four kinds to everybody, surrounded by young vegetables and with salsa verde (page 174).

☐ *Italian version of Pot au Feu.*

For about 10

Summer Veal Stew

2½–3 lbs boned breast of veal (make stock from
   bones)
1 large onion, chopped
butter or oil to brown meat in
1–2 oz flour
a dash of white wine or cider
stock or water, salt, pepper
parsley, slice of lemon peel
1 lb button onions, peeled and blanched for 10
   minutes in boiling salted water
1 lb young fresh peas

Preheat the oven to Reg 2½/310°. Cut the veal
into neat 1″ cubes. Brown the meat in a large
flameproof casserole. Remove it to a plate. Add
the onion and let it soften. Return the meat,
sprinkle with the flour and stir until it thickens.
Add the wine or cider, and stock gradually, and
let it bubble 2–3 minutes. Add seasoning,
parsley tied in a bunch, and a slice of lemon
peel. Cover and cook in the oven for 1–1½ hours.
Then add the shelled peas and onions, and cook
until both are tender. Remove parsley and lemon
peel and serve from the casserole with plain new
potatoes or rice.

The sauce is very much improved at the end by
the addition of an egg yolk beaten with lemon
juice and slowly added. Do not let it boil.

For 6

Osso Buco

2 whole veal shins, including bones, sawn across
   into 1½″ pieces
2 tablespoons olive oil
2 anchovies
1 small glass white wine
1 lb tomatoes
2 bay leaves
a bunch of parsley, celery tops, sage or rosemary
salt, pepper
To finish: 1 clove garlic, few sprigs parsley
              2 strips lemon peel

Brown the meat all over in oil, in the casserole
it is to be served in. The meat pieces should all
stand side by side with the bone upright. Add
the chopped anchovies, let them cook a minute,
then add the wine and let it bubble up.
Meanwhile skin and chop the tomatoes. Add
them to the meat, together with the bunch of
herbs and enough light stock or warm water to
come half way up the meat. Season with salt
and pepper and bring to simmering point before
covering and putting the casserole into a moderate
oven Reg 3/325° for 1½ hours. Turn the pieces
of meat once. Just before serving remove the
bunch of herbs and chop the parsley, garlic and
lemon peel very finely. Sprinkle it over the meat
and serve with Italian rice, risotto milanese or
noodles, giving each person a fair share of marrow
bones.

☐ *English butchers don't always understand what
you need veal shin bones for and unless it is cut
correctly the dish will not work. So tell him exactly
how you want the bones — cut across into slices
(looking somewhat like oxtail) with 1 to 1½ inches
of marrow-bone through the middle of each. There
should be a decent amount of meat on each, and one
shin should make four good slices.*

For 4

Vitello Tonnata

2 lbs leg of veal, boned and rolled
12 anchovy fillets
7 oz tin tunny fish
3 carrots
2 onions
1 stick celery
1 small glass white wine
2 tablespoons wine vinegar
bouquet thyme, parsley and bayleaf
salt, pepper, olive oil
½ pint stock
lemon juice
tablespoon of capers

Make cuts in the veal with a sharp pointed knife, and push half an anchovy fillet into each one as you make it. When it is well larded with anchovies put it in a fireproof casserole on a layer of sliced carrots, onions and celery. Add the white wine, vinegar, herbs, salt (not much because of the anchovies), pepper and stock. Braise the veal, covered, at Reg 3½/3350 for 1½ hours, turning it once.

Allow to cool in its liquid, remove it to a dish, put in the tunny fish and allow the liquid to reduce for 20–30 minutes.

Skim off any excess oil and sieve the sauce through the fine blade of a moulin-légumes together with any remaining anchovies.

Gradually stir a tablespoon or two of olive oil into this sauce — like mayonnaise it can curdle, so take it slowly.

Finally add lemon juice and stir in the capers, it should be a fine, fairly sharp pale pinky-beige sauce.

Carve the veal into thinnish slices and arrange them one at a time on a serving dish, giving each one a spoonful of the sauce. Spread the remaining sauce over the top, and allow to stand for several hours or overnight.

For 8

Steak and Kidney Pie

For the pastry
4 oz self-raising flour
4 oz plain flour
4 oz butter (or lard if you prefer)

For the filling
2 lbs chuck steak
½ lb ox kidney
bay leaf, 1 medium onion
1½ oz seasoned flour
water, 1 egg
2 oz dripping
pinch salt, water

Make the pastry and leave it to rest in a cold place. Preheat oven to Reg 7/425°. Trim the steak and kidney and cut it all up into nice pieces. Toss the meat in seasoned flour (you can add a pinch of dried mustard to the salt and pepper if you like) and brown it in good dripping. Brown the chopped onion. Mix the steak, kidney and onion, adding a bay leaf. Put it in a 12″ pie dish with a pie funnel in the centre. Add water to come almost, but not quite, to the top of the meat. Cover with pastry. Decorate and glaze with beaten egg, to which is added a pinch of salt and dash of water. After 15 minutes reduce heat to Reg 4/350°, after another 10 minutes look to see if the pastry is coloured yet. If it is, cover firmly with damped double greaseproof paper to prevent the pastry burning. Give the pie 1½–2 hours cooking in all. This is a much better way of making steak and kidney pie than recipes which tell you to pre-stew the meat.

☐ *If you can add a pigeon or two it is a great luxury and much improves the flavour.*

For 6

Steak and Kidney Pudding

For the pudding:
8 oz self-raising flour
4 oz shredded beef suet
salt
water
For the filling.
1 lb decent stewing steak
3 lambs kidneys or 4–6 oz ox kidney
2 oz seasoned flour
stock
1 medium-sized onion, chopped
¼ lb mushrooms, sliced (if liked)

Trim the meat and cut it into neat pieces. Skin, core, and slice the kidneys. Roll meat and kidney in seasoned flour. Add onion and mushrooms (if liked). Make the pastry by mixing suet, flour and salt with a little cold water. Roll it out and, keeping a piece for the lid, line a greased pudding basin. (This basin should be large enough for the pudding to increase in size a little during cooking.) Put in the meat, etc., adding a little more seasoning and cold stock almost to cover. Shape the lid, damp the edges of the pastry, and seal firmly. The pudding should be at least one inch below the top of the basin. Cover with greased paper, then foil, or a cloth, and tie well (see page 225). Cook in a large pan of boiling water (with a lid) for 5 hours. Keep the water boiling and well topped up. You can cook it half one day and half the next if necessary. Serve it turned out of the basin with more gravy and plain boiled potatoes, carrots or cabbage, and mustard.

☐ *Some people prefer to leave out the onions and mushrooms. Cook it less long if you use better quality meat.*

For 4–6

Blanquette de Veau

2 lbs shoulder or breast of veal
2 bayleaves
12 peppercorns
2 onions, 4 carrots
salt
4 tablespoons good stock (if available)
2 oz butter
1 oz flour
½ lb mushrooms (optional)
2 egg yolks
1 small lemon
4 tablespoons cream

Cut the veal into one-inch squares, removing the fat. Put in a saucepan, cover with cold water, bring to the boil and let it simmer with two bayleaves and a few peppercorns for ¾ hour. Now add the sliced onions, a piece of lemon peel, a few carrots and some salt. Four tablespoons of good stock can also be added at this stage. Simmer on for another 1¼ hours. Melt the butter in another pan, stir in the flour and one pint of the hot veal broth, strained. Add the cleaned mushrooms and cook for ten minutes. Then, off the heat, add the strained pieces of veal, the egg yolks beaten with the juice of a small lemon, a little more stock if needed and the cream. Heat thoroughly, letting the egg yolks thicken slightly, taste for seasoning and serve with a fresh-looking vegetable such as French beans or fresh peas.

For 6

Buying cheap English veal for a blanquette is quite all right as long as it is well trimmed. But this is difficult to do when the meat is raw, even with a very sharp knife, because of the abundant gristle and hidden pipes. However, if you cut it into large pieces — if a shoulder, take out the bone, and if breast cut into three or four chunks — and then blanch it for five or ten minutes and refresh in cold water, this both solidifies the meat and removes some of the scum. The veal can then be trimmed of unwanted pieces and cut into neat shapes. Keep the liquid in which the veal was blanched; together with the bones and trimmings it makes a good jellied stock.

How to Carve a whole Leg of Lamb or Pork

Sharpen your long-bladed carving knife, have ready your carving fork and a spoon for the juices.

1. Put the joint with the rounded meatier side (outside) uppermost. Shading indicates the bone.

2. Remove the shank bone (a) with a small knife if the butcher has not already done so. Using your fork to steady the joint, start slicing away from the knuckle (b). Make thin even slices and alternate them with closer-grained vertical slices from the front of the leg at (c).

3. When the 'eye' appears (a small oval disc of fat in the middle of all the lean) (d) turn the joint over.

4. Take off nice big flat slices from this new side (e) keeping the joint steady with your fork. Continue to carve slices from these three surfaces by turns until you reach the bone. Don't start serving until you have some of the meat from all three sides.

N.B. Carving the meat from a V-shaped cut in the middle is the most wasteful method of dealing with a leg of lamb.

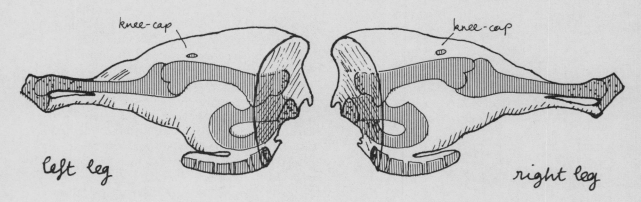

knee-cap   knee-cap

left leg   right leg

1

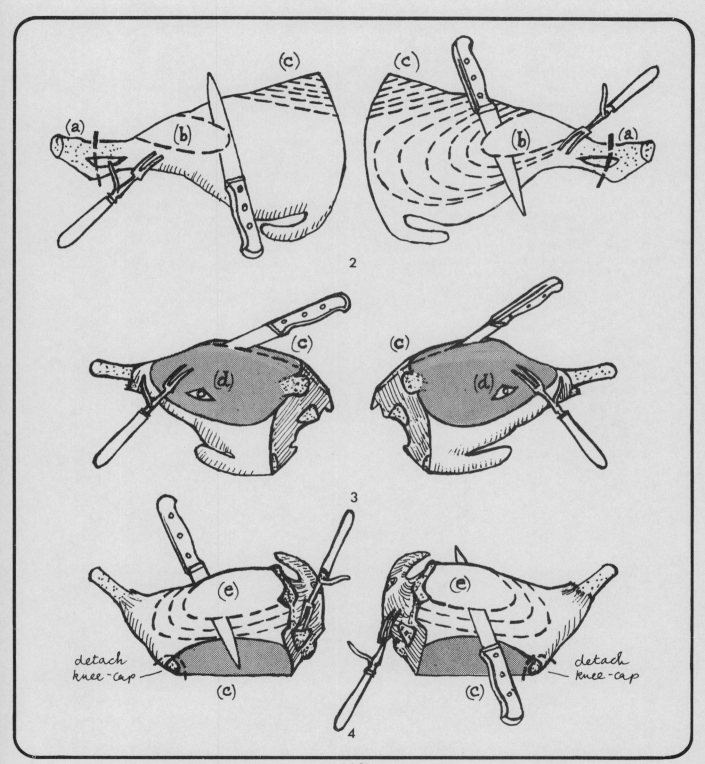

detach
knee-cap

detach
knee-cap

2

3

4

119

How to Carve a whole Shoulder of Lamb

The astonishing fact is that, if you carve it correctly, a shoulder of lamb provides enough good slices to feed eight or nine people.

1. Place the shoulder, left or right, with the knuckle to the left (shaded lines show position of bones).

2. Carve vertical slices from behind the elbow (a) parallel to the edge of the blade-bone and working towards it. Raise the joint off the plate with the fork or you will blunt your knife on the plate. Carve more vertical slices from the front of the blade-bone (b). These will be fattish slices, so find out who likes a bit of fat and give these slices to them.

3. Cut a few vertical slices from (c). Hold the knuckle with your hand to steady the joint.

4. Turn the joint over, and, starting halfway across the underside, carve large thin horizontal slices. This is a very good and juicy part, so don't start serving the meat until you have reached this point. There is plenty of meat under here: when you have reached the bone take a few horizontal slices from (d), the underside of the first leg-bone.

Left Shoulder

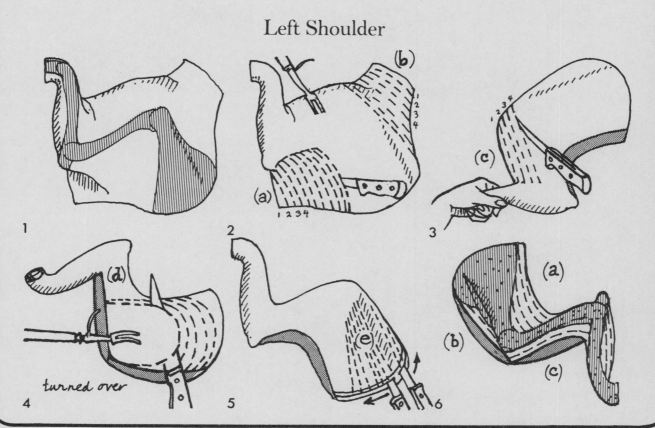

5. Turn the shoulder over again and insert the knife horizontally between the bone and the meat and slide it from the side of the vertical ridge in the middle of the shoulder-blade to the edge of the joint. This loosens the meat and enables you to carve nice vertical slices parallel to the ridge (e).

6. Finish by carving a few more vertical slices at (a), (b) and (c).

You will be left with nothing much but bones.

Right Shoulder

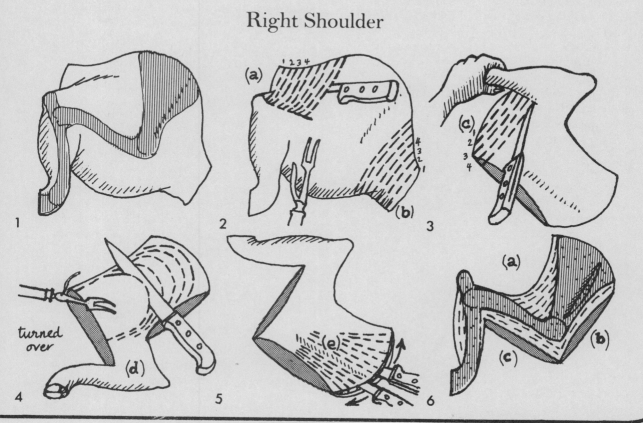

Lamb Polo

1 lb dried apricots
2 boned shoulders lamb
  (ask the butcher to do it for you)
4 onions, chopped
4 oz cooking butter (2 oz are for the rice)
2 teaspoons ground coriander
1 teaspoon ground cinnamon
2 teaspoons ground cumin
salt and freshly ground pepper
2 lbs rice

Pour one pint of boiling water over the apricots and allow them to soak for an hour or two. Start cooking the rice in the Persian way (page 57). Trim most of the fat from the meat, and cut it into one-inch squares.

Melt half the butter in a large flameproof casserole, soften the chopped onions and brown lightly, stirring all the time. Turn up the heat and add the lamb. Brown all over very thoroughly and add the spices. Fry them, stirring well, for two or three minutes, then add the apricots with the water in which they soaked, plenty of salt and plenty of pepper. Add enough water just to cover the meat and simmer, covered, for 1½ hours, or until tender, stirring from time to time. Serve with Persian rice.

☐ *This is a Persian recipe; it has a beautiful, spicy, strange flavour and smell. It can well be made the day before as it is improved, if anything, by being kept and reheated.*

For 10–12

How to Carve a Saddle of Lamb or Mutton

A saddle is not an economical joint, it just looks very magnificent and tastes extremely delicious. To an inexperienced carver it is a complete puzzle, practically all bone with some long thin pockets of meat, and a lot of waste. If you just cut all the middle out you may find you don't have enough to go round, but with skilful carving you should be able to feed 8 to 10 people. Carve with the tail end to the left and the skin side up, and cut quite a few slices before you start handing it round.

1. The first cut is very important. Make it parallel to and at least 1″ from the backbone (a) to (b).

2. Cut slices to make a wedge shape at (a) and (b) as shown. Cut a few little slices (c), for those who like fat.

3. Continue to cut fairly thick slices as shown, turning the dish if necessary, long slices from the loin end and short slices from the chump or tail end. The projecting haunch bone (d) will gradually be uncovered.

4. Turn the joint over, still working on the same half, and carve long thin slices from the fillet (e) to (f). This is the best part and should go to favoured guests. There are some small chunks of well-done meat to be found at (g).

5. Finish one side before you start carving the other. A good carver makes a clean job of it and leaves very little but bones.

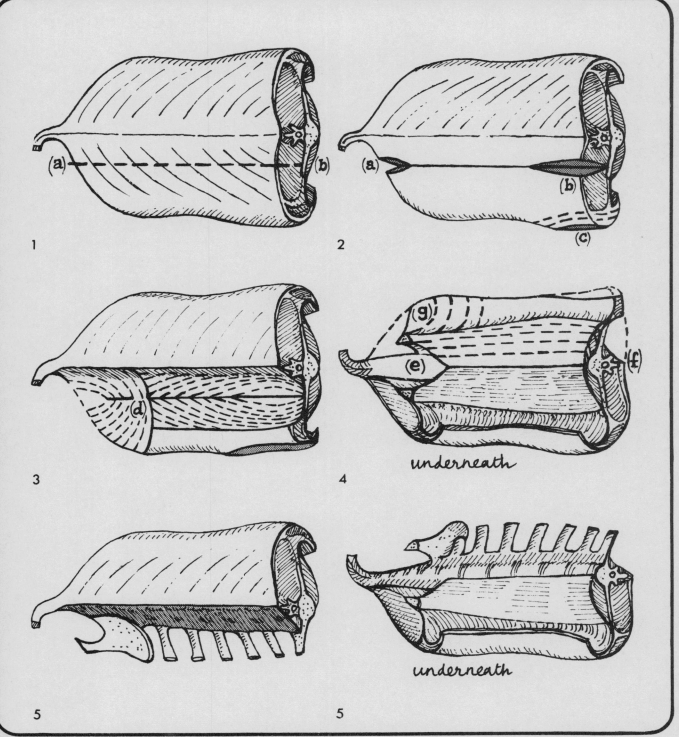

1

2

(a)   (b)

(a)   (b)

(c)

3

(d)

4

(g)

(e)

(f)

underneath

5

5

underneath

Guard of Honour

A pair of best ends of lamb, chined (consisting
   of about 8 cutlets each)
4–6 oz breadcrumbs
1–2 shallots, peeled and chopped
1 egg beaten in a little milk
½ teaspoon grated lemon peel
parsley and thyme, chopped
salt and pepper

Make up the guard of honour as shown. Chop
or mince the trimmings, having removed some of
the fat. Mix them with the breadcrumbs, herbs,
seasoning, lemon peel and enough egg and milk
to bind them. Preheat the oven to Reg 5/375°.
Put the two prepared pieces together as shown
and fill the cavity with the stuffing. Skewer the
pieces together with 2 skewers and cover the
bones with silver foil to prevent them burning.
Rub a little oil over the outside of the lamb,
sprinkle with salt and roast for 1 hour, or if it is
stuffed 1½ hours. To serve cut down between the
bones and give each person two cutlets and some
stuffing.

☐ *This is equally good made with or without
stuffing, and served plain or with red currant jelly.*

For 8

To Make a Guard of Honour

1. Take a pair of best ends of lamb, each
consisting of 6–8 chops. Tell the butcher what
you want them for, so that he can trim the bones,
but don't let him separate them.

2. Skin them, if necessary.

3. On the inside score a line across the ribs
about 2½″ down. Cut the meat out between the
ribs as far down as this line. Keep the trimmings
for stuffing or gravy-making.

4. Fit the two sides together interlocking the
ribs as shown. Fill the cavity with stuffing if you
like, or serve it, when roasted, with watercress
in the cavity. Cover the rib bones with silver
foil while cooking. Skewer the two sides together
if using stuffing.

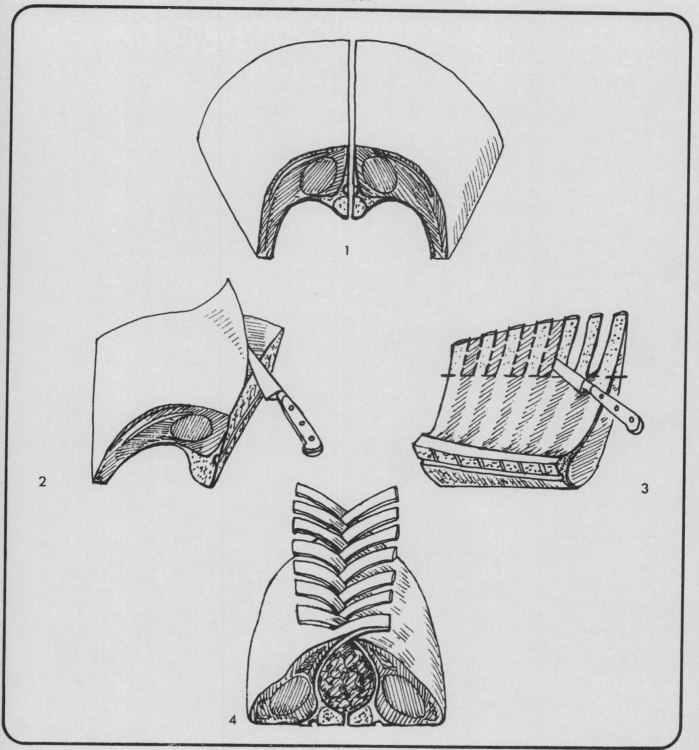

1

2

3

4

Shoulder of Lamb with Avgolemono Sauce

1 shoulder lamb
4 cloves garlic
2 lbs broad beans
2 egg yolks
juice 1 lemon
salt and pepper
a little chicken stock
butter or oil for roasting

Ask the butcher to chop the shoulder down through the bone, but not right through the meat underneath, to make slices one inch thick. The shoulder is now easy to carve into slices but still in one piece (see diagram). Put in a roasting pan, fat side up, with the peeled cloves of garlic in the cuts. Spread the joint with a little butter or oil, sprinkle with salt and pepper, and roast at Reg 5/375° for ¾–1 hour, basting two or three times.

Meanwhile cook the shelled broad beans in boiling salted water and drain, keeping some of the water they cooked in. Beat together the egg yolks and lemon juice and add about half a cup of the bean liquid. When the lamb is cooked remove it from the roasting pan and keep it warm on a dish in the oven. Remove the garlic and skim off the fat from the juices in the pan, before stirring them into the egg and lemon sauce. Put this sauce in a pan over a very low flame, add the broad beans and about two tablespoons of stock, season and thicken very gently — it takes a long time — without ever boiling.

Slice up the shoulder, pour on the sauce, and serve with plain rice or baked potatoes and a simple salad.

☐ *This is a Greek dish and very delicious; the lemon counteracts the richness of a fat shoulder very well.*

For 6

Epigrams of Lamb

1 lb breast of lamb
1½ oz butter, melted
1 egg, beaten
pinch thyme
1 cupful fresh white breadcrumbs
salt and freshly ground pepper
Béarnaise sauce (page 248), or tomato sauce
  (page 253)

Remove the bones, gristle and some of the fat from the cooked lamb while it is still warm, and cut into neat fingers or squares when cold. Mix the melted butter with the beaten egg, thyme and seasoning. Dip each piece of lamb into this mixture, then into fresh breadcrumbs.

Grill under a moderate heat until browned both sides, and serve with Béarnaise or tomato sauce. They make crisp little morsels which should be enjoyed by children.

☐ *This dish is quite luxurious and rich, and yet is made out of the most humble piece of meat that has already done a stint in the cooking of Scotch Broth. It is definitely better if it is eaten fairly soon after it comes out of the broth.*

For 2–3

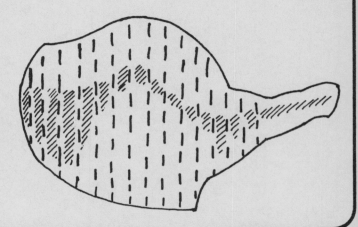

Boiled Leg of Lamb and Caper Sauce

1 large leg New Zealand lamb
1 swede or turnip
1 leek, 1 onion, 2 carrots
2 tablespoons sea salt, less if using ordinary salt
for caper sauce:
salt
1 oz butter, ½ oz flour
3 or 4 tablespoons lamb cooking liquid
1 tablespoon capers
1 tablespoon caper vinegar
thin cream or top of the milk

Cover the leg of lamb with cold water in a large saucepan, and bring it slowly to the boil. Skim impeccably, add the peeled whole vegetables and salt. Simmer, covered, very slowly so the water just turns lazily in the pan, and keep skimmed. It will take 1¾–2 hours. Strain well before serving. Make a sauce with the butter, flour, three to four tablespoons of lamb broth, strained, and the caper vinegar. Add the capers and a little cream, and if you like you can add the onion that cooked with the lamb, chopped fairly small. Season the sauce and serve in a jug: it should be the consistency of cream. Boiled potatoes are best with this dish, or perhaps turnips, cooked in with the meat for the last 25 minutes.

☐ *If you buy New Zealand leg of lamb towards the end of summer it is very cheap and on the large side. Boiled, it tastes almost as good as the mutton that used to be available, and served with caper sauce it is perfect.*

For 6–8

Navarin

2 lbs best end of lamb (or mutton if you can get it)
2 tablespoons butter
salt, pepper
a teaspoon of sugar
2 tablespoons flour
½–¾ pint water, warmed
a bouquet of herbs
½ lb very small onions
1½ lbs new potatoes, or small old ones, peeled

Ask the butcher to separate each chop and cut off the ends. There should be 3 or 4 neat little chops for each person. Melt the butter in an ovenproof casserole, and brown the meat on both sides. Sprinkle with salt and pepper, and clear a little space at the bottom of the casserole. Sprinkle the sugar there, and watch it until it caramelises. This is very important as it gives the finished dish its golden colour. Next sprinkle the flour over the meat and stir it round well. Add the warm water and mix it well with the meat. Add the little onions and the bouquet and put the lid on the casserole. Let it simmer on top or in the oven (Reg 2/300°) for an hour. After this time remove as much fat as you can. Push the potatoes into the meat and return the pot, covered, to the heat, for at least another hour. Serve when the potatoes are soft and golden (remove the bouquet).

☐ *You can add turnip and carrot cut small, with shelled peas and beans at the same time as the potatoes. It then becomes Navarin Printanière.*

For 4

Lancashire Hot-Pot

2–3 lbs middle neck of lamb, cut into chops and
    trimmed of fat
8 medium potatoes, peeled and thickly sliced
3 medium onions, sliced
3 lambs kidneys, skinned, cored and sliced
4 oz mushrooms, sliced if large
12 shelled oysters are traditional but not vital
1 oz dripping
1 oz flour
¾ pint water
salt and freshly ground pepper
½ oz butter

Preheat the oven to Reg 3/325°. Make the hot-pot
in a tall round pot, of iron or earthenware. Use half
the butter to grease the inside of the pot, put in half
the sliced potatoes, and season them. Brown the
chops in some hot dripping in a frying pan, and lay
them over the potatoes. Season, and cover with a
layer of onions also fried in dripping, followed by
the kidneys, mushrooms, and oysters if you have
them, seasoning each layer. Finish with a layer of
overlapping slices of potato. Fry the flour in the
frying pan with a little more dripping, and gradually
add ¾ pint boiling water, stirring to remove the
sediment from the bottom of the frying pan. Cook
a few minutes to thicken a little and strain over the
contents of the pot. Season the top layer, dot with
butter and cover. Cook, covered, for two hours, and
for a further ½ hour uncovered to brown the top.
Serve very hot with pickled red cabbage, its
traditional accompaniment.

For 6

Moussaka

1½ lbs cooked lamb or beef, finely chopped or
    minced
3 large onions, sliced
1 lb aubergines
olive oil for cooking
½ pint stock, bouillon or gravy
3 tablespoons tomato purée
salt and freshly ground pepper
for the top:
3 or 4 egg yolks
¾–1 pint seasoned milk

Make the top first, as it takes up to an hour to cook;
it combines so well with the aubergine flavour that
it is worth making this top rather than the alternative Béchamel sauce.

Combine the beaten egg yolks and seasoned milk
and put to thicken in the top of a double boiler,
or bain-marie; don't let the water boil or the sauce
will curdle. Stir with a wooden spoon from time to
time, while you prepare the other ingredients. When
it is like thick custard let it cool and thicken even
further.

Preheat the oven to Reg 4/350°. Meanwhile slice
the unpeeled aubergines thickly on the slant and
fry them gently in plenty of olive oil; they should be
just transparent, not browned. As they cook, lift
them out and line the bottom of a deep oval casserole
with some of them.

Fry the onions in more oil until brown. Put half the
minced meat into the casserole on top of the aubergines, then the onions then more aubergines and
the rest of the meat. Press firmly down. Mix the
tomato purée and seasoning into the heated stock
and pour over the meat. Spoon the custard-like top
over all and cook for about one hour at Reg 4/350°.

For 5–6

Greek Meatballs

1 lb fresh minced beef and lamb, mixed
2 eggs
1 clove garlic, crushed
1 medium onion, finely chopped
handful coriander leaves or parsley, chopped
½ teaspoon cinnamon
1 teaspoon salt and plenty of freshly ground pepper
3-inch piece stale French bread, or thick slice any
   home-made type white bread
butter and oil for frying
milk or water

Put the meat, eggs, garlic, onion, herbs and seasonings in a bowl, and mix. Soften the bread, crusts
removed, in milk or water. Squeeze dry and crumble
into the mixture. Mix again thoroughly — with
your hands is the easiest way. On a floured board
roll into walnut sized balls and fry in a mixture of
butter and oil for five to six minutes, turning
frequently. Serve with a fresh tomato sauce.

For 4–5

Shepherd's Pie

1 ½ lbs minced beef, or lamb (fresh or left-over)
1 large onion
1 clove garlic
2 tomatoes
2 carrots
stock, water, parsley, bayleaf, thyme
tablespoon tomato purée
1 ½ lbs potatoes
¼ pint milk, 1 ½ ozs butter
salt and pepper
olive oil, or dripping
dessertspoon flour, ½ oz butter, for thickening

Put three or four tablespoons olive oil or dripping
in a wide shallow pan and heat gently. Chop the
onion and garlic finely and add them to the fat.
While they are frying, peel the tomatoes and chop
them finely. When the onions start to brown, add
the tomatoes and cook fast, stirring, until all the
water has evaporated and the sauce starts to brown.
Now add the meat and carrots, grated on the coarse
side of the grater. Fry fast for ten minutes more,
if using raw meat, turning the meat over often.

If using left-over (cooked) meat, warm through
gently. Now add half-stock, half-water to come
almost to the top of the meat, but not to cover it.
Add thyme, salt and pepper, bayleaf, tomato purée
and a handful of chopped parsley. Left-over meat
needs no further cooking, but if using fresh meat,
simmer for an hour and a half, adding more stock as
needed and stirring from time to time. Work a
dessertspoon of plain flour into a nut of butter
(about half an ounce) and drop little pieces of this
paste into the mince, stirring, to thicken it. If you
thicken it at the beginning it tends to separate and
your mince has a lot of Spanish looking tomato-
coloured oil on top. After adding the flour, cook on
for 20 minutes. Put the meat into a pie dish. Cover
with creamy mashed potatoes made exactly as on
page 164. Bake in a moderate oven, Reg 5/375°, for
25 minutes until nicely brown and tempting.

For 6

Fried Pork Fillet

1 small pork fillet
juice of ½ lemon
salt and freshly ground pepper
butter for frying

Slice the pork fillet into little rounds about quarter of an inch thick. There will seem a lot, but they shrink in cooking. Between two pieces of grease-proof paper beat the little rounds of meat flat with a rolling pin. Season with lemon juice, plenty of fresh ground black pepper and a little salt. Melt the butter in a frying pan, and when it starts to brown slide in half the little escalopes of pork. As soon as the edges become whitish, flip the pieces over. They should fry quite quickly and be delicately browned and juicy after three or four minutes on each side. Slide on to a hot dish and fry the remaining pieces. When they are done and removed to the hot dish, squeeze any remaining lemon juice into the pan and add a little hot water (sherry is good too if you have it). Pour the pan juices over the meat and eat with a carefully made purée of creamy potatoes. These little escalopes are just as good in flavour as veal and much juicier.

☐ *Pork fillet is also called pork tenderloin. It is a totally lean piece of meat, and a good buy because there is no waste at all.*

For 2

Stuffed Pork Fillet

1 small pork fillet
1 small Italian, or other spicy sausage
2 oz mushrooms, chopped and sweated in butter
1 beaten egg yolk
parsley, chopped
salt and freshly ground pepper
2 rashers streaky bacon
butter for roasting
little dry white wine or cider

Preheat oven to Reg 5/375°. Score the fillet down the middle twice, lengthwise, taking care not to cut right through. You can now flatten it out like an oblong piece of pastry; bang it even flatter with a rolling pin.

Skin the sausage and mix the contents in a bowl with the egg yolk, chopped mushrooms, sweated in butter, chopped parsley and seasoning. Put this stuffing in a line down the middle of the flattened fillet. Fold the fillet over the stuffing and fasten into a long sausage shape with string or toothpicks. Cover the joint, which should be pressed together well, with the bacon slices, rinds removed, to keep the meat moist (see diagram opposite).

Cover with foil and roast with a little butter at Reg 5/375°, for 40–45 minutes, removing the foil for the last ten minutes. Remove the string or toothpicks and cut the meat into little round slices, each prettily enclosing a nugget of stuffing, and serve with a thin gravy made with the pan juices and a little dry white wine or cider. The fillet can be dry if overcooked, but always tastes very delicious.

For 2–3

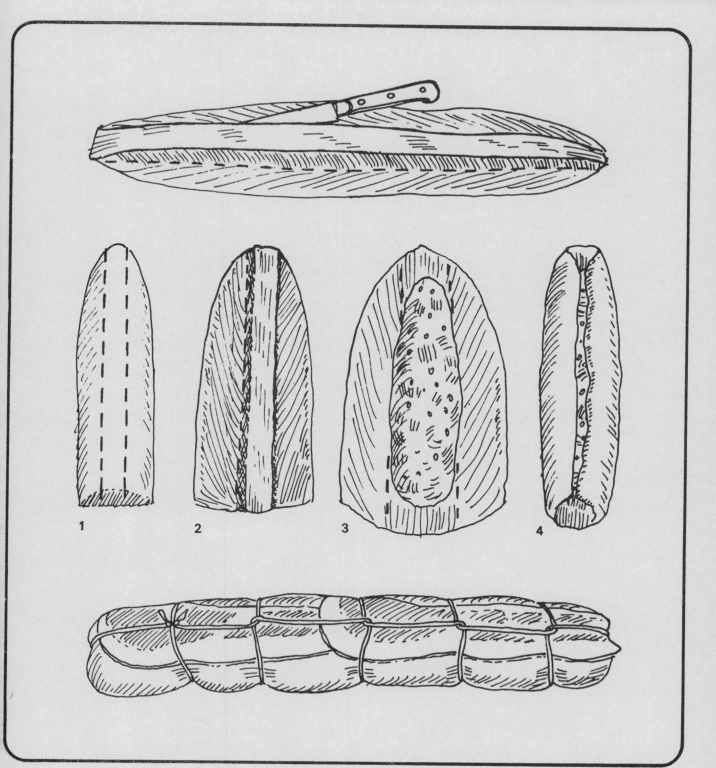

1 2 3 4

Pork Spare Ribs

2 lbs really cheap proper spare ribs, largely bones

For the marinade
juice of 1 large lemon
1 tablespoon olive oil
chopped fresh herbs (chives, marjoram, thyme
    rosemary)
salt, black pepper
1 clove garlic, crushed
1 large teaspoon Barbados (soft brown) sugar

Ask the butcher to cut the ribs in half across.
Mix the ingredients for the marinade together
and pour them over the pieces of meat. Leave it
to soak in for at least 1 hour, turning them about
from time to time.

If you have a barbecue or charcoal grill cook
the ribs over a grid, wiping excess moisture off
them first.

If you are roasting them in the oven, set it at
Reg 6–7/400°–425°, turn the pieces once, and
baste with the marinade. Allow them ½ hour.
Serve with salad, Barbecue sauce (page 247),
French bread and spring onions.

☐ *Very messy to eat, but easiest with hands and no
knives and forks*

For 4

Roast Hand of Pork

4–6 lbs hand of pork
a clove or two of garlic
salt, pepper, sprig of rosemary
oil

Preheat the oven to Reg 3/325°. Make sure the
butcher has scored the skin all over. (If he has
not a Stanley handyman's knife is the best sharp
knife for this.) Insert the garlic and the sprig of
rosemary, between the meat and the fat and rub
the fat all over with salt. Roast, basting often
for 3 hours or more. It should be well done and
very crisp on the outside. Remove to a warm
place to stand for at least ½ hour before carving.
Serve with apple sauce and gravy.

This cheap but rather fat joint is good hot or
cold.

For 4–6

How to Carve a Hand of Pork

1 & 1a. Remove crackling, and cut it up
separately.

2 & 2a. Carve horizontal slices from the top of
the joint, making the slices as thin as possible,
as the grain is complicated and thick slices would
be a bit chewy. Continue till you reach the bone.

3. Turn the joint over, and carve as many fine
slices as you can.

4. Carve away from the sides of the bones. Use
the knuckle for making stock as it does not have
much in the way of carveable meat.

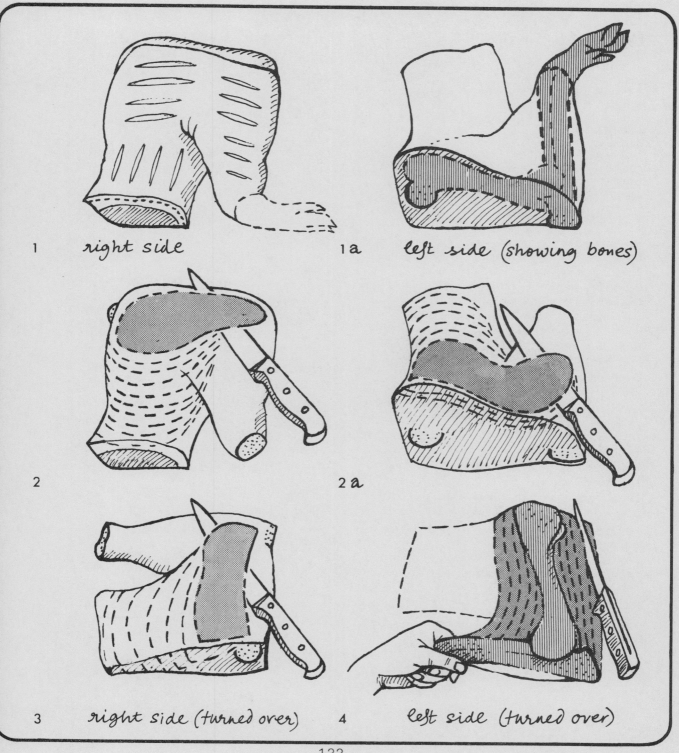

1   right side

1a   left side (showing bones)

2

2a

3   right side (turned over)

4   left side (turned over)

Pork and Beans

1 lb dried haricot beans
2 lbs salt belly of pork, lean end or 2 lbs hand
   of bacon or gammon
1 onion
2 tablespoons vinegar
2 tablespoons brown sugar
2 tablespoons treacle
2 tomatoes
1 teaspoon mustard
pepper, salt

Soak the beans, and if necessary the pork or
bacon too (ask the butcher). Parboil the beans in
plain unsalted water for ½ hour or more,
depending on how fresh they are (see the note in
the introduction to vegetables). Add the pork in
a piece and the whole onion, just cover with cold
water and simmer until the skins of the beans
begin to split, about 1½ hours. Then drain,
keeping the liquid, put the beans in a buttered
casserole and add the vinegar, sugar, tomatoes,
peeled and chopped, the boiled onion which you
chop roughly, black treacle, mustard and pepper.
Add a little salt only if the beans need it — there
may have been enough in the pork or bacon.
Remove the skin and put the meat in with the
beans. Add 2 or 3 tablespoons of the cooking
liquid and bake, covered at Reg 4/350° for 2
hours, then remove the lid and bake for a further
hour or more, until the beans are soft and tender
and the liquid creamy. Add more liquid during
cooking if it is needed.

☐ *This reheats extremely well.*

For 4–6

Pork and Cabbage

1½ lbs fresh belly of pork
1 savoy cabbage
½ lb boiling sausage
a little lard or pork fat
1 oz butter
1 oz flour
stock or milk for the sauce (about ¾ pint)
parsley, salt, pepper

Remove the skin from the pork with some of the
fat. Sprinkle the remaining fat with a little salt
and roast the meat with a little lard or pork
dripping at Reg 4/350° for ½ hour. Towards the
end add the sausage twisted into short lengths.

Quarter and core the cabbage and shred it
coarsely. Blanch it in boiling salted water for 5
minutes.

Make a parsley sauce with the butter, flour and
stock and the chopped parsley. Season well.

Drain the cabbage and put it into a casserole.
Lay the part-roasted pork and sausages on top;
you can cut the pork into serving pieces first,
and pour on the parsley sauce. Cover and cook in
a slow oven, Reg 2/300° for 1 hour.

☐ *This is rather a rich and filling dish. It reheats
well.*

For 4–6

Poor Man's Cassoulet

2 ½ lbs meaty end of fresh belly of pork
1 lb dried haricot beans, soaked overnight
1 onion, peeled
1 lb tomatoes, skinned and chopped
1 clove garlic, crushed
salt and freshly ground pepper

The pork belly should be boned and cut in one-inch slices. Roast these slices in a medium hot oven, Reg 5/375°, for 15 minutes. Put the beans in a pan with the onion and cover by an inch with cold water. Bring to the boil and simmer 45 minutes. Put the tomatoes in a casserole with the lightly roasted pork and its juices, the crushed clove of garlic, the beans, onion and half the liquid in which they were cooked. Add salt and pepper and cook in a low oven, Reg 3/325°, for two hours, keeping closely covered. This is better if made the day before and reheated. The juice should be rich and creamy.

For 6

Pork Kebabs

2 lbs leg of pork, off the bone
oregano
fresh lemon juice
freshly ground pepper
olive oil
salt

Even in the cheapest Greek restaurants they do use leg of pork rather than a cheaper cut, because it is so much better.

Cut the pork into little cubes and sprinkle liberally with oregano, lemon juice and pepper. Allow it to soak up these flavours for a couple of hours, turning the cubes over from time to time. Thread the cubes on skewers and shake off as much lemon juice as you can. Brush with oil and grill fast for five minutes, turning frequently. Sprinkle with salt and pepper and eat with a salad of green bottled chillies, lettuce and raw onions, and with plain rice. The bottled chillies can be found at most continental provision stores and delicatessens.

For 4–6

Cassoulet

1 lb haricot beans
pieces of pork skin or bacon rinds cut in large
   squares
4 large onions
4 cloves
1 large carrot
2 large bouquets of herbs
several cloves garlic
1 lb salt pork
1–2 lbs blade, spare rib or hand of fresh pork
whole or ½ shoulder of mutton (depending on
   number of people to be fed)

a small duck, or 1–2 wild duck
4 large tomatoes
1 lb Toulouse or other boiling sausage
salt, pepper
6–8 oz fresh breadcrumbs

Soak the beans overnight. Take a large iron pan with a lid, or a deep thick earthenware one. Line it with the pork rinds, including those from the salt pork. Drain the beans, put them in as well, cover with more fresh water, add 1 onion stuck with 4 cloves, the carrot, the bouquet, 4 cloves garlic, and the salt pork cut into big cubes. Bring gently to the boil, skim and simmer in the oven or on top until the beans are nearly done but not splitting (about 1½ hours).

Meanwhile set the oven at Reg 3/325°. Cut the boned lamb and pork into largish pieces, and roast them with the whole duck, for ¾–1 hour, while the beans are cooking. Strain off the fat, and use two or three tablespoons to fry the remaining three onions, peeled and chopped. Keep the rest of the fat for later. When the onions are soft and golden add the peeled and chopped tomatoes. Add the rest of the gravy from the meat tin, and plenty of salt and pepper. While this is cooking cut the duck into six pieces. Cut the sausages into pieces as well if they are big.

Drain and reserve the liquid from the beans, throw away the original onion, carrot and bouquet and re-fill the pot in which the beans were cooked, or use a new larger one, as everything has to go in this time. Put the pork rinds first, then a layer of beans, then meat, sausage, duck, onions and tomatoes, then beans with a fresh bouquet and two or three cloves of crushed garlic, then the remaining meats and

vegetables. Finish with some beans and a good cupful of their liquid, and finally strew the top thickly with fresh white breadcrumbs and drip a little roasting fat on to the breadcrumbs. Put it back to cook uncovered in the oven at Reg 2/300° for 1½ hours.

Traditionally, at least three times during the cooking you push down the breadcrumbs as they turn golden and sprinkle more breadcrumbs on. This makes a really delicious thick crust, and is a very important part of every cassoulet. Add more liquid if the whole thing seems to be going dry.

A fresh green salad is all that you need to follow.

☐ *The traditional French recipe uses preserved goose (confit d'oie) but it is perfectly acceptable to use wild or tame duck instead. It is not cheap but very filling for a large lunch on a cold day. If you cannot buy pork or bacon rind separately use strips cut from the outside of the pork in this recipe.*

For 8–12

Boiled Bacon

any cheap cut of green or smoked bacon ($\frac{1}{2}$ lb per
   person, more if there is bone or a lot of fat)
2 medium onions per person
3 medium carrots per person
bayleaf, sprig parsley
whole cloves
breadcrumbs
Demerara sugar

Green is milder than smoked, and since only the butcher or grocer know how salty either is (and even he may not), green is less risky, and less likely to need long soaking. Large cuts nearly always need soaking several hours or overnight. The cheapest cuts are hock, which has quite a lot of fat, and collar which is leaner. Hock is better eaten cold; a large piece, weighing eight or nine pounds, is good for parties.

Timing: small pieces, 1–3 lbs, need 1–1$\frac{1}{2}$ hours. Large pieces, 3 lbs and over, need 30–35 minutes to the pound. To see if it is cooked, push a skewer into the meat. If it goes in and comes out easily it is ready. Bacon is better slightly over- than under-cooked. Soak the bacon in several changes of water if necessary. Tie firmly with white string if it is a ragged piece. Just cover with cold water, in a pan large enough to hold all the vegetables and herbs. If the piece of bacon is small, 2 lbs and under, put the peeled onions in at the beginning of the cooking, with the herbs; if the piece is large put the herbs in at the start but add the onions 1 hour before the end. Let the water come slowly to the boil, then simmer gently. Add the scraped carrots half an hour before the end of the cooking. At the same time remove the bacon, letting the vegetables go on cooking in the liquid.

Remove the string from the bacon and gently peel away the rind. Criss-cross the fat in a diamond pattern, with lines about an inch apart. Mix equal parts of soft breadcrumbs and Demerara sugar, enough to cover the scored fat. Press the mixture into the fat with your hands. Stick a clove into the centre of each diamond. Put the bacon in an oven-proof dish with two tablespoons of the cooking liquid to prevent it sticking. After 20 minutes in a moderate oven, Reg 5/375°, the sugar and bread-crumbs should have combined to make a firm sweet crust. Serve with the vegetables, drained and arranged on the dish with the bacon, either whole or sliced, and with parsley sauce if liked. Whole boiled potatoes are good with this too, and if you have a good firm variety you can cook them in the bacon stock with the carrots. Keep the stock for pea soup etc.

Salt Pork

If you buy salt pork at Sainsbury's or other super-markets, you can be sure it will not be over-salty, because they are consistent about the amount of time the meat stays in the brine. However, many small butchers keep pieces of meat in the brine-tub indefinitely to preserve them; it is essential to find out, when buying from a butcher with a vast brine-tub, just how long each piece of pork has been there, how salty it is, and how long a soaking it will need. Do not be put off by the butcher's suggestion of bringing the meat to the boil in a pan of water and then throwing this water away. This does not work on very salty pork; it does need soaking, overnight at least.

Salt Pork with Peas

2 lbs salt pork belly (lean end), skin removed
1 large onion, sliced
6 carrots, sliced lengthwise
2 bayleaves
bunch of parsley and thyme, tied with a thread
8 oz yellow split peas
salt if needed

Soak the pork, overnight if necessary. Put it in a large saucepan, cover with cold water and bring to the boil. In the meantime prepare the vegetables. Add them and the herbs to the pork and simmer for two hours, covered. Remove the vegetables and add the split peas to the water; taste for salt and simmer until the peas are cooked, about one hour. Some people put the peas in a cloth bag and hang it over the side of the pan in the water to cook. It does prevent them from dissolving into a mush. If they do disintegrate, strain off the liquid before serving the peas on a dish round the piece of pork.

☐ *This is a filling peasant dish.*

For 6

Cold Pickled Pork, or Salt Pork

A hand of salt pork with its trotter, boned, tied and rolled (about 4–6 lbs when ready)
2 onions
2 carrots
2 bay leaves
a sprig of thyme, some peppercorns
1 clove garlic

Depending on the strength of his brine, the butcher will take 2–5 days to salt the pork for you. If he has a hand of pork already salted, ask him to bone, tie and roll it in a sausage shape for you. Soak it for 6–12 hours when you get home, no matter how perfect the butcher says it is. Change the water once or twice. Put it in a casserole or baking tin with the trotter, bones (if you have them), carrots, onions, herbs, garlic and pepper and just cover with water. Cover the dish and bake in the oven Reg 3/325° for 3 hours.

Leave it to cool in its own liquid for 1 hour, then put it in a bowl, with greaseproof paper over it and a weighted board or plate on top of that. Keep stock for soup. Next day the pork is ready for cutting. Eat with salads and as you would ham.

☐ *Belly of salt pork can be cooked in the same way. Remove the bones when nearly cool. Wrap in grease-proof paper and press till cold.*

For 10–12

Pork, Beef or Chicken Korma

1 ½ lbs pork or beef cut into squares, or 2 lbs raw
  chicken joints
for the marinade:
1 teaspoon ground turmeric
1 clove garlic, crushed
1 5-oz carton plain yoghurt

1 clove garlic, 1 onion
butter for frying, salt
5 whole cloves
5 whole cardamoms
1 cinnamon stick of about 1 inch

Marinate the meat in the yoghurt, mixed with
turmeric and a crushed clove of garlic, for an hour
or more. Slice the onion and the whole clove of
garlic and fry lightly in butter in a flameproof
casserole without browning. Add the spices, fry a
few minutes longer, than add the meat and its
marinade. Season with a little salt.

Cook covered in a slow oven, Reg 2/300°, for 1½
hours for chicken or pork, two hours for beef.

☐ *This curry is absolutely not hot, but is mild and
spicy and very delicious contrasted with a hot one.*

For 4–6

Gratin of Ham and Potatoes

½ large onion, chopped
1 clove garlic, crushed and chopped
nut of butter
1 tablespoon oil
4 oz slice ham
2 eggs
½ pint milk
2 oz Gruyère, grated
1 oz Parmesan, grated
salt, freshly ground pepper and nutmeg
1 lb potatoes

Preheat oven to Reg 5/375°. Heat a little butter and
the olive oil in a small frying pan and soften the
onion and garlic for 10–15 minutes without browning.
Add the ham cut into sticks like large matches,
heat through and keep warm.

Meanwhile beat the eggs into the milk, and add the
grated cheese, salt, pepper and a touch of nutmeg.
Peel the potatoes and grate them coarsely; squeeze
out the water with your hands (there will be more
than you think). Mix the whole lot together in a bowl,
turn it into a buttered oval gratin dish, and dot the
top with butter. Bake in the top of the oven for 30–
35 minutes; finish off by browning under the grill.

☐ *This is a very good lunch for a winter's day.*

For 4

Couscous

1 lb couscous
1–2 lbs lean stewing lamb (neck, fillet or
    shoulder)
3½ lbs boiling chicken (not too old and tough)
½ lb chick peas (soaked overnight)
1 turnip, 1 onion, 1 carrot
12 dried apricots (or 2 handfuls of raisins) soaked
1½ lbs vegetables, from among the following:
courgettes, peas, runner, french or broad beans

2 red or green pimentoes, 1 cauliflower
½ lb tomatoes, peeled and chopped
a sprig of mint
salt, pepper, olive oil, water, butter
harissa (or cayenne red chilli), ground ginger,
saffron, paprika

TO MAKE THE STEW

Cut the meat into convenient pieces and put it
with the whole chicken, pre-soaked chick peas,
onion, carrot, turnip, salt and pepper into the
bottom half of the *couscousier*, or a large
saucepan. Just cover with water and add a little
olive oil. Simmer, covered, for 2 hours. One
hour before the end start cooking the couscous
(see method below). ½ hour before the end add
the fruit, tomatoes, cut-up vegetables and mint,
with saffron or ginger if wished. Before serving
drain off most of the liquid which can be served
separately as an extra sauce or kept for reheating
at another meal. Pile the meat, vegetables and
cut-up chicken on a dish and serve the couscous
and sauce in separate bowls.

TO MAKE THE SAUCE

Take ¼ pint of the liquid from the stew, and add
cautiously a little harissa or cayenne or chilli for
a fiery sauce, or paprika with tomato purée for a
milder one, in which case use ½ pint of liquid as
people will take more.

TO COOK COUSCOUS

Start 1 hour before the stew is finished. Turn the
couscous into a bowl and moisten it with 1 or 2
cups of water — it will go rather solid. Mix it
very well with your hands, to make sure there
are no lumps at all. Put it in the top half (with
the holes) of your steamer or *couscousier* and set

it over the slowly cooking stew or boiling water
for ½ hour, without a lid. Do not press it down.

When ½ hour is up, turn it back into the bowl
again and add 1–2 cups of cold water with a little
salt and pepper. Stir well, this time with a
wooden spoon (it will be hot) and make sure
there are no lumps. Return it lightly to the
steamer. After another ½ hour over the simmering
stew or water it should be ready, light and
fluffy with each grain soft and separate. Finish
by stirring in an ounce or two of butter and turn
it into a warm dish.

For 6–8

Notes on Couscous

Sausages or Sausage Meat

Caul fat (optional) 1 tablespoon vinegar
1½ lb belly of pork
2 tablespoons fine fresh breadcrumbs
a handful of parsley, finely chopped
1 level teaspoon ground mace
a large pinch of ground coriander
a large pinch of black pepper
½–1 teaspoon salt
2 rashers lean bacon
2 tablespoons finely chopped onion
2 oz lard

Basically a North African dish, it translates rather well into English, now that the actual proper grain, or couscous, is available in many shops, not only delicatessens but also health food shops, as is harissa, for the sauce. Moreover it is not at all difficult to cook if you have a *couscousier* or perforated steamer which fits tightly over a pan in which you can boil water or cook a stew. The steamer doesn't need a lid, but it does need to fit tightly into the pan below. You can fix a cloth all round the join of the two pots to help keep in the steam if need be. Ideally the meat and vegetables cook below the couscous, but if the lower pan is too small to hold everything, the stew can cook separately, and the couscous cooks just as well over water. Don't worry about it falling through the holes, it stays together in a mass.

Soak the caul fat in hot water with a tablespoon of vinegar. Put the pork, skinned and boned, and the rashers of bacon twice through the fine blade of the mincer. Mix it with the breadcrumbs, parsley, spices and salt. Soften the finely chopped onion in half the lard and add it to the mixture.

To make the sausages, dry and skin (if necessary) the caul fat and stretch it by easing it with the flat of one hand and the fingers of the other. Cut it into 4″ squares. Shape the sausage meat into little sausage shapes, wrap them in caul fat, like little parcels. When you want them, fry them very slowly in lard or pork dripping.

Caul fat is not very easy to get, but sausage skins can be obtained if you know of a butcher who makes his own sausages. You then only have the problem of filling them, which is possible with a mixer with a sausage-filler. Otherwise make skinless sausages which, however, tend to be dry.

☐ *10 times better than average bought sausages.*

Makes just over 1½ lbs.

Toad in the Hole

6 large sausages
6 slices streaky bacon
for the batter:
4 oz plain flour
salt
2 eggs
½ pint milk
2–3 tablespoons oil or good pork dripping

Make a pudding batter by sieving the flour and salt into a bowl, make a well in the centre and add the eggs, breaking the yolks with your spoon before you start stirring. Add the milk gradually, stirring in the flour little by little until half the milk is added; keep going until all the flour is taken up and the mixture is smooth. Then add the rest of the milk and beat for five or ten minutes. Stand the batter in a cool place for one hour. Preheat oven to Reg 9/475°. When batter is ready, skin the sausages, heat the oil or dripping in a baking tin, fry the bacon two or three minutes, then add the skinned halved sausages. Put the tin in the oven for five minutes, then pour on the batter and cook for five minutes at Reg 9/475° and 35–40 minutes at Reg 7/425°.

For 4

Sausage with Lentils

1 cotechino or poaching sausage, of ¾–1 lb (available from delicatessen shops)
¾ lb small green lentils
2 cloves garlic
1 stick celery, chopped
butter
salt

Soak the lentils for three or four hours, then wash them and place in a pan of cold water with the peeled cloves of garlic and stick of celery. Bring slowly to the boil, skim and simmer gently for 1–1½ hours, adding salt half-way through, when they have started to get tender. Three-quarters of an hour before you want it ready, put the sausage, pricked all over with a needle, into a pan of cold water. Bring it gradually to the boil and poach in slowly simmering water for three-quarters of an hour.

Strain the lentils, keeping the liquid for soup, and add a large nut of butter. Serve with the sausage cut in slices and a good glass of rough red wine.

For 4

Sausages with White Wine Sauce

1 ½ lbs spicy French or Italian sausages
glass white wine
1 ½ oz butter
scant 1 oz flour
½ pint milk (infused with onion, bayleaf and peppercorns)
salt and freshly ground pepper
mashed potatoes *or* cooked haricot beans

Make half a pint of Béchamel with one ounce of butter, and the flour and milk. Season with salt and pepper. Soak the sausages in lukewarm water for a few minutes. This helps to prevent them from bursting. Dry them, prick all over and fry gently in the remaining half ounce of butter until practically done, pouring the fat off from time to time. Add the wine, and when it is reduced by half, take out the sausages and keep hot, or arrange them on a mountain of mashed potatoes, or plain, cooked haricot beans. Add the Béchamel to the wine in the frying pan, stir it well and pour over the sausages. This sauce is a good addition to bangers and mash, but the bangers need to be a bit special to be worth it.

For 4

Hamburgers

1–2 slices home-made type bread
1 lb minced beef
1 small onion, chopped
1 clove garlic, finely chopped
parsley, thyme, pinch nutmeg
salt and freshly ground pepper
oil and butter for frying

Soak the bread in water, squeeze dry and crumble into a bowl. Add the meat, onions, garlic, herbs and seasoning and mix thoroughly. Shape into 12 small, flat round cakes on a floured board. Heat oil and butter in a large frying pan over a moderate heat and fry the hamburgers for three or four minutes on each side, depending on how well you like them cooked. They can be pink and juicy inside, or brown right through. Serve with fried onions, or plain, or with fresh tomato sauce (page 253). They are much cheaper than frozen ones, a good deal less than half the price, and they taste better.

For 4

Tripe

Veal tripe is best, but ox-tripe is more commonly sold. It can be bought prepared to varying degrees, so find out from the butcher how much longer it needs to be cooked. It is sold completely raw (don't buy it like this if possible); blanched and scraped; prepared or 'half-cooked' (which is the best way to buy it) and cooked.

If you do buy raw tripe, wash it very well and then blanch it (bring to the boil in salted water and refresh in cold water). Then simmer the blanched tripe for three hours in salted water with carrots, onions, celery, a bayleaf and some peppercorns, by which time it is 'half-cooked'.

Half-cooked tripe is ready to be turned into a stew or braised in a rich sauce.

Fully cooked tripe is often egg-and-breadcrumbed and fried. Tripe should be eaten 'al dente', with a slight bite, like spaghetti; overcooked it becomes flabby, undercooked it is tough and rubbery. There are several different textures to the tripe, the honey-comb probably being the best bit, but it is a good idea to mix it with some of the other pieces.

Always wash tripe well before cooking and dry it carefully, as it holds a lot of water which can spoil a rich sauce.

Tripe is so cheap compared with most other kinds of meat that you can afford to be a bit extravagant with its dressing up; so if the recipe demands a glass of wine and a dash of brandy, don't hold back, it is worth it.

Tripe and Onions

2 lbs prepared tripe
3–4 Spanish onions, peeled and sliced
6 bacon rinds, or a small piece of salt pork or ham
bayleaf, mace
enough milk and water, half and half, to cover the tripe and onions (1–1 ¼ pints altogether)
salt and freshly ground pepper
2 oz butter
scant 2 oz flour
4 triangular pieces fried bread

Put the well-washed tripe, in a piece, with the sliced onions, into a flame-proof casserole or large lidded saucepan with the seasoning, bayleaf and mace and the ham, pork or bacon rinds. Just cover with water and milk, season, bring to the boil, cover the pan and simmer gently for 45 minutes. Fish out the onions with a slotted spoon, and if the tripe is not yet tender, let it go on cooking. Sieve the onions, and strain the cooked tripe. Make a pint of Béchamel with the flour, butter and some of the strained liquid from the tripe, add the onion purée and season well. Cut the drained tripe into strips or small squares, smother it with the sauce, in the casserole in which it cooked. Reheat in the oven and serve very hot with triangles of bread fried golden in a mixture of oil and butter, or pork dripping.

☐ *This is a very traditional English way of cooking tripe.*
Very often people don't really enjoy tripe until they have eaten it two or three times, but once acquired the taste is there for good, and those who do appreciate it, appreciate it very much; there is something deeply soothing about the flavour.

For 4

Italian Tripe

2 lbs prepared tripe, half cooked
   washed and dried
1 tablespoon olive oil
4 oz salt pork belly, cut in small chunks
1 onion, 1 clove garlic, chopped
large glass white wine
2–3 tomatoes, skinned and chopped
1 tablespoon tomato purée
salt and freshly ground pepper
bouquet of bayleaf, parsley, rosemary and thyme
4 tablespoons grated Parmesan
1 cup fresh breadcrumbs, fried golden in butter

Heat the olive oil in a flameproof dish, deep enough to cook in, but shallow enough to go under the grill. Brown the onion and salt pork slowly. Add the tripe cut in one-inch squares, and the garlic and white wine and simmer, uncovered, until the liquid is reduced by half — after about 15 minutes. Add the tomatoes, tomato purée, herbs and seasoning, cover the pan and simmer until the tripe is just tender, about 30–45 minutes. The sauce should be fairly thick, but add a little water if it starts to stick at the bottom. Preheat the grill. When ready, remove the herbs, stir in three tablespoons of Parmesan, strew the top with the breadcrumbs and the remaining Parmesan, and grill until piping hot all through and lightly browned on top.

For 4

Portuguese Tripe

1 ½ lbs prepared tripe, carefully washed and dried
1 onion, sliced into rings
4 tablespoons olive oil
1 tablespoon flour
1 lb tomatoes, skinned and chopped
2 cloves garlic, crushed
few sprigs parsley
sprinkling dried marjoram
salt and freshly ground pepper
2–3 green chilli peppers, cut in strips, seeds removed
dash of white wine

Fry the onions in the oil, in a flameproof casserole, until the rings have separated and become transparent. Add the tripe, cut in small pieces, and brown lightly. Cook it rather fast at this stage or the tripe will get very juicy and won't brown. Add the flour, tomatoes, garlic, herbs, salt and pepper, chillies and wine, and simmer covered in a slow oven, Reg 1½/290°, for one hour. This is a very good rich moist stew with a hot flavour; it comes originally from Portugal, via Dahomey, but has been considerably modified. If you use bottled chillies, use six or seven as they are milder than fresh ones.

For 4

Grilled Tripe

1 lb thick dressed tripe, well-dried and cut into
   fingers
4 tablespoons oil
juice ½ lemon
pepper, salt
parsley
breadcrumbs for coating

Cut the ready-prepared tripe into strips about ½″ by 2″. Marinate them for 1 hour in the oil, and lemon juice with salt, pepper and parsley. Just before you want to eat them drain them, coat with breadcrumbs and grill gently until brown, about 8–10 minutes each side. Serve with salad and grilled or fried tomatoes.

For 2

Ox-Tongue

1 ox-tongue, salted and if possible smoked, of about
  3 lbs (Sainsbury's have these often)
3 carrots
3 onions
1 stick celery
1 fresh pig's trotter (if salted, soak with the tongue)
parsley, thyme, bayleaf
peppercorns
mustard sauce (page 251)

Soak the tongue for 24 hours changing the water once or twice. Put it in a large casserole with the sliced vegetables, add the pig's foot and enough water to cover. Throw in the peppercorns and the bunch of herbs, bring gently to the boil and simmer in the oven in a covered casserole at Reg 2/300° for $3\frac{1}{2}$–$4\frac{1}{2}$ hours. Take out of the liquid and skin while the tongue is still very hot. Put it on a dish and serve hot with mustard sauce.

If you want it cold, strain and reduce the liquid in which it cooked to about one third, so it will set to a firm jelly when cold. Taste it for salt; if it is too salty you must dilute it and add aspic. Some cooks prefer to lay the tongue out on a plate, top side up, and glaze with the almost-set jelly, but you can roll it up, squeeze it into a straight-sided round dish, fill the spaces with the reduced cooking liquid, press with a weighted plate for 24 hours, and turn it out before serving. Some people think it looks prettier like this in a jellied shape, and that laid out on a dish it looks as though it will say 'ouch' when you cut it.

For 6

Calves' Tongues with Salt Pork

$\frac{3}{4}$ lb salt pork belly (lean end, not soaked)
4 calves' tongues
1 onion
1 stick celery
2 carrots
sprigs parsley
peppercorns

Put the cleaned chopped vegetables in a large saucepan with the parsley and peppercorns, tongues and freshly salted pork, rind removed. Just cover with water, bring to the boil and simmer really slowly for $2\frac{1}{4}$–$2\frac{1}{2}$ hours, with the water just moving gently. The salt from the pork is absorbed by the tongues as they cook.

When they are tender take them out and skin them, as soon as they are cool enough, starting underneath the tips and removing the skin from front to back in large pieces. Remove any bones, trim them, and put into a hot dish with the salt pork, removed from the bone and cut into large cubes (about two inches across). Sprinkle with chopped parsley and serve very hot with parsley sauce or mustard sauce (page 251) and plain boiled potatoes.

☐ *This recipe came from the butcher. The calves' tongues become an appetising pink from the salt in the pork. Sheeps' tongues can also be cooked this way.*

For 4

Brains in Batter

2 calves' or 3 sheep's brains
flour for dusting
fritter batter
salt and freshly ground pepper
oil or fat for deep frying

Heat the oil or fat in a deep-frying pan. Prepare the brains as described. Cut the brains into halves or, if you prefer, into four. Dry, and dust with seasoned flour. Using a spoon, coat the brains with batter and fry carefully to a golden brown. Serve with tomato sauce.

For 2

The Preparation of Brains
Calves' brains are the best; you need one set per person. Lambs' brains are much smaller, so buy three sets for two people. Soak the brains in tepid water for half an hour or more. Remove the skin and membranes and all the red threads. Blanch in simmering salted water, acidulated with lemon juice, for fifteen minutes or more. If they still seem too slippery and fragile to handle you can firm them up by chilling in the refrigerator for an hour or so, or even freezing in the ice-compartment before slicing or cooking them in batter etc.

Brains in Black Butter

Prepare the brains as above but as soon as they are cooked drain them very well, slice them and serve them very hot with black butter (page 248) poured over them.

Brains in White Sauce

4 lambs' or 2 calves' brains
2 oz butter
1 oz flour
¼ pint milk, infused with a sliced onion, 8 peppercorns and a bayleaf
good pinch nutmeg
salt and freshly ground pepper
juice of ½ lemon

Prepare the brains as on this page. They should be perfectly white. Remove the stem and slice each brain in half. Make a well flavoured sauce with half the butter, the flour and the milk, seasoned with nutmeg, salt and freshly ground pepper. Melt the remaining ounce of butter in a frying pan and gently fry the brains for three or four minutes, seasoning with salt and pepper. Add the sauce to the brains, simmer four minutes more, stirring very carefully. Transfer it carefully to a heated serving dish, sprinkle with lemon juice and serve.

For 4

Brains Vinaigrette

4 sets lambs' brains
stock
vinaigrette dressing
parsley, capers

Soak and skin the brains. Poach for 20-30 minutes in good stock and allow to cool in their own bouillon.

When they are quite cold remove them carefully and allow them to drain for 5 minutes. Serve sliced with a good vinaigrette poured over them and sprinkled with chopped capers and parsley.

For 4

Grilled Liver on a Skewer

¾ lb liver, lambs' or calves', sliced thickly
1 onion
1 red or green pimento
2 tablespoons olive oil
juice of ½ lemon
thyme
salt and freshly ground pepper

Prepare one hour before you start to cook. Cut the liver into squares about ¾ inch across. Cut the onions and pimentoes into pieces about the same size. Mix the olive oil and lemon juice, salt, pepper and thyme. Marinate the liver, peppers and onions in this for an hour.

Take out the pieces of meat and vegetables and put them on skewers, alternating meat, onion and pepper. Grill under a fairly fast heat, turning from time to time. Serve with plain boiled rice, to which you can add the juices from the grill pan.

For 2–3

Liver with Sour Cream

2 large onions, finely chopped
oil for frying
1 lb pig's liver, cut into ½" cubes
5 oz carton of sour cream
1 tablespoon flour
½ pint water
marjoram, parsley, salt

Fry the finely chopped onions in a little oil until they are transparent. Add the liver and fry, turning often, with the onions for 5 minutes. Mix the sour cream with the flour, add the water slowly, stirring, and add this to the liver and onion, cooking and mixing for another 5–10 minutes. Add the marjoram. Keep warm till ready to serve, and only add salt and pepper just before doing so, otherwise the liver becomes tough. Sprinkle with parsley. Serve with boiled or mashed potatoes, and sweet-sour gherkins or cucumber salad.

For 4

Liver with Raisins

2 lbs liver (pig's or lambs') thinly sliced
1½ oz butter
1 onion, chopped
2–3 rashers bacon, or salt pork
salt, pepper
1 tablespoon wine vinegar
1 dessertspoon Demerara sugar
2 tablespoons seedless raisins (previously
   soaked in water)

You need a large frying pan with a lid for this dish. Season the slices of liver with salt and pepper, and fry briefly in the butter. Remove the slices and keep them warm. Cut the bacon or salt pork into small pieces and fry lightly with the onion in the same pan. Add the vinegar, sugar and raisins. Return the liver to the pan, and cook gently, with the lid on for 1 hour. Serve with mashed potatoes.

☐ *Some people hate liver cooked for a long time in any form, but for those who like it this is a good recipe.*

For 6

Liver Provençale

1 lb lambs' liver, cut in thin slices
olive oil
2 cloves garlic
small bunch parsley
flour
butter
wine vinegar
salt and freshly ground pepper

Chop the garlic and parsley finely. Pat a little flour, seasoned with salt and pepper, into the liver to absorb the moisture. Heat half a tablespoon of oil in a really heavy frying pan. Meanwhile in a saucepan melt a good dollop of butter, without browning, and add the chopped garlic and parsley.

When the oil is really hot, with a blue haze rising, put in the slices of liver, flip them over and remove them to a hot dish. They should not have more than one or two minutes' cooking altogether. Take the frying pan off the heat and add the butter and garlic mixture. Add a dash of vinegar, let it sizzle up and pour it, still sizzling, over the liver.

Serve immediately with a purée of potatoes or turnips.

For 4

Rognon de Boeuf Saignant

1 ox kidney
2½ oz unsalted butter
small bunch parsley
salt and freshly ground pepper

Cut the kidney into half-inch slices, removing all the fatty core. Chop the parsley.
Heat one ounce of the butter in a heavy frying pan. When it is really hot, with a blue haze rising, put in the slices of kidney. Sauté for two or three minutes, moving them around in the pan. Turn them over and cook the other side in the same way. Meanwhile melt the rest of the butter in a small pan with the chopped parsley, without letting it brown. When the slices of kidney are browned on both sides, put them in a heated dish, throwing out the butter in which they cooked. Pour the freshly melted butter and parsley over, sprinkle with salt and freshly ground pepper and serve immediately. They will be very pink inside and very tasty; the red juice which they make mingles well with the butter. Serve with watercress and puréed potatoes.

For 4

Pigs' Kidneys with Lovage

2 pigs' kidneys
salt and freshly ground pepper
pork dripping, or oil and butter
juice of ½ lemon
1 tablespoon lovage, finely chopped, or celery leaves
 or celery salt

About half an hour before you will eat them, slice the kidneys finely, removing all the fatty core, and sprinkle with salt and pepper. Leave for 25 minutes. Melt the fat, or oil and butter, in a thick frying pan, so that the bottom is liberally covered. Raise the heat and fry the kidney slices briskly, a few at a time, so that each slice gets an even contact with the heat. As soon as both sides have changed colour from dark red to pale brown, put the pieces in a heated serving dish.
Finish by sprinkling with lemon juice and chopped lovage. Serve at once with their own juices and mashed potato.

☐ *Lovage, once you have it, is very easy to grow and is perennial like mint. It is similar in flavour to raw celery leaves; if you haven't any lovage use celery instead.*

For 2

Kebabs with Lambs' Kidneys

4 lambs' kidneys
4 rashers bacon, rinds removed
1 large onion
6 firm tomatoes
1 pimento, seeds removed
12 small mushrooms
12 basil leaves
juice of $\frac{1}{2}$ lemon
olive oil
salt and freshly ground pepper
two bayleaves
thyme

Skin, core and slice each kidney into four. Cut the
bacon into one-inch squares. Quarter the onions
and part the pieces, halve the tomatoes, cut the
pimento into one-inch squares, remove the mushroom stalks. Put the meat and vegetables, including
the basil leaves, in a bowl, and sprinkle with lemon
juice, plenty of olive oil, salt, pepper and thyme.
Add the bayleaves and marinate for about
half an hour. Divide everything between eight
skewers, alternating the ingredients and putting the
basil leaves against the cut side of the tomatoes.
Grill or barbecue, brushing with more oil, turning
frequently. They take five or ten minutes. Serve
with plain rice and a green salad. Mix the left-over
marinade (and the juices from the grill-pan if you
are indoors) into the rice before serving.

For 4

Kidneys with Lemon Juice

4 lambs' kidneys, skinned and cored
3 cloves garlic
juice of $\frac{1}{2}$ lemon
dash white wine
salt and freshly ground pepper
sprig parsley, chopped
oil for frying

Chop the kidneys into pieces about $\frac{3}{4}$ inch thick.
Heat a heavy frying pan until it is very very hot.
Chop the garlic and when the pan is ready pour in a
little oil, just enough to cover the bottom, and throw
in the garlic. To this add the kidneys and sauté
them three or four minutes, moving and turning
them with a wooden spoon or fork all the time. Add
the lemon juice, wine, chopped parsley and seasoning. Let it sizzle up and serve immediately with rice.

For 2

Kidney Pilaff

4–5 lambs' kidneys
1 onion, sliced
1 tablespoon olive oil
1 tablespoon butter
2 bayleaves
sprig of thyme
2 tablespoons tomato purée, moistened with a little
    stock
salt and freshly ground pepper
1 dessertspoon wine vinegar

Sauté the onion in oil and butter, in a sauté pan,
without browning. Skin and core the kidneys and
chop them into thin slices across. Sauté with the
onions, bayleaves and thyme, for five to six minutes.
Add the tomato purée and stock, and the vinegar,
salt and pepper. Stir in and heat through. Serve with
plain rice.

For 2

Sweetbreads

Fricasseed Sweetbreads

1 lb poached sweetbreads, kept warm
1 pint of stock in which they were poached (see opposite)
1 oz butter
1 oz flour
juice of 1 lemon
2 egg yolks
salt and freshly ground pepper
parsley, chopped
½ lb mushrooms (optional)

The preparation of sweetbreads

This preparation applies whatever the recipe, and to both lambs' and calves' sweetbreads.

Wash under a running tap, or soak in frequently changed salted water for one to three hours, until they are no longer pink but pearly white. Put into a pan of cold, salted water and bring slowly to the boil; boil two or three minutes, remove and cool at once in cold water. This stiffens them, making them easier to handle. Skin and remove all the lumps of gristle you can. Press between two plates for an hour.

The main methods of cooking from this point are: Poaching — poach in stock until tender, then use in a fricassée. Frying — (1) slice the sweetbreads; flour, egg-and-crumb and fry gently. Serve with tomato sauce (page 253); (2) slice, dip in fritter batter and fry gently; (3) slice and sauté quite simply in butter, for 10–15 minutes. After they are cooked, make a quick sauce in the pan with cream and a few mushrooms previously sautéed in butter, or serve them plain, sprinkled with lemon juice.

Strain one pint of the stock in which the sweetbreads were poached and make a sauce with the flour and butter and strained liquid. Mix the lemon juice with the egg yolks, season with salt and pepper and add to the sauce, away from the heat, stirring attentively; once it is mixed in, the sauce can no longer curdle. Let it thicken, then pour the sauce over the sliced sweetbreads and sprinkle with parsley. Serve with boiled or mashed potatoes.

You can add ½ lb mushrooms, first cooked in the stock, to the sauce.

For 4

POULTRY AND GAME

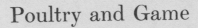

Poultry and Game

It really is worth buying boiling chickens; it may seem more difficult because of the time factor, but, thinking ahead, you can put a nice fat hen in a pot with some herbs and vegetables, cover it with water and put it to simmer very gently while you go out. It can sit there for hours, gradually becoming tender, and it makes large amounts of delicious broth. It is worth going further to find a bird that has had a happy life, but even a battery hen has a remote resemblance to chicken, once carefully cooked. All poultry is now fairly cheap, since it is reared on such a vast scale.

When you buy a fresh chicken, don't forget to take home the giblets (and if you buy a frozen one don't forget to look inside before you cook it, as polythene does not make a good stuffing); the giblets are invaluable for gravy or stock or to improve the flavour of the sauce that goes with the chicken, and the liver is a good addition to most stuffings.

Game, both for casseroling and roasting, is getting scarcer and more expensive every year, but still seems to be cheaper in the country. It is worth remembering that the birds are only young and plump at the beginning of the season, and become increasingly thin and tough as the winter wears on. Young pigeons are available only from March to October, and even in those months make certain you have not got dad or grandad from the year before. The same applies to wild bunnies, though tame rabbits are not allowed to go on hopping about long enough to get tough.

Full instructions are given for the drawing, plucking and trussing of birds, and the drawing and skinning of rabbits or hares, for anyone lucky enough to get a present of game, but a pheasant run into by a car is unlikely to make good eating, poor thing, because of the bruises.

To Pluck and Draw and Truss a Bird

As with rabbits and hares, game-birds from friends tend to arrive fully clad. In the case of most game, and depending on the weather, it should hang for a week to ten days before being plucked. Hang, head uppermost, in a cool airy place. Pigeons are eaten fresh, but can be kept hanging in their feathers for a few days until they are wanted.

The chief problem with plucking, for someone who hasn't done it before, is controlling the feathers, so choose a small room with an easily swept floor (on a still day it can be done out of doors). Sit down with the bird on a table in front of you and a large carrier bag or cardboard box at your feet or on your lap.

Hold the bird by one wing and start under the wings, pulling a few feathers at a time with a sharp pinching tug. Always pull in the direction they are pointing, not against the grain, or you may tear the skin. Carry on plucking from the wings and lower neck, steadily leaving the skin bare and working towards the tail. When you come to the big strong wing feathers pull them out one by one. Don't be tempted to cut them, as you will be left with awkward stumps. Drop each handful of feathers into the box or bag as you pull it out. A mound of pheasant feathers is a pretty sight, but one puff of air, even if it's only somebody laughing, and they are all over the place. There is no need to pluck the neck or head.

When you have finished, there will be a few tufts of down here and there, so light a twist of paper or a taper and turn the bird round a few inches above it to singe off every whisker that remains.

Drawing

Lay the plucked bird breast down and feel for the place where the neck joins the shoulders. Cut through the skin about two inches above this point. Put your knife in under the skin and cut through the neck where it joins the shoulders. Draw out the neck, leaving a flap of skin for covering the hole. Carefully pull out the crop, without breaking it (it is a bag full of grit and grains), and the windpipe. Keep the neck for the giblet stock, and throw the head away. Put your finger into the hole between the shoulders and run it all round the inside of the bird, as if it was a knife loosening a pudding in a basin.

Turn the bird on its back and just under the tail you will find the vent Cut all round this, right through the skin. You can then pull this away and put your hand, or fingers if it is a small bird, right inside to pull out the loosened innards. Look for the gall bladder attached to the liver. It is oval, small, dark brown and full of very bitter yellow liquid. If this bursts it is the ruin of the bird, as the strong taste doesn't easily wash away, so cut away the gall bladder first. Cut out the gizzard (a hard, dark reddish object) and slice it almost through, but stop at the grey skin, which is a bag with more undesirable contents. Throw this away but keep the healthy reddish outside part, plus the liver and heart. Throw everything else away, and wash and wipe the inside of the bird.

The neck, liver, heart and gizzard make giblet gravy. Cut off the bird's feet, pulling out the tough tendons from feet to thighs as you do so, if possible.

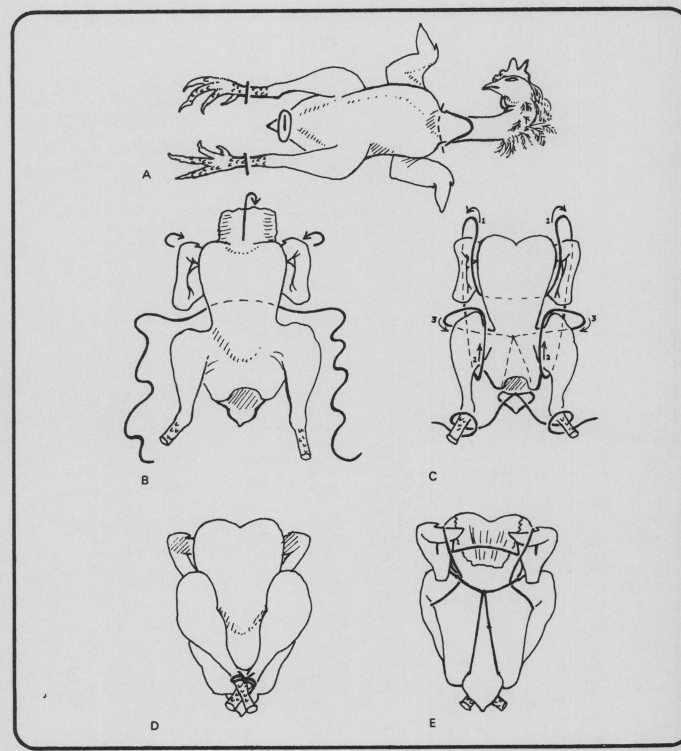

Trussing

This method does not use skewers.

(A) Lay the drawn bird on its back with its tail towards you and make the cuts shown in the diagram; tuck the front flap of skin at its neck over the neck hole and down over the back. Flip the pinions (the last joint of the wing) inwards and tuck them behind the shoulders.

(B) Take about 3 feet of string and pass it under the bird's shoulders, the loose ends being one in each hand on each side of the bird.

(C) Pull the string up under the wings of the bird, over the shoulders, down the back of each wing, past the elbows, past the legs. Pull it up under the thigh joints and, without letting go, pull it all tight, and flip the bird over onto its front. Tie a knot in the middle of the back, and turn it over again.

(D) The bird should now be looking much neater, plumped up with its legs drawn up to its wings. Bring the two ends of the string down the back and knot them over the parson's nose.

If you want to stuff the bird, do it now.

(E) Bring the ends of the string from the knot on the parson's nose and tie the drumsticks firmly together, below the breastbone.

Poule au Pot de bon Roi Henri

1 cabbage, 1 lb carrots
½ lb turnips, 4 sticks celery   1 onion
1 large boiling fowl, not too fatty
1 bacon hock (preferably smoked)
2 slices stale white bread
6 oz ham or boiled bacon with its fat
3—4 sprigs parsley, 3—4 sprigs tarragon
1 clove garlic, salt, pepper
plenty of nutmeg
2 fresh eggs and 2 oz butter
or the eggs from inside the fowl and its own
    fat melted down (economy)

Prepare the cabbage, cut it in half, and put it in a very large saucepan with the scraped carrots, turnips, celery and onion. Cover with 6–7 pints cold water. Stuff the chicken with a stuffing made by chopping the boiled bacon or ham, the bird's liver and the heart very finely. Mix with the grated bread, chopped herbs, garlic and beaten eggs. Add salt, pepper and nutmeg, and the melted butter, and stuff the bird with this mixture. Skewer it well or sew it up to prevent the stuffing escaping. Put it in the pot, bring it to the boil, skim, and simmer for 1½ hours. Add the bacon hock and simmer another 1½ hours or less if the chicken is small. Serve the strained bouillon, skimmed of most of its fat and with a handful of finely chopped parsley or cooked rice thrown in. You can serve it with the vegetables but they are pretty soggy by now. Traditionally pieces of bread toasted in the oven are served with it, but new bread or fried bread croûtons are good too (croûtons are not necessary if you have added rice).

The next course is the chicken with its delicious stuffing and the boiled bacon hock, followed by a salad or accompanied by a green vegetable such as beans.

For 8

Boning a Chicken or Duck

Find a knife with a short thin blade and sharpen it extra well. Turn the drawn chicken over and cut along the middle of its back from neck to tail (1). Sliding your knife hard up against the carcass of the bird, work your way round one side, slowly pulling the meat away with your fingers to expose the line for your next cut (2). When you encounter the leg, feel with your free forefinger for the ball and socket joint and slide the point of your knife into it to free it. Continue cutting round, disengaging the wing, but cutting outside the fine flat bone that lies beneath it on the carcass. When you have cut round to the flat side of the breastbone, start on the other side of the back in the same way. Cut the skin from the ridge of the breastbone very carefully indeed as it is paper-thin here. Lift out the carcass, leaving the parson's nose on it. You can remove the upper leg and wing bones (3) by sliding your fingers and knife down close to the bone and cutting firmly through the joint. Remove the wing tips completely, skin, bone and all, or you can leave the last two wing bones and the drumsticks (shown as dotted outlines) where they are. The flesh can now be flattened out, skin side down, seasoned and sprinkled with wine, and any rich stuffing put in the centre (4). The bird is wrapped round this and made more or less into a chicken shape again, and the opening tied, skewered or sewn together (5). You can roast this stuffed chicken or simmer it in stock.

A pâté mixture of pork and veal with perhaps a few pistachio nuts and a good proportion of fat makes an excellent stuffing. Serve it cold, with the threads removed and the seam-side down. Cut it right across in slices like any pâté. You can bone a duck in exactly the same way. If you sew the opening rather than tying it, the bird miraculously goes back into shape while it is cooking.

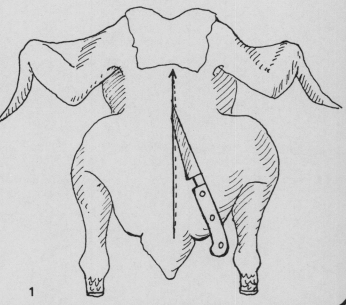

1

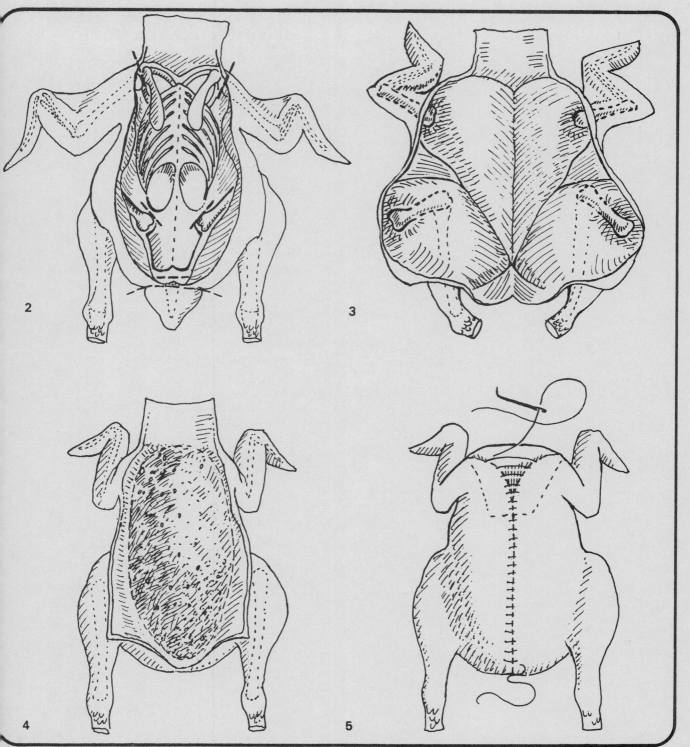

2

3

4

5

159

Fried Chicken

1 small chicken, cut in 8 pieces
3–4 tablespoons oil
1 lemon
salt, pepper
1 clove garlic
1 onion
parsley
2–3 tablespoons plain flour
pork dripping or butter and oil for frying

Make a marinade with the oil, lemon juice, salt, pepper, sliced garlic and onion, and sprigs of parsley torn up small. Marinade the pieces of chicken in this for 2–3 hours. Take the pieces out, dry them and shake them well with flour, seasoned with more salt and pepper, in a paper bag.

Heat pork dripping or oil to a depth of about 1" in a heavy saucepan or sauté pan. When it is very hot put in the pieces of chicken and brown them evenly on all sides. Then cover the pan and turn down the heat, cooking the chicken gently and turning the pieces from time to time, for $\frac{1}{2}$ hour or until the chicken is cooked.

Serve with quarters of lemon. If you prefer the chicken to be very crisp on the outside take the lid off the pan again 15 minutes before serving.

For 4

Chicken with White Wine Sauce

1 chicken cut in 8 or 10 pieces
4 shallots, 1 oz butter
2–3 tablespoons oil, flour
salt, freshly ground pepper
1 glass white wine
6 juniper berries
2 cloves garlic
3 good strips orange peel
a large bunch of thyme
1 glass stock made with the giblets

Dust the pieces of chicken with flour, salt and pepper. Brown in fat and oil in a heavy pan or flameproof casserole. Do this fairly slowly, about 5 minutes each side. Remove the pieces to a plate. Soften the chopped shallots in the butter and oil. When they start to brown return the chicken, pour on the wine and let it bubble. Add the stock, crushed juniper berries, sliced cloves of garlic, orange peel, thyme, salt and pepper.

Simmer uncovered on top of the stove for $\frac{3}{4}$ hour, turning the pieces of chicken from time to time and tipping the pan to mix the sauce. When tender remove the thyme and taste for seasoning and serve sprinkled with chopped parsley.

☐ *This is also good with rabbit.*

For 4–5

Chicken Curry

1 small roasting chicken
3 onions, peeled and chopped
1 clove garlic peeled and chopped
½ teaspoon ground turmeric
½ teaspoon ground chilli
½ teaspoon salt
2 teaspoons ground coriander
½ teaspoon cumin
¼ teaspoon each ground cinnamon, cloves and
    cardamom
pinch black pepper
4 tablespoons yoghurt, olive oil

Heat the oil in a saucepan with a lid, and sauté the
onions and garlic for a few minutes. Add the chicken,
cut in pieces and skinned, and the turmeric, chilli
and salt, and sauté until the chicken is lightly
browned, five to seven minutes. Add the coriander,
cinnamon, cloves, cardamom, cumin and yoghurt,
and fry three minutes more. Simmer covered for one
hour, adding a little water if necessary. Serve with
plenty of rice and Raïta and Dhal.

For 4–5

Chicken and Leeks

1 small chicken
4 small leeks
1 oz butter
4 oz long grain rice
1 pint milk
salt and freshly ground pepper

Clean the leeks and cut into one-inch pieces. Soften
in the butter for five to ten minutes without letting
them even start to brown. Cut the chicken into four
large pieces and skin them. Leave the carcass for
stock.

Butter a casserole and arrange a layer of leeks in
the bottom, add two pieces of chicken, sprinkle
on half the rice, then repeat the layers again, leeks,
chicken and rice. Add half a teaspoon of salt and pour
over enough milk to cover everything (about a pint).
Cover closely and cook in a slow oven, Reg 2/300°,
for 1–1½ hours depending on the chicken. This makes
a lovely winter lunch.

For 4

Chicken Croquettes

a few mushrooms peeled and chopped, if
    available
½ lb left-over chicken, chopped up (no skin or
    gristle)
Béchamel —1½ oz flour, 1½ oz butter, just under
    ½ pint milk
1 egg yolk
salt, pepper
flour
1 egg, beaten
dry breadcrumbs
deep fat

Fry the mushrooms, if any, in butter. Make the
sauce, which should be very thick, and season it.
Add the chicken and mushrooms and egg yolk.
Stir over low flame until the mixture is really
thick. Put it on a flat dish to cool and solidify
(leave all day, or overnight). Take a floured
board and shape croquettes (like fat sausages).
Dip in beaten egg, then breadcrumbs, and fry in
smoking hot deep fat, until golden. Serve with
tomato sauce.

□ *These are also very good made with left-over
pheasant or turkey.*

For 4

How to Carve a Turkey, Large Chicken or Capon

Sharpen two knives, one with a 6″ blade and one
with a 9″ blade and have ready your carving fork
and a spoon for the stuffing. Remove all strings
and skewers.

1. Remove the merry thought or wishbone by
feeling your way carefully round its outside edge
with your short knife, and snicking the sinews
where it joins the bird's shoulder-bones. This
helps to carve fine, straight breast slices.

2. Place the bird with its legs to the left, stick the
fork firmly into the drumstick, make cut (a) and
pull the drumstick towards you so that you can
cut through the ball and socket joint. Slice
through to remove thigh and drumstick.

3. Carve slices from the thigh and more slices
from the drumstick.

4. Using your long-bladed knife and leaving the
wing where it is, so that the bird does not tip
over, carve careful vertical slices starting halfway
down the breast at (b). A horizontal cut (c)
across the top of the wing through to the carcase
helps to make neat slices and keep the wing
intact. The reason for starting halfway down the
breast and making your cuts vertical rather than
slanting is that any meat remaining after you
have carved what you need stays nice and moist
under its skin.

5. Remove the wing as you did the leg, levering
it away with the fork and snicking through the
joint with your short knife. Cut off wing-tips if
they have been left on by the butcher, and
divide the wing in two if it is a large bird.

6. Carve the other side as before but keeping the
meaty side towards your guests and tilting the
bird towards you with the help of your fork.

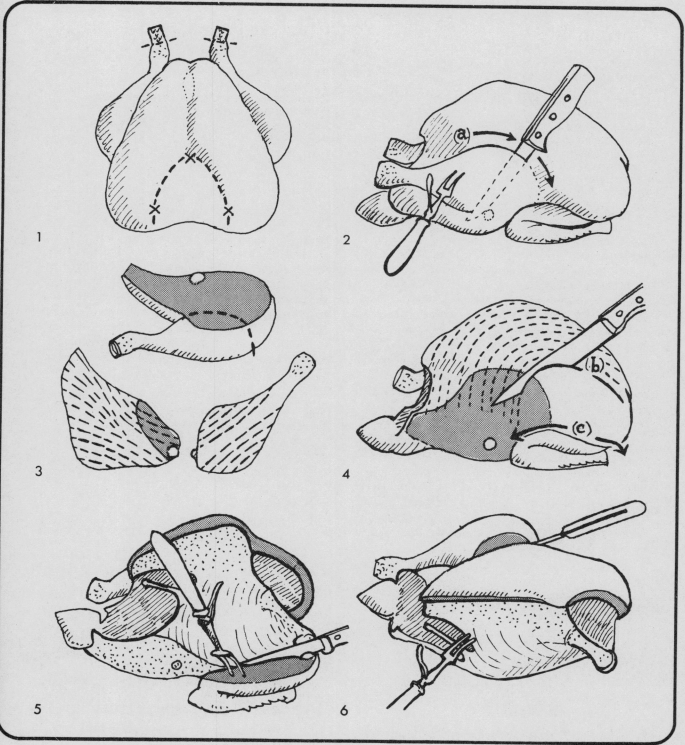

1

2

3

4

5

6

Chicken Pie

1 small boiling chicken
2 carrots, 1 onion
8 peppercorns, 1 bayleaf, salt
1 oz butter, 1 oz flour
juice of ½ lemon
chopped parsley
6 rashers bacon
4 oz mushrooms
plain pie pastry (page 256)
top of the milk

Cover the chicken with water in a large saucepan, bring slowly to the boil, skim and add the sliced vegetables, bayleaf, peppercorns and salt. Simmer for 1½ hours or longer, until the bird is tender. Allow to cool a little in the cooking liquid. Preheat oven to Reg 7/425°. Make a sauce with the butter, flour and ¾ pint of the strained, hot chicken broth. Throw in the mushrooms whole and simmer for eight minutes. Check for seasoning. Skin the chicken and cut it into pieces. Roll the bacon rashers, rinds removed, and keep together with toothpicks while you fry them gently for 15 minutes. Remove the toothpicks.

Mix the chicken pieces, chopped parsley and lemon juice into two thirds of the mushroom sauce, keeping the remaining sauce aside, and turn the mixture into a pie dish. Lay the bacon rolls on top and cover with pastry. Brush with top of the milk and bake at Reg 7/425° for ten minutes and then at Reg 4/350° for 20 minutes or longer. Serve with the extra sauce.

☐ *A bright green vegetable such as sprouts, broccoli, or best of all fresh peas, sets off the pale interior of the pie. It is also delicious eaten cold.*

For 4–6

Chicken Paprika

An elderly chicken, jointed in small pieces
2–3 onions, chopped
2 tablespoons oil and butter, or chicken fat
2 tablespoons paprika
¼ pint sour cream
salt to taste

Brown the pieces of chicken in oil and butter or chicken fat, in a flameproof casserole, remove them to a dish and fry the onions in the same fat. Stir in the paprika, let it cook for a minute, then return the chicken, season and cover very tightly with foil and the pan lid. Leave to simmer very slowly or put in a low oven, Reg 2½/315°, for 1–1½ hours, depending on the age of the chicken. When it is tender, thicken the copious juice with half the sour cream just before serving (don't let it boil).

Serve each helping with an extra dollop of sour cream and a sprinkling of paprika on top. Boiled noodles tossed in butter are lovely with this dish.

For 4

Chicken Livers with Sage

1 lb chicken livers, cut in pieces
1 oz butter
2 slices bacon, rinds removed, cut in pieces
salt and freshly ground pepper
3 or 4 fresh sage leaves, chopped, or 1 teaspoon
    dried sage
sherry

Melt the butter in a small iron pan, and sauté the pieces of bacon for a minute or two. Add the chicken livers, a little salt, pepper and sage and cook five minutes, stirring them about a bit. Remove the chicken livers and bacon to a hot dish and keep them warm, while you add a dash of sherry and a similar amount of water to the pan, and let it sizzle for a minute, stirring to release the sediment. Pour the juices over the livers and serve

For 4

Chopped Liver

1 lb chicken livers
6 oz chicken fat or oil
2 large onions, sliced
2 large hard-boiled eggs
pepper, salt

Melt the fat in a frying pan. Add onions and soften them. Just before they get brown add the chopped chicken livers. Stir until the livers are well cooked. Put the mixture into a chopping bowl with the hard-boiled eggs, season, and chop to a fine paste (or put through mouli, or pound). Serve cold, rolled into little dumplings, with rice salad, or spread on toast or biscuits.

For 4–6

Chicken Fat

If you have a nice large fresh boiling fowl you will find it has large areas of good yellow fat around the back opening. These can be rendered down to produce some really fine frying fat with a delicate flavour.

Cut off any parts that are discoloured, put the rest in a bowl, standing in a pan of water and let it simmer until all the fat has run out. Strain it to remove any bits of fibre, and chill.

Roast Duck

3 lb duckling with giblets
½ an orange
leaf of sage
salt, pepper, oil
a bouquet of herbs
onion, carrot

Preheat the oven to Reg 3½/335°. Put the orange, sage and a sprinkling of salt and pepper into the duck. Rub the outside with oil, and sprinkle on some salt. Put the giblets, all but the liver, into a saucepan, with water to cover, and the bouquet, onion and carrot, and salt and pepper. Simmer while you roast the duck. Lay the duck upside down in a roasting tin and roast, basting occasionally for ¾–1 hour. Turn it over the right way up and drain off most of the fat which has run from it. Pour the giblet stock into the pan and give it another hour, basting as you go, until the skin is crisp and dark gold. Put it on a warm serving dish and make the gravy in the following way.

Remove most of the fat from the roasting tin with a large spoon. Put it over a low heat and put in the liver to cook whole. When the juices are bubbling add a sprinkling (just a touch) of flour and ½ glass of wine if you can spare it. Then add a little water and cook, stirring, turning the liver over from time to time. Remove the liver to the serving dish and serve the gravy in a sauceboat, having tasted it for seasoning. Leave the duck to stand in a warm place for at least ½ hour before carving.

For 4

How to Carve a Duck or Goose

You can deal with a small duck by cutting it into 4 portions as described for a small chicken (pages 106–7). A larger duck or a goose will need to be carved.

Sharpen your short poultry knife and your long carving knife, use the short one for jointing and the long one for carving slices. Remove all string and skewers.

1. Remove the wishbone by carefully feeling your way round its outside edge with your short knife and snicking through the sinews at the shoulder joints.

2. Turn the bird over onto its breast and insert your knife under and behind the leg, which lies well underneath the bird (a). Prize it away with your fork, sever the ball joint with the point of your knife and continue the cut towards the tail-end of the bird (b) as there is a nice piece of meat here to include with the leg.

3. Cut the leg in two; the joint is off to the side so feel for it carefully.

4. Turn the bird the right way up and make vertical slices with the longer knife, carving the bird from about quarterway up its breast (c). These will be thin slices that end just above the wing. When you have finished the breast remove the wing. It has hardly any meat on it but somebody might like to chew it.

5 & 6. Carve the second side as you did the first, keeping the meaty side of the bird towards the guests.

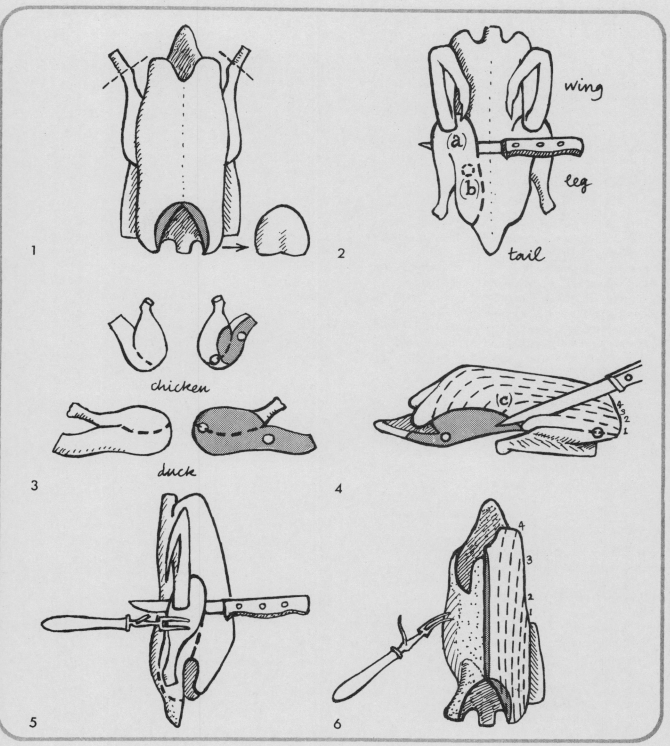

1

2 wing

leg

tail

(a)
(b)

3 chicken

duck

4 (c)

5

6

Stuffed Duck for a Party

1 7 lb duck
1 glass brandy
1 glass white wine } (if possible)
salt, pepper, marjoram, thyme, parsley, pistachios
    (if possible) truffles if you have any
1 fresh pig's foot
1 carrot
1 onion
½ lb pigs' liver or chicken livers
¼ lb bacon rashers (rinds removed)
¾ lb pie veal

*Choose 2 things from any of these, according
to the amount you have to spend, and
availability.*
1 pigeon
1 very small roasting chicken
½ lb cooked tongue in 1 piece
½ lb cooked ham or boiled bacon in 1 piece
1 small rabbit
2 cloves garlic

Start two days before the party. Bone the duck according to the diagram on page 158 for boning a chicken, leaving its lower leg bones in, and wings. Salt and pepper its inside and sprinkle with brandy or wine. Leave to rest while you prepare the stuffing and stock. Put its bones into a large saucepan with a bouquet of herbs, the pig's foot, the carrot and onion, and add to it any other bones and scraps you may encounter from making the stuffing — e.g. rabbit, pigeon, or chicken bones. Aim to make almost 1 gallon of stock, which will give 20 people delicious consommé for a first course.

Make the stuffing. Stiffen the liver by cooking it in a little butter before mincing it with the bacon rashers and pie veal. If you are using pigeon, chicken or rabbit, take the slivers of meat from the tenderest parts and mince the rest putting the bones in the stock-pot. Marinade the slivers in brandy.

If you are using the tongue, ham or bacon, cut strips about ½" square and 4" long. Mix the minced meats well and add salt, pepper and crushed or finely chopped garlic. Add chopped parsley, thyme leaves and marjoram if you have it. Add pistachio nuts and truffles if you are feeling the party is worth it. Add brandy and wine and 2 ladles of stock, which should be getting good by the time you have done all this boning and mincing. Taste a teaspoon of the mixture for seasoning after frying it in a little butter. Drain the liquid from the marinading

strips into the minced mixture. Stuff the duck with alternate layers of mince, and fillets, or strips of meat. Sew it up. Cool about 1½ pints of stock and place the duck in it. Use an oval tin or steel fishkettle with a lid if you have such a thing, if not use a baking tin and cover it with silver foil, but the shape of the finished duck will spread in a tin, so tie tapes round it. Braise it in the oven 1½ hours covered, Reg 3/325°. Finish by draining off the stock, but keep it separate and turn up the oven to Reg 5/375° for the duck to brown, uncovered, for ½ hour. Allow it to cool completely before removing threads. Scrape the sediment from the pan with the stock from the cooking of the duck, this will improve its colour and flavour. Strain it through a sieve and put it to cool in the fridge. There will be a great deal of fat on it. Also strain the consommé from the big pan and put it to cool.

NEXT DAY. Remove the threads from the duck and take all the fat from the cooking stock, which should be jellied enough to use as a glaze. Pour a little at a time over the duck, to coat it with a nice shine. Decorate if you like, with strips of green cucumber skin, slices of tomato or red pimento, and pieces of white cucumber. Serve with its dark jelly chopped up all round it, and slice it as you would a loaf of bread. Serve the soup first, clarified with egg white if need be Add as much sherry to it as you can for flavour.

For 20

Old English Pigeons

2 plump pigeons
6 medium onions, chopped
salt, sugar, pepper
bouquet of herbs (parsley, bay leaf, thyme)
juice of 1 lemon
½ oz butter
½ oz flour

Buy the pigeons well in advance (as this recipe entails marinating them for 3–6 days). Make a mixture of equal parts of salt and sugar, about a dessertspoonful of each and rub it well into the birds, inside and out. Leave them in the refrigerator or cool place (covered with a cloth and turning occasionally) for 3–6 days. Take them out, wash them well and dry them. Put them into a bowl, or casserole with a tight fitting lid, with the chopped onions, herbs and a little salt and pepper. Cover tightly with foil, or a cloth and greaseproof paper and steam (as you would a suet pudding) in a large covered pan of constantly boiling water for 4 hours. (Young birds may be done after 2–3 hours, so test occasionally.) A great deal of gravy is produced by the onions and birds, by the time they are done, which you turn into a sauce with the flour, butter and lemon juice. Remove the pigeons and onions to a warm dish and discard the bouquet. Work the flour and butter together thoroughly and add bit by bit to the gravy stirring constantly over a low heat till the sauce thickens. Add the lemon juice and check seasoning. Serve birds, cut in half with sauce and onions poured over them.

For 4

Braised Pigeons with Celery Sauce

4 young pigeons
flour
2 heads celery
2 onions
2 oz bacon in a piece
butter
1 glass red wine
thyme, bayleaf
3 or 4 tablespoons cream
1 tablespoon beurre manié
a little salt and plenty of freshly ground pepper

Cut the celery into half-inch pieces and chop the onions coarsely. Cut the bacon into rough dice. Heat the butter in a flameproof casserole, add the bacon, and when it is sizzling brown the pigeons, dusted in flour, in the fat for a few minutes, until they are coloured on every side. Remove them to a plate and put the vegetables into the casserole to sweat, covered, for a few minutes. Lay the pigeons on top and pour the heated wine over everything. Add herbs, salt and pepper, cover and simmer on top of the stove or in the oven at Reg 3/325°, so that the liquid is almost, but not quite, boiling, for about 1½ hours, or until the pigeons are tender. Put the birds on a hot dish and keep warm with the vegetables, scooped out of the sauce with a perforated spoon. Skim most of the fat off the juices and thicken them with the beurre manié, stirring all the time. The juice is copious, most of it coming from the celery. Finish the sauce by stirring in the cream, and taste for seasoning. Pour it over the birds and vegetables and serve puréed potatoes.

☐ *An alternative method is to put a pint of fresh shelled peas and a lettuce into the pot, instead of the celery, about 25–30 minutes before the end of the cooking.*

For 4

Grouse Pudding

1 old grouse
¾ lb chuck or skirt of beef
1 onion, with a clove in it ⎫
1 carrot, sliced   ⎬ To make stock
a bouquet of herbs, salt ⎭ with bones of
   and pepper   grouse
¼ lb mushrooms, tossed in butter or bacon fat
1 oz seasoned flour
6 oz self-raising flour ⎫
3 oz shredded suet   ⎬ Suet pastry
Salt, a little water   ⎭

Start several hours, at least six, before dinner. Strip the grouse from its carcase, leaving the legs and wings whole, quarter the breast meat. Cut the beef into thin slices. Make stock by covering the onion, carrot, herbs, salt and pepper, grouse carcase and beef trimmings with cold water and simmering, covered, for 2 hours. Let it cool, and strain it.

Make the pastry with the suet, flour, pinch of salt and water. Take ¾ of it to line a greased pudding basin. Wrap each cooked mushroom (quartered if large) in a strip of the beef, which has been tossed in seasoned flour. Put grouse and beef alternately in the lined basin and almost cover with strained stock. Cover with remaining pastry, damping the edges to make it stick. Cover the top firmly with doubled greaseproof paper or silver foil, tucked under basin's rim and tied with string. Have a large pan ready with boiling water and put the basin into it, so that the water comes about ⅔ of the way up the basin. Cover the pan and keep it boiling for 4 hours, replenishing with boiling water as need be.

To serve, heat the remainder of the strained stock and cut a wedge from the pastry lid. Pour in the boiling stock, mixing with the pudding contents, so that each serving is well gravied.

For 4

Casseroled Partridge with Cabbage

2 oz pork fat, fresh or salt, pork dripping or lard
2 old partridges
2 carrots, peeled and sliced
1 small onion, peeled and sliced
1 savoy cabbage
4 oz bacon or salt pork
a bouquet of herbs, pinch of mace or grate of nutmeg
4 pork chipolatas, or boiling sausages
salt, pepper, dash of white wine
½ pint stock
½ oz flour, ½ oz butter worked together

Cut the pork fat into cubes, and put it in a large iron or earthenware casserole to give out its fat or alternatively melt the lard or dripping. As the fat begins to run, dust the partridges with flour and brown them on all sides, turning frequently. While they are browning slice the onion and carrots and shred the cabbage finely.

When the birds are golden brown, remove them to a plate and keep them hot while you soften the onion, bacon and then the cabbage in the same fat in a separate pan. Turn them over a few times until they are glistening and starting to brown. Cover the bottom of the casserole with carrot slices, place the birds on top, bury them in the cabbage, onion and bacon, and season well with salt, pepper and mace or nutmeg. Add the bouquet and the wine, and let it sizzle, then add enough stock or water almost to cover the birds. Put on the lid and leave in the oven, Reg 2/300° for 3–4 hours. 1 hour before the end brown the sausages, and put them in the casserole with the partridges. Serve each person with half a partridge, a sausage and some cabbage and gravy thickened with beurre manié before serving. If it suits you to cook them more slowly use Reg 1/275° for 4 hours or more. They are done when the legs pull easily from the bodies. They will stay moist if you keep them buried in the cabbage.

For 4

To Skin A Rabbit or Hare

If you have never skinned a rabbit or hare the sight of one of these otherwise welcome gifts on the kitchen table, with fur intact, is rather upsetting. It must be skinned before it can be cooked, and this is really (once you've done it four or five times) quite easy and not too awful. If you can't face it you will have to take the whole thing to a butcher, but think of the time saved if you can do it yourself. A hare should be well hung (head down) but a rabbit should be gutted as soon as possible. Lay the animal on several layers of newspaper. Take a sharp pointed knife, find the lower tip of the breast bone and slit the skin right through. Make an incision from the tip of the breastbone to the base of the tail. This can be done without looking the first time, if your sense of direction is accurate. Do be sure you have gone through the skin, or you will have to do it again to extract the innards. Having made this incision pick up the animal, front legs in one hand, back legs in the other, belly to the newspaper, and shake; the intestines will drop on to the paper. Boldly pull any that remain, until you find you are dealing with relatively familiar pieces like liver and kidneys; take these out and put them aside. Throw the intestines away. Then get on with the skinning. Starting with the original incision, peel the skin away towards the spine on each side. Flip the back legs inside out, as if you were taking off very difficult stockings. Sever the legs at the heel joint (the bend above the foot) and cut off the tail. The back and the middle of the animal should now be skinned.

Pull the skin up towards the head, flipping out the front legs as you did the back, and severing the legs at the first joint above the foot; go on pulling the skin towards the head. The easy way out is not to skin the head, but to chop it off as soon as the neck is clear. However, if you feel you need the head, which makes good stock, you must carefully cut round the ears and eyes, and pull the whole skin over the head, ending at the mouth.

With the rabbit or hare now naked, make an incision between the back legs and clean it well under a running tap. Break the membrane across the rib cage, take out the heart and lungs and wash it all very well. Before cooking a rabbit, it is a good idea to get rid of the slime left after skinning, and also the sour grass taste of a wild rabbit, by soaking in fairly heavily salted water for an hour. This also helps to whiten the flesh. A hare will need a good rinsing, as it always seems to be so much bloodier than a rabbit.

Jointing is fairly simple. The back legs are severed where they join the backbone, and then divided along the centre of the pelvis. The next piece (the saddle) continues till the ribs begin. The ribs have the front legs and shoulder joined on, and again can be split down the centre. The head is not used except for making stock. The kidneys can be left in the saddle, but the liver should be kept aside, as it helps to make a good sauce. The heart can be left under the ribs, or used with the head for stock.

Rabbit Stew

1 small rabbit
6 oz fresh belly of pork
1 onion, finely chopped
butter and oil for frying
1 glass white wine
1½ lbs tomatoes, peeled and chopped
1 bunch parsley, tied with thread
1 clove garlic, chopped
salt and freshly ground pepper
parsley and garlic to finish

Remove the rind and cut the pork into cubes; sizzle it in the oil and butter in a sauté pan until the fat begins to run. Add the onion and soften it, browning only slightly. Add the jointed rabbit and brown the pieces thoroughly. Bring the wine to the boil in a small pan. Pour it over the rabbit and add the tomatoes, parsley, garlic, salt and pepper. Turn the heat down and simmer uncovered, stirring from time to time and turning the pieces of rabbit, for 1–1½ hours until the rabbit is tender.

Serve in a gratin dish, spooning the pork and tomatoes over the rabbit and sprinkle with freshly chopped parsley and garlic.

For 4

Notes on Rabbit

The only cheap rabbit is that which you shoot yourself, or deep frozen Polish, Australian or Chinese. All these need long slow cooking (unless the rabbit you shoot yourself is a tiny one and therefore young).

Good butchers stock large, tame, tender young hutch rabbits. These are delicious, need little cooking, and are rather expensive. They cost more per pound than roasting chicken or shoulder of lamb.

If you do use these rabbit recipes on a wild English or foreign rabbit, double the cooking times.

Sauté of Rabbit with Mustard

1 tender young rabbit, jointed, and its liver
butter and oil for frying
2 shallots, sliced into rings
2 rashers bacon, rinds removed, cut in pieces
1 glass white wine
generous sprig thyme
salt and freshly ground pepper
parsley, chopped
coffee cup thin cream, or top of the milk
2 teaspoons Dijon mustard

Melt enough butter and oil in a large shallow frying pan or casserole to cover the base of the pan. Fry the shallots for a minute, add the bacon, then turn up the heat and brown the rabbit pieces, keeping the liver aside. Add the wine and let it bubble a little, turn down the heat, add the thyme, salt and pepper, and let the rabbit cook, covered, until it is tender, which should be within half an hour or even less if it is a really young one. Remove the sprig of thyme.

Fry the liver separately in butter, chop or slice it and mix it with the cream and mustard. Pour this over the rabbit pieces, heat through, reduce by boiling if necessary, and serve sprinkled with parsley.

If you have a tough or large rabbit, cook it much longer. Flour the pieces before frying, and after the wine has bubbled up add half a pint of warm stock, which can be made from the head and giblets of the rabbit. Simmer until tender and then proceed as before to finish the sauce. If the sauce is not thick enough, add an egg yolk or beurre manié, or reduce by boiling rapidly.

Rabbit Escalopes

2 fillets from either side of the backbone of a large,
  tender rabbit
seasoned flour
1 egg, beaten
fine dried breadcrumbs
1 tablespoon each of butter and oil
butter
dash of sherry

Ask the butcher to take the fillets from the rabbit
before he joints it. If he refuses, take it home whole,
and with a sharp, pointed knife cut a line as near
the spine as you can, all along the back. Keep the
knife against the bone and carefully remove the
fillet. The underbelly, which is thin and flappy, will
come too; cut this off. Turn the fillets underside up,
so the silvery side is below, and cut lengthwise
almost through but not quite. Lay them on a piece
of well-oiled greaseproof paper, cover with another
piece and then bash, with either a proper steak
beater or a rolling pin. They will flatten out considerably to a neat pear shape.

Take them out of the paper, dip in seasoned flour,
then beaten egg, then crumbs. Fry gently in butter
and oil for about five minutes each side.

Remove them to a warm plate while you drop
another tablespoon of butter into the pan, raise
the heat, and as it froths add a dash of sherry. Stir
it quickly and pour a little of this good gravy on
each escalope.

☐ *This is only feasible if you have a large rabbit.
Use the rest for a pâté, stew, pie or jelly.*

For 2

Roast Saddle of Hare

1 saddle of hare, preferably marinated for two days
  as this makes it more tender and tasty
  and improves the flavour of the gravy
flour
4 rashers bacon
butter, beef dripping or pork fat
water
salt and freshly ground pepper
¼ pint single cream or top of the milk

Take the hare out of the marinade and wipe it dry.
Remove the silvery membrane over the back with a
sharp knife. Preheat the oven to Reg 7/425°. Melt
about half an ounce of butter in a frying pan. Dust
the saddle with flour, brown it on all sides in the
butter, take it out and wrap in bacon rashers. Roast
in butter for 20–30 minutes, basting often. Add
half a glass of water five minutes before it is cooked.
Take off the bacon and put the hare with the rashers
on a hot serving dish to keep warm.

Pour off some of the butter from the roasting tin,
or scoop it off with a metal spoon. Add a minute
sprinkling of flour to the juices in the tin; let it
bubble a moment and stir in the cream. Heat gently,
taste for seasoning, and pour the small amount of
thickish sauce over the saddle.

Carve in lengthwise strips parallel to the backbone
and serve with puréed potatoes or celeriac or hot
beetroot.

☐ *Some people include the back legs to stretch the
saddle further.*

For 2–3

Jugged Hare

1 hare, jointed and cut up
seasoned flour
2 tablespoons lard or dripping
1 large onion
4 carrots
1 stick celery
bunch of parsley and thyme
4 cloves
8 peppercorns
stock, salt
1 tablespoon beurre manié
small glass port, or 1 tablespoon redcurrant jelly

If you like, you can marinate the hare for 24 hours in the marinade for game. Wipe the joints dry and flour thoroughly all over. Heat the lard in a flameproof casserole and fry the joints quickly to brown them. Put them aside and put the sliced onion and the carrots and celery, cleaned and sliced, into the pan. Cover and allow to sweat for ten minutes. Replace the hare, add the herbs, cloves and peppercorns, and pour in enough stock just to cover. Add a little salt and simmer, covered, for one and a half hours, in the oven at Reg 2/300° or on top of the stove.

Remove the joints to a dish. Strain the liquid and reduce by almost half. Stir the beurre manié into the hare liquid making a smooth, thick sauce. Stir in the port or redcurrant jelly, put the hare back into the casserole or onto a nice white oval dish, and pour the sauce over.

Before serving allow it to stand in a hot place, without cooking, for ten minutes, to let the sauce and meat marry together again and the flavour develop.

For 4

Marinade for Game

¼ pint vinegar (wine or cider)
½ pint red wine
grating of nutmeg
bayleaf, sprig of thyme
2 large onions, finely sliced
salt and peppercorns

Mix everything together and pour it over the game in a china or glazed earthenware dish. Turn the meat over from time to time; you can leave it there from one to fourteen days.

Vegetables

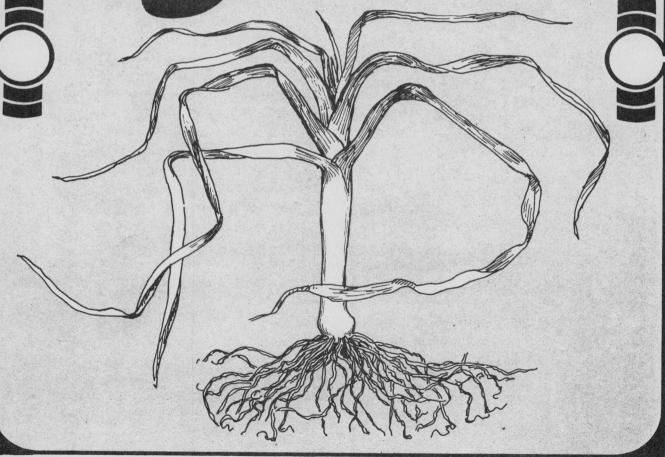

Vegetables

The only way to buy fresh vegetables, unless you want to pay the earth for them, is in season, and to buy them often so that they can be eaten absolutely fresh. There are dozens of different vegetables to be seen trundling in muddy lorries towards Covent Garden on any dark winter morning; parsnips, cabbages, sprouts, beetroots, carrots, endives, celeriac, swedes, celery, Jerusalem artichokes, red cabbage, turnips, winter spinach, onions, leeks, cauliflowers, spring greens and curly kale are all grown in Britain and are far, far cheaper to serve than the smallest handful of imported French beans. So, of course, are all the pulses that are so comforting on a cold day. Lettuces seem to struggle up all the year round, but they do become more expensive in winter and taste of less.

The best vegetables are home-grown, and at least home-grown herbs are a possibility for everyone, since they can be planted out quite happily in the smallest window-box. Parsley is almost always on sale, so it makes sense to concentrate on the more unusual herbs, tarragon, basil, lovage, even thyme, rosemary, sage and chives which can be made to feel at home on a city windowsill.

Since tomatoes are only in season for a few months (home-grown ones from August to October), it is worth remembering that tinned Italian tomatoes always make a good substitute in cooking. They are grown in blazing sunshine and have a beautiful sweet flavour even after they have been in a tin.

Most books on nutrition suggest peeling vegetables thinly, as many of the vitamins lie close to the surface and thick peeling disposes of too many of them; for economy this is important too, though it is not a rare sight to see even quite experienced cooks carving off the peel of potatoes, carrots, turnips, parsnips and so on in great chunks.

Nutrition books also suggest conservative (loaded word) cooking of green vegetables such as broccoli, cabbage, peas, beans and brussels sprouts. Their method is to use from half to one inch of water so the vegetables are virtually cooked in steam. But if you just cover them with salted water and cook them for the minimum time, they come out tasting and looking so much better and fresher that people are bound to eat more to make up for vitamins that have escaped. Once they are cooked, drained and smothered in butter they should be eaten straight away; they do not keep hot well, and lose their flavour and colour very fast.

With salads, there are two vital things that go wrong. One is that the salad is washed but not properly dried before the dressing goes on — the result, a soggy wasteland of tasteless wet green. Second, instead of being over-generous with oil and lubricating the salad to give it a wonderful unctuousness that contrasts with the crisp leaves, the vinegar (which should be wine or even cider but NEVER malt) is overdone and the result gives the palate a violent shock. Put the dressing on a green salad at the last possible minute, it goes listless so fast. A handful of sprigs of parsley, tarragon or chervil with stalks removed are a good addition to a green salad. Tomatoes aren't; make two separate salads instead of one jumbled one. Watercress makes a very good salad to accompany game or a juicy piece of beef, and is nearly always cheap.

Roast Jerusalem Artichokes

1½ lbs Jerusalem artichokes
lard or pork fat

Cook them like roast potatoes, parboiling for 2–5 minutes before putting into the hot fat. Baste them, put them in the oven and cook on the shelf below the meat, or put them in the roasting tin round the meat. They don't take as long as roast potatoes, about 30–40 minutes; they should be turned over carefully and basted once or twice.

☐ *Very good with roast pork. You can also cook parsnips like this.*

For 6

Aubergine Fritters

4 large aubergines
fritter batter (page 56)
salt
deep oil for frying

Cut the aubergines in lengthwise slices, sprinkle with salt, and allow them to drain for half an hour or more. Wash and dry the slices and coat them with batter. Heat the oil in a deep frying pan and deep-fry the aubergines to a golden brown. Drain very well before serving.

These are excellent with lamb.

☐ *This recipe is also fine for courgettes.*

For 6–8

Brussels Sprouts with Chestnuts

1 lb brussels sprouts
2 oz butter
½ lb chestnuts
salt, pinch of sugar
stock (about ½ pint)

Skin and cook the shelled chestnuts in the stock with a little salt and sugar, until they are tender (about ½ hour). Clean and trim the sprouts, cook them in salty boiling water until done (not too soggy) — about 10–15 minutes, according to their size. Drain well and melt half the butter in a pan and sauté the sprouts in it for about 10 minutes. Serve them mixed carefully with the chestnuts and any of their juice which remains. Take care not to crush the chestnuts or sprouts as you mix them. Leave them for 5–10 minutes in a warm place before serving.

☐ *A winter dish, and traditionally served with turkey.*

For 4–6

Broad Beans in their own Sauce

2–4 lbs broad beans, depending on their age
½ oz butter
½ oz flour
top of the milk
1 tablespoon finely chopped parsley, chervil or
    savory
lemon juice
salt

Pod the beans. If they are young and tender include a section of the pod around some of them. If they are old and tough make sure you remove the crescent attached to the bean, and even their outer skin.

Bring salted water to the boil and throw them in. When tender, strain, keep the beans warm and reserve the liquid. In another pan melt the butter, make a white roux with the flour and gradually stir in a cup of the liquid, the top of the milk and the chopped herbs of your choice. When you have a smooth sauce add the beans and a squeeze of lemon, season with salt if necessary, and serve.

For 4

Broad Beans in Oil

1½ lbs broad beans, small and fresh
6 spring onions
3 tablespoons olive oil
½ lemon
salt and black pepper

Cut up the broad beans with their pods still on. Any that look tough or ropey should be shelled. Roughly chop the firm parts of the onions. Heat the oil in a thick saucepan, put in the beans and spring onions and sweat them very gently with the lid on for 10 or 15 minutes. Add the juice of half a lemon and half a cup of water, salt and pepper, and cook uncovered until soft, about an hour. If necessary add a little more water. They should be very tender with an intense flavour. Good hot or cold.

For 4

Hot Beetroot with Garlic

5–6 small beetroots (the smallest you can buy)
1 clove garlic
olive oil
salt, sugar, chopped parsley

Boil the beetroots with 1″ of stalks and their tails left on. Very small beetroots need about ½ hour's gentle boiling, larger ones need longer — up to 2 hours. Peel them while still hot and heat the slices of garlic in the oil in a flat fireproof dish which you can take to the table.

Slice the beetroot into the oil and sprinkle with a little fine salt, sugar and parsley. Moisten it all with a little more oil, and leave to keep hot. Serve as soon as possible or the beetroot begins to lose its shine. It is also, if kept moist, nice cold this way.

For 6

Hot Baked Beetroot

1 lb raw beetroots
salt, fresh ground pepper
butter
a squeeze of fresh lemon juice
¼ pint cream (optional)

Wash the beetroots but do not break the skin or peel or cut them in any way. Put them in a brown paper bag and bake them in a very low oven, if you are using it for a stew or other slow-cooking dish, for about 3–4 hours at Reg 1/275°. Otherwise boil them in their skins in salted water until tender (2 hours). When they are soft (easily pierced with a skewer) skin them while they are still hot, slice them and lay the slices in a buttered gratin dish. Dot with butter and sprinkle with salt, pepper and lemon juice and heat them gently. Just before serving you can pour on some warmed cream or more melted butter and lemon juice. Sprinkle with parsley and serve as an hors d'œuvre or with hot sausages or game (roast pigeons, hare, etc.).

For 4

Chang's Cabbage

1½ lbs cabbage, green or white
2 tablespoons oil
few drops soy sauce
1 teaspoon salt
3 teaspoons sugar
2 tablespoons vinegar

Mix the salt, sugar and vinegar together. Slice the cabbage as finely as you can, discarding the tough stalks and outer leaves. Wash well and then shake as dry as possible in a cloth, as you would salad. Heat the oil in a large frying pan over a fairly high heat, and when it is really hot (but not burning), fling in the cabbage. Keep it moving about with a wooden fork, if you have one, or a spoon. As soon as it is all covered with oil, shake a few drops of soy sauce over it, then pour on the vinegar mixture. Let it cook a minute or two and serve at once, hot, crisp and juicy.

Children don't always like this, but adults like it as a change from universal plain boiled cabbage (though cabbage is not nearly as universal as it used to be, and boiled correctly it can be a really beautiful and delicious vegetable).

☐ *This is a sweet-sour cabbage, very Chinese but rather good with Shepherd's Pie or chops. It is also very quick — cooked in seconds.*

For 6

German Red Cabbage

1 medium-sized red cabbage
1–2 oz butter, 2 cloves garlic
1 large cooking apple, peeled and cut up
2 medium onions, peeled and sliced
bunch of thyme, parsley, and a bayleaf
grated orange rind or juice
1 teaspoon caraway seeds
pinch cinnamon, pinch nutmeg
salt and pepper
2 tablespoons brown sugar
small glass red wine (left-over is best as it becomes slightly vinegary)

Preheat oven to Reg 2/300°.

Take the large damaged outer leaves off the cabbage, quarter it and shred as finely as possible, discarding the centre core. Melt the butter in a flameproof casserole, add the cabbage and cook gently, covered, for five minutes. Add the apples, onions, garlic, a little grated orange rind, herbs, spices, salt and pepper. Mix everything together well, sprinkle on the sugar, add the wine, cover and put in the oven, for up to three hours. Check half-way through that it is not drying up, and if it is add a little hot water. This reheats very successfully, and is possibly even better for it.

☐ *A rich and filling dish.*

For 4–6

Cabbage with Noodles

1 medium-size white cabbage
1 onion
2 oz butter
salt, black pepper
½ lb dry noodles

Drop the washed, cored and quartered cabbage into boiling salted water and cook 5 minutes. Drain well. Meanwhile chop the onion finely and soften it in the butter in a large pan or casserole, then add the cabbage and stir well. Cover and cook 30–40 minutes, turning from time to time, until soft and golden. Season with salt and plenty of black pepper while the cabbage is cooking. Drop the noodles into boiling salted water and when they are just tender drain them well. Time it so that they are ready together. Mix into the cabbage and add a little more butter. Serve on its own or with meatballs or pork chops.

For 6–8

Frances's Cabbage

1 medium-size cabbage, any sort
1 oz butter
1 rasher bacon, diced
2 oz sultanas
a pinch each of cinnamon, nutmeg, cayenne
1 dessertspoon brown sugar
1 dessertspoon wine vinegar

Shred the cabbage, chop it up and leave to soak for 1 hour in cold water. Melt the butter in a large pan, throw in the well-drained cabbage, vinegar, bacon, sultanas, brown sugar, cinnamon and nutmeg, pinch of cayenne. Cook slowly, covered, for 1 hour, turning occasionally. It needs little or no salt.

For 4

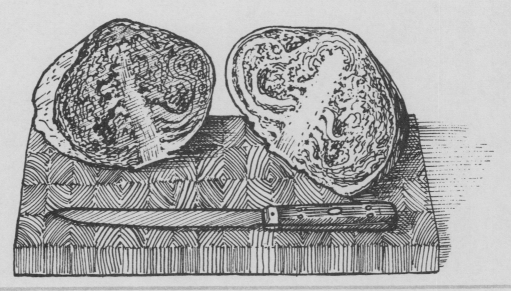

Cabbage with Sour Cream and Dill

1 cabbage
1 5 oz carton sour cream
1 teaspoon dill seeds
salt
freshly ground pepper

Quarter, core and wash the cabbage. Drop the pieces into boiling salted water and cook until just tender. Drain well and return to the pan with the sour cream, dill, a little salt and plenty of freshly ground pepper. Heat gently and cook, stirring to separate the pieces of cabbage from each other, until the water that drains from the cabbage has evaporated and the still greenish, but no longer bright green, leaves are bathed in a creamy sauce. Serve with pork chops or sausages.

☐ *Very successful with children who don't usually like cabbage.*
For 4

Coleslaw

½ small white cabbage, shredded finely
2 new or 1 old carrot, grated
1 or 2 sticks celery, shredded lengthwise into matchsticks
1 eating apple, grated

For the dressing
½ teacup of vinaigrette dressing
½ teacup of mayonnaise made with lemon
a little top of the milk

Mix the grated and shredded vegetables together in a china bowl. Add the vinaigrette dressing, made with a pinch of sugar, and turn and mix it well. Leave it to become absorbed for a little while. Thin the mayonnaise with the top of the milk and mix this in well too. Taste for seasoning. It should be a soft pale creamy salad, almost sweet, but with a slightly crisp vinegary bite.

☐ *This keeps well overnight, so if you are making it for a party it can be one of the things you can make in advance. You can alter the proportions of cabbage, etc., but don't be tempted to spoil it by adding onions, or herbs, not even parsley. It is very good with hamburgers or frankfurters*

For 6

Carottes Rapeés

1 large garden carrot for each person
6 tablespoons olive oil
1 ½ tablespoons white wine or cider vinegar
pinch of sugar, salt, and freshly ground pepper

Grate the carrots finely; make a dressing with the oil, vinegar, sugar, salt and pepper and turn the grated carrot in it until every shred is glistening.

In France they might serve this half and half with celeriac rémoulade (this page) or a salad of very finely shredded red cabbage tossed in a dressing heavily loaded with Dijon mustard.

For 5–6

Celeriac Rémoulade

2 heads celeriac
mayonnaise:
2 egg yolks
¼ pint oil
vinegar (white wine or cider)
salt and freshly ground pepper
mustard powder

Make a very mustardy mayonnaise by combining a spoonful of the mayonnaise with at least a teaspoonful of mustard powder, and mixing it very well into the rest.

Peel the celeriac and cut it into thin strips or shred it on a mandoline. Mix in the mayonnaise quickly. It is quite common to blanch the shredded celeriac before adding the mayonnaise but this can make it soggy and spoil the flavour.

For 8

Italian Carrots

1 lb carrots, old or young
1 oz butter
½ teaspoon salt
½ teaspoon sugar
1 dessertspoon flour
¼ pint water

Cut the cleaned carrots into thin strips. Melt the butter in a thick saucepan with a close-fitting lid. Sweat the carrots gently in the butter for about five minutes. Add salt and sugar and sprinkle on the flour, mixing it well with a wooden spoon. Then gradually add the water, clamp down the lid tightly, and leave to simmer slowly for twenty minutes. The carrots will be very tasty and covered with a thick golden sauce.

☐ *This recipe is also perfect for tiny young turnips and for celery.*
If you cook celery in this way, blanch it first in boiling salted water for five minutes.

For 4

Courgettes in Butter

1½ lbs courgettes
2 oz butter
chopped parsley (or chervil, mint or chives)
salt and freshly ground pepper
lemon juice

Wash the courgettes and peel them if necessary.
Cut in half-inch rounds or quarter them lengthways,
then cut these slices in half.

Bring a pan of salted water to the boil and cook
the courgettes for five minutes. Drain well and return
to the rinsed and dried pan with the butter.
Sprinkle with whichever herb you choose and simmer
gently, without browning, until the courgettes are
tender, 10–15 minutes. Season, and add a squeeze of
lemon if you like.

For 4

Courgettes au Gratin

6 small courgettes
4 medium tomatoes, peeled and chopped
1 clove garlic
parsley, chopped
salt and freshly ground pepper
1 oz butter
2 tablespoons oil
½ cup dried breadcrumbs

Don't peel the courgettes unless they are elderly.
Slice into thick pennies and strew with salt, leaving
them in a colander or on a tilted plate for an hour or
so, to drain off some of their moisture.

Heat the oil and butter in a large frying pan, and toss
the dried courgettes, a few at a time, without
browning them. Keep them warm. Melt a little
more butter and oil and cook the chopped tomatoes,
garlic, salt, pepper and parsley, until you have
a thickened purée. Add the courgettes and turn the
mixture into a gratin dish. Cover with the breadcrumbs, dot with butter and cook in a hot oven,
Reg 7/425°, for half an hour.

For 4 (or 2 if served as a course on its own)

Crudités with Aïoli

6–8 carrots
2 green peppers
2 heads chicory
1 cucumber
6 sticks celery
6 tomatoes
2 heads fennel
aïoli (page 246)

This can be made with any fresh crisp vegetables. Simply clean and cut them up, the carrots, peppers, chicory, cucumber and celery into sticks about two inches long, the tomatoes into quarters, the fennel into slices.

Put the vegetables, each sort in a group, on a large dish that just holds them all. Cover and chill lightly; serve crisp and fresh with a powerful aïoli, as the first course to an otherwise rich meal. Eat them with your fingers, dipping each piece into a dollop of aïoli on your plate.

For 6

Chick Peas

You cannot skimp the soaking of chick peas — they must be soaked overnight. Wash them first, then put them in a bowl large enough for them almost to double in size. Cover well with water and after their soaking cook them gently in the same water. A pinch of bicarbonate of soda softens the water and shortens the cooking time (rain water is, in fact, the best thing to cook all pulses in). Add no salt until the peas are almost tender. Cooking time depends on the age of the peas: new, they can take as little as half an hour, old, up to two hours.

Hummus with Tahina

½ lb chick peas, soaked overnight
¼ pint tahina paste (made of sesame seeds and bought in tins or bottles from Greek or Cypriot shops)
2 juicy lemons
2 cloves garlic, crushed
salt
olive oil

The chick peas must be cooked very well (this page); drain them and reserve their liquid. Greeks then roll them with a rolling pin (in a large plastic bag) until they are pulverised, which gives an uneven texture but you can mouli or liquidise them, moistened with a little of their liquid. When they are crushed, add more of the cooking liquid, the tahina paste, lemon juice, crushed garlic and salt. The taste must be adjusted to the way you like it, some like more lemon, some more garlic and so on. Serve, moistened with a little more oil, on a plate, with a few spring onions and some good hot bread. Eat this as a simple lunch dish or a first course.

For 6

Bulgour

½ lb coarsely ground wheat (from Greek or Health
   Food shops)
¼ lb Italian vermicelli
1 pint hot stock, bouillon or water
2–3 oz butter
salt
pepper
sprinkle of parsley

A deep, round earthenware dish with a lid is good
for cooking this in. Otherwise, use a largish pan
with a lid. Melt the butter in the pan. Break up
the vermicelli, and brown it in the butter, stirring
with a wooden spoon. Add the ground wheat
(bulgour) and stir while it rapidly absorbs the
butter. Pour in the hot stock or water, stir well
and, putting the lid on, turn the heat as low as
you can. Let it cook undisturbed for 12 minutes,
when all the liquid should be absorbed. Stir again,
and replace lid. Remove from heat and leave it
alone for another 12 minutes. Stir it again and leave
it for 5 minutes. Serve with seasoning of more
pepper than salt, sprinkled with parsley, and if
liked, a spoonful of yoghurt with each helping.

☐ *Similar to couscous, it goes well with stews.*

For 6–8

To Cook Dried Beans or Lentils

white, green, red, brown or black, large or small
   beans, 3 oz per person
water
bouquet of parsley, thyme, bayleaf, celery stalk and
   garlic if liked
salt

Soak the beans for several hours, at least four and
at most twelve or overnight; any longer and they will
start to ferment. Drain and put in a saucepan with
enough cold water to come two inches above the
top of the beans. Add *no salt* but put in the herbs
and garlic (and a piece of salt pork or bacon if you
like). Bring slowly to the boil and cook gently until
the beans are tender, a minimum of one hour and
up to two, depending on how long ago they were
picked and dried. If they take longer than this the
chances are they will never be tender.

Add salt about 15 minutes before draining the
beans. Keep the liquid for soup. They are now
ready for whatever you want to do with them. They
can be served as they are with plenty of freshly
chopped parsley and butter; or bathed in a sauce of
tomatoes and onion cooked in oil with a cupful of
their own liquid; or stirred into a creamy sauce
made with butter, flour and their own liquid, plus
chopped parsley; or you can leave out the
parsley but add chopped boiled bacon or ham.

Cold, they make very good salads with vinaigrette
dressing and raw onion, tuna fish, green beans or
just parsley.

Haricot and French Bean Salad

½ lb large white haricot beans (dried)
1 onion
2 cloves garlic
1 lb French beans
1 tablespoon white wine vinegar
5–6 tablespoons olive oil
½ Spanish onion
parsley, chopped
salt and freshly ground pepper

Soak the beans for about 5–6 hours. Put them in a pan and cover well with cold water, put in the peeled onion and the cloves of garlic. Bring slowly to the boil, skim and simmer for about ¾ hour. Add salt and simmer on for a quarter of an hour or so. When tender but not mushy, drain and cool. Cook the French beans, broken in pieces if they are too long, in boiling salted water for 10–15 minutes. When just tender, strain and refresh quickly under the cold tap. Drain very well. Mix the two kinds of beans together. Make an oily dressing with plenty of freshly ground pepper, and mix it in carefully so as not to break up the haricots. Strew some rings of Spanish onion on top and some chopped parsley if you like.

☐ *This is a very pretty dish*.

For 6

Dhal

½ lb small orange lentils
1 onion ⎫
1 clove of garlic ⎬ peeled and chopped
1 oz butter, or margarine and oil
1 teaspoon tomato purée
½ teaspoon coriander powder
½ teaspoon cumin seed
salt

Cover the lentils (they don't need soaking) with double their volume of water. They will cook quite quickly and absorb most of it. In another pan, fry the onion and garlic lightly in the butter until transparent. Add the tomato purée, spices and some salt. Stir. Add the lentils, which should not be too runny. Mix all well together and cook until the flavours are absorbed by the lentils (5–10 minutes). This will reheat well. If it is too stiff, add hot water.

☐ *For eating with curries*.

For 4

Purée of Split Peas

1 lb green or yellow split peas
1–2 oz butter
1 bay leaf and sprig of thyme tied together
salt
water or stock
1 small onion, finely chopped

Wash the peas and soak them overnight, especially if you don't know how old they are (although if you are in a hurry you can cook them straight away). Put them in a pan with enough cold water or stock to cover them by 1″. Add a walnut of butter and the herbs. Let them simmer, covered, over a low heat, adding more hot water or stock if necessary. Don't let them dry out too much or they will burn. Add salt when they are half-cooked. When they are completely cooked (after about 1½ hours) remove the herbs, sieve the peas, and stir in the finely chopped onion, which has been softened in the remaining butter. Reheat it very gently, with a little more stock if necessary.

□ *This is very good with sausages instead of the usual mashed potato. It is also delicious on its own with croûtons fried in butter as a filling first course.*

For 6

Traditional Pease Pudding

½ lb split peas, soaked overnight
1 large potato
2–3 pints bacon stock

Cut the potato in cubes and put it with the peas in a bag, or tied in a cloth, and stew it in the bacon stock. When soft, after about 1½ hours, mash or sieve the peas and potato and eat hot or cold. Keep the liquid in which they were cooked, and if there is any pease pudding left mix it in a bowl with a few tablespoons of the stock. Then return it to a saucepan with the remaining stock and you have some nice soup.

□ *If you are having salt pork or boiled bacon you can cook this in the same pot. Up North it is eaten with fish and chips.*

For 3–4

Benahavis Lentils

1 lb brown or green lentils (soaked overnight)
1 onion
1 large carrot
thyme, bay leaf
salt, pepper
1 whole head of garlic
olive oil
2–3 rashers bacon or 2–3 ozs salt pork
¾ lb black pudding
¾ lb spiced continental sausage

Wash the lentils and start cooking them in plain water, to cover them by about 1–1½″. Peel and chop the onion and carrot and add the herbs, tied in a bunch.

Keeping it intact, fry the entire head of garlic in olive oil in a small frying pan, until it is almost black all over. Put it in with the lentils, chop up the bacon or salt pork and fry them in the same oil for a minute or two. Add them and the oil to the lentils, cover and simmer until the lentils are tender; they should absorb most of the liquid. Remove the lid if there is too much liquid when they are nearly cooked, and let them simmer on until of a thick porridgy consistency. Cut the black pudding and sausage into 1″ lengths and fry them lightly, then add them to the lentils. Season with salt and pepper and serve, giving those who like it a clove of garlic, which is soft and fragrant but not pungent by this time.

For 6–8

Three Bean Salad

4 oz dried red kidney beans
4 oz dried haricot beans
4 oz flageolets or chick peas
6 chopped spring onions
8 tablespoons olive oil
1–2 tablespoons red wine vinegar
salt, chilli pepper (about as much as you would use of ordinary pepper)

Soak the beans overnight in separate bowls and cook them separately as some take longer than others. Add salt towards the end of cooking time. Drain, allow to cool and then mix all together with a dressing made of the olive oil, vinegar, salt and chilli pepper. Allow to stand for an hour or so to absorb the dressing, stir in the chopped onion, which should not be chopped until the last minute, and sprinkle with freshly chopped parsley.

☐ *This salad is very pretty but extremely filling. Serve it with lamb or as a starter to an otherwise light meal.*

For 6

Leeks in Red Wine

10 leeks, the same size and not too large
2 tablespoons olive oil
1 glass red wine
½ pint boiling water or stock
salt

Trim the leeks and wash well. Drain and shake them as dry as possible. Heat the oil in a wide shallow pan with room for all the leeks side by side. Gently brown them all over, pour on the wine and let it bubble a minute or two. Add salt and boiling stock or water, cover the pan and cook until the leeks are tender (test by piercing the root end with a sharp knife).

Take out the leeks with a perforated spoon and put them on a hot serving dish. Reduce the liquid a little and pour it over. These are particularly good with roast meat or chicken.

For 4

Leeks Vinaigrette

1 ½ lbs of the smallest leeks you can buy
5 dessertspoons olive oil
1 ½ dessertspoons white wine vinegar
salt and freshly ground pepper
Dijon mustard
garlic

Clean and trim the leeks, keeping the firm white part and the best of the green.

Bring a pan of salted water to the boil, drop in the leeks and let them cook until just tender. Put in a colander and leave to drain and cool.

Mash a clove of garlic with salt, mix with a teaspoon of mustard and plenty of pepper. Add 1½ dessert-spoons of vinegar and mix in thoroughly. Now add the oil, mixing gradually — it thickens like mayonnaise. You will need about 5 dessertspoons of oil but taste from time to time until it is right. When the leeks are thoroughly drained, lay them on a plate all in the same direction. Pour on the dressing and turn them a couple of times. They look very good on a white oval or oblong dish.

☐ *Serve these as an hors d'oeuvre or salad.*

For 2–4

Mushrooms à la Grecque

¾ lb fresh button mushrooms
4 tablespoons olive oil
4 tablespoons water
juice of ½ lemon
1 teaspoon coriander seeds
salt and freshly ground pepper
bayleaf, thyme, parsley

Boil together in a wide shallow pan the oil, water, lemon juice, coriander seeds, seasoning and a large bunch of herbs, for ten minutes. Clean the mushrooms, and if they are small add them whole to the liquid, if large, quarter them first. They must be closed and round; open ones absorb too much liquid, and exude too much so they end up sloppy.

Simmer the mushrooms slowly for ten minutes, stirring, then remove them to a dish and reduce the liquid a little. Pour it over the mushrooms, when the herbs and coriander seeds will be stranded on top. Leave them there, they look lovely and improve the flavour. Let the mushrooms get cold and eat with coarse brown bread and unsalted butter. They do shrink terribly but they don't need to be eaten in large quantities. Serve them with other salads as an hors d'oeuvre. They are good with cold cooked lentils in an oil and vinegar dressing, or with courgettes done in the same way as the mushrooms but with tomatoes instead of water added to the sauce.

For 4

Raw Mushroom Salad

½ lb tiny button mushrooms
¼ pint sour cream
½ lemon
salt and freshly ground pepper

Trim the mushrooms, and if they are the slightest bit bruised or brown, peel them. As you peel each one, rub it with a cut lemon. When they are all ready slice each one down into very thin slices. Keep the stalks on so that each slice shows a tiny mushroom in section.

Put them into a white china or earthenware bowl and mix in the sour cream; season lightly. This should be a very delicate salad. If you like you can add a little more lemon juice to sharpen it up.

☐ *This is one of the prettiest salads there is.*

For 3

Mushrooms with Brown Rice

½ lb mushrooms
4 oz brown rice
1 oz butter
parsley
3 cloves garlic
salt and freshly ground pepper

Soak the brown rice in salted water overnight, strain and rinse. Put it in fresh salted water and cook gently until tender, 15–20 minutes. The grains should still be separate and have a slight bite to them.

Meanwhile slice the mushrooms and put them in a sauté pan with the butter. Let them cook very, very slowly so that the juices all run out; stir from time to time. Chop the parsley and garlic finely. Stir the drained rice and the parsley and garlic into the mushrooms, season, let it get really hot and then serve with stewed lamb or beef or roast lamb.

For 4

Field Mushrooms

mushrooms
butter
top of the milk
salt
pepper

Clean and slice the mushrooms, melt the butter in a frying pan and fry them gently. As they absorb the butter, add a saucerful of creamy milk. Continue cooking for about ten minutes; they will then take more milk. This, rather than being absorbed, will thicken a little, leaving the mushrooms in a delicate creamy sauce. Add salt and pepper to taste and eat at once with egg and bacon or toast.

Pommes de Terre Rissolées

2 lbs new potatoes the size of a walnut
2–3 oz butter, preferably clarified or unsalted
coarse salt

Scrape the potatoes, and dry each one thoroughly on a cloth. Melt the butter in a large heavy saucepan and fry the potatoes, turning them over and over so they brown evenly. When they are nicely golden turn the heat right down and cover the saucepan. Let them cook gently like this for an hour. When the potatoes are tender, and easily pierced with a skewer, turn up the heat and shake the pan until they are crisp on the outside. It may take several minutes, so take care not to burn the butter at this point. As soon as they are crisp, sprinkle with plenty of coarse salt, and serve. They don't always end up absolutely crisp, but they do always end up absolutely delicious.

☐ *This is a recipe for small new potatoes; very good with any plainly roasted or braised poultry or meat.*

For 6

Champ

2 lbs potatoes
¼—½ pint milk
butter
salt and pepper
10 spring onions
bunch parsley

Peel and cut up the potatoes, and cook them with plenty of salt for a bit too long, until they are really soft but not disintegrating. It takes about 25 minutes. Meanwhile chop the spring onions and parsley as finely as you can, and heat the milk. When the potatoes are done, drain them and mash them with the boiling milk, pepper and more salt if necessary, plus butter if you like. When they are finely puréed add the chopped onions and parsley and mash these in. The potatoes should still be moist enough to fall off the spoon when you give it a shake.

This is an Irish potato dish which you could practically eat on its own. It is also very good with fish or any plain roasted meat.

For 6

Rösti

2 lb cold boiled potatoes (kept overnight in refrigerator or cold place to dry them out)
2–3 tablespoons butter
a dash of olive oil
salt, pepper

Grate the potatoes through a coarse grater. Let them stay in a light mass while you melt the oil and butter in a heavy frying pan. Tip the potato heap in to the pan, and press it down gently so that you can get a lid on. Season well and cook over a brisk heat at first and then turn down to medium, for 10–15 minutes, making sure it is not burning, (a) by sound (b) by smell. Remove lid, loosening the cake with a spatula and sliding a little more butter or oil down the side if necessary. Shake the pan until it rustles on the bottom, which is after a few minutes. Serve turned upside down on to a heated dish, and cut in wedges like a cake.

For 4–6

Potato Crisps

1 large potato
salt
deep oil for frying

Peel and slice the potato as thinly as possible. This is quickly done on a cucumber slicer or mandoline.

Wash the potato slices under the cold tap as you cut them, to remove the loose starch granules, and keep them all in cold water until you have finished the slicing. Then dry well in a cloth, shaking them as if you were drying a salad. Keep them in the cloth until ready to start frying.

Heat the oil in a pan with a deep-frying basket; when a blue haze rises test one slice. If it comes straight up to the surface, sizzling, the oil is ready. Lift the basket out of the oil, holding it over the pan fill it with two handfuls of crisps, and lower it back into the oil. If you put in too many crisps there is a great danger of the oil boiling over, so be very careful at this point and whisk the basket out if the oil starts to rise too far. As soon as the crisps *start* to colour lift the basket out of the oil while you count ten, then put it back again. As they turn golden lift them out, let them drain, and put them in a dish lined with kitchen paper to dry, sprinkling with fine salt.

They keep crisp in polythene bags.

German Potato Dropscones

¼ lb potatoes, peeled
¼ lb plain flour and 1 heaped teaspoon baking
    powder, or ¼ lb self-raising flour
2 eggs, separated
1 tablespoon oil or melted butter
¼ pint or less of milk
salt

Grate the raw potatoes. Squeeze out some of their liquid and put them into a bowl. Mix at once with the flour and baking powder. Incorporate the egg yolks, butter or oil, milk and a little salt. Whip the egg whites stiffly, and fold into the mixture. Heat and grease the griddle (see dropscones, page 230).

Drop spoonfuls of the mixture on to the griddle, giving them about three minutes on each side. Serve with eggs and bacon. They are also good spread with butter.

☐ *Eat these for breakfast or tea.*

About 20 scones

Really Crisp Fried Onions

Spanish onions
salt
flour
deep fat or oil

Slice the onions into thin rings and separate each one. Sprinkle lightly with fine salt and let them stand for an hour or so, for the moisture to drain off. Toss them in flour and drop them into hot fat or oil (with blue haze rising). As soon as they are golden brown take them out and drain them on kitchen paper. Eat as they are or with hamburgers etc.

Little Glazed Onions

1 lb little pickling onions
2 tablespoons butter
2 heaped teaspoons sugar

Neatly skin all the onions and boil them in salted water until tender (about 15–20 minutes). Drain them very well. (This part can be done in advance and they will be then very well drained if left standing in a colander.) Melt the butter in a shallow heatproof serving dish, tip in the onions and sprinkle them with sugar. Cook them on a medium heat, turning them from time to time until they are all yellow and shiny. This takes about 20–30 minutes. Serve as they are, in the same dish.

☐ *Very good with roast game or lamb.*

For 4

Sweet Corn Fritters

10 oz of corn kernels, cooked and stripped off
   the cobs (or a 12 oz tin of corn kernels)
2 oz flour
1 egg
¼ pint double cream
walnut of butter
6 rashers of bacon
salt, pepper

Drain the corn kernels. Put the flour in a bowl. Make a well in the centre, break in the egg and stir it into the flour until it is smooth. Then add salt, pepper and cream and the sweetcorn. Heat a nut of butter in a frying pan. Fry the bacon in the butter and then keep it hot while you drop tablespoons of the sweetcorn mixture carefully into the sizzling fat. Fry over a moderate heat — turn it down if the fat starts to smoke or darken. You can do three or four fritters at a time. When the underneath is brown and set turn them over carefully and brown the other side. Eat hot, though they are quite good cold.

☐ *If you are using tinned corn, avoid the sort which includes strips of pimento.*

For 6 or more

Sorrel Purée

1 lb sorrel
½ oz butter
½ oz flour
a pinch of salt
a pinch of sugar

Optional
1 egg
a dash of cream or top of the milk

Strip the thin red stems from the sorrel leaves, which have been well washed. Shake them fairly dry and put them as they are in a saucepan over a lowish flame, stir occasionally. As you stir they will change colour, soften and turn to a purée. Mash the butter and flour together (beurre manié) and drop little pieces of the mixture on to the sorrel; stir, and it will thicken somewhat. Add the salt and sugar to taste. It is ready to eat at this point but you can further improve its texture and consistency by stirring an egg or two into it, and adding a dash of cream.

☐ *This is very good with fish and can be treated either as a sauce or a vegetable or used as an omelette filling. You don't usually find sorrel in shops but it is one of the easiest vegetables to grow, and as long as you prevent it from flowering you can eat it almost all the year round. Moreover it is a perennial, so once planted (from seed) you have it for ever. Make sure it is French sorrel, not wild English, which is more bitter.*

For 4 (a little goes a long way)

Salade au Lard

Chicory, young spinach leaves, dandelion, endive, or watercress
Vinaigrette dressing
1 rasher of bacon per person

Wash the salad leaves and dry well. Trim the rind off the bacon and cut into little sticks about half an inch long. Fry the rinds slowly in a frying pan to extract the fat; when it starts to run remove the rinds and fry the bacon pieces until crisp and brown, while you are making a slightly vinegary dressing; don't add much salt, the bacon will do this.
Toss the salad in the dressing and at the last moment pour the bacon and its fat over everything. Mix well and serve with the bacon still hot.

For any number

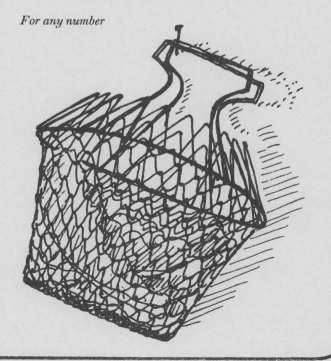

Spinach or Swiss Chard Gratiné

1 lb Swiss chard or spinach
2 medium-size onions, sliced
3 tablespoons olive oil
¼ lb mushrooms, dried or equivalent of fresh (optional)
2 cloves garlic
2 eggs
2 tablespoons grated cheese (Parmesan if possible)
salt, pepper, chopped parsley
½ cup breadcrumbs

Remove large stalks for another recipe (see this page) wash and shred leaves, cook with a little salt without shaking the wetness off the leaves in a covered pan for about 10 minutes, stirring occasionally. Turn into a colander and press dry. Brown onions in olive oil in a saucepan. Add mushrooms, drained chard, garlic (crushed) and parsley. Cook for 5 minutes, then allow to cool. Beat eggs with cheese, salt and pepper. Mix with cooled chard, turn into a buttered gratin dish, or shallow casserole, sprinkle with breadcrumbs and bake for 20 minutes at Reg 4/350°.

Can be eaten hot or cold.

For 4

Spinach and Chick Peas

½ lb chick peas
salt
1 lb spinach
1 tablespoon paprika
2 tablespoons olive oil
1 slice bread
1 onion, chopped
3–4 tomatoes, peeled and chopped
1 clove garlic

Soak the chick peas overnight and cook as on page 186. When they are tender, fry the slice of bread golden in oil. Put the fried bread on one side while you fry the onions, then the tomatoes. Wash the spinach, shake it and sprinkle it with salt. Heat two tablespoons of oil in a large pan, add the paprika and stir it in. Add the spinach and when it is lightly fried, put the mixture into a saucepan with the chick peas, onions and tomatoes.

Pound the clove of garlic, add the fried bread and pound it thoroughly. Add this mixture to the chick peas. Cover and simmer for half an hour, when you will have a fragrant vegetable stew, thickened and interestingly flavoured by the pounded fried bread.

☐ *Very good for a cold day.*

For 3–4

Spinach with Tomato Sauce

1 lb spinach
½ lb tomatoes
salt and freshly ground pepper
pinch sugar
1 small onion, chopped
1–2 oz butter
butter and oil for frying

Wash the spinach very well, shake off most of the water and cook in a covered pan with the moisture still clinging to the leaves, until tender, 10–15 minutes. Drain off the water it has made, chop and stir in the butter and a little salt.

While the spinach is cooking, skin and chop the tomatoes. Sweat the chopped onion in a little butter and oil, without browning, for 10–15 minutes. Add the tomatoes, salt, pepper and sugar to taste. Let it simmer into a rough purée, stirring from time to time.

Serve the spinach with a little dollop of tomato sauce in the centre of each helping, so it looks like a red and green fried egg.

It is a suprisingly good combination of tastes.

For 2

Spinach Tart

2 lbs fresh spinach
1 oz butter
1 oz flour
½ pint creamy milk
2 cloves garlic
1 oz grated Parmesan
butter
salt and freshly ground pepper
9 oz flan pastry (page 38)

Make the pastry well in advance and keep it in a cool place. Cook the washed spinach in the water still clinging to the leaves, with a good sprinkling of salt. Make a smooth Béchamel sauce with the butter flour and milk; season it and add the crushed cloves of garlic and most of the cheese. Drain the spinach when it is well cooked, squeezing out the water very thoroughly, and chop slightly. Meanwhile butter a 7–8 inch flan case and line it with pastry. Bake this shell blind (page 38).

Mix the spinach into the sauce, pour into the flan case and sprinkle with the remaining cheese. Bake at Reg 4/350° for 15–20 minutes and brown the top briefly under the grill, dotting it with butter first.

☐ *This is a very good hot lunch dish; eaten cold it is marvellous for a picnic.*

For 4

Ratatouille

3 aubergines
3 onions
3 courgettes
2 lbs tomatoes
2 green or red peppers
3 cloves garlic
¼ pint oil
marjoram, salt, pepper

Sprinkle the quartered and sliced aubergines with salt. Allow them to drain in a colander or sieve while you prepare the other vegetables. Slice the peeled onions and the courgettes into thin slices. Skin the tomatoes and chop roughly. Cut the peppers into strips, removing every seed. Peel the cloves of garlic and squash them. Start cooking the onions gently in the oil, without browning them. When they are transparent add the garlic and the aubergine shaken to remove the drops of moisture that form on the slices. After 5–10 more minutes add the peppers and courgettes and a little more oil if necessary. Keep stirring the vegetables gently to prevent them sticking at the bottom. After another 10–15 minutes add the tomatoes, marjoram and pepper. Taste for salt — there was some on the aubergines and you may not need much more. Cook until everything is tender and you have an aromatic stew with the individual vegetables still distinguishable.

For 8–10

Turnip Tops

4 healthy turnip tops (or 1 lb turnip tops)
salt
water
oil
lemon juice

Keep the turnips for another day and look at the leaves. Reject any yellow or tough ones. Strip the stalks off all the others, and wash them well.

Bring a pan of salted water to the boil, fling in the turnip leaves, boil until tender, 15–20 minutes. Tip into a colander, drain and press dry, and chop them up a bit. Put them in a hot china dish and pour oil and lemon juice over them before serving.

Do the same with spring greens and curly kale.

For 4

Turnips in Cream Sauce

6 small young turnips (about 1 lb in all)
2–3 oz butter
salt, pepper
sugar, nutmeg
1 tablespoon flour
½ pint milk
a little chopped parsley

Put the peeled turnips in a pan of cold salted water to cover. Bring it to the boil and after 2 minutes remove the turnips and run cold water over them. Drain them and put them in a pan large enough to allow the turnips to lie in one layer. Add about ½" of warm water, 1 tablespoon butter, a pinch of salt, and a sprinkling of sugar. Cook fairly briskly, turning them about from time to time, until all the water has evaporated, and you are left with just the butter. Keep the turnips warm while you make a sauce with the rest of the butter, flour and milk. Season it with salt, pepper and nutmeg and cook until thick and smooth. Tip the turnips into it, with all their buttery juice. Serve sprinkled with parsley.

☐ *Very good with roast lamb or duck.*

For 4

Baked Swede

1 swede, peeled and cubed
2 oz butter
½ teaspoon salt
½ teaspoon sugar

Butter a small casserole with a close-fitting lid. Sprinkle the salt on to the cubed swede, and put it into the casserole, dotted with the remaining butter. Sprinkle with the sugar, cover very tightly with foil and the lid, for you add no water, and bake in a low oven, or the bottom of a warm oven, for 1½ hours.

☐ *People with an aversion to mashed swede seem to gobble this up.*

For 4

Mashed Swede

1 large swede
salt and pepper
sugar
1 oz butter
orange juice

Peel the swede, removing all the fibrous pieces. Cut into one-inch cubes, cover with cold water, add salt and cook 20–25 minutes. Drain the swede, mash carefully, add pepper, a little more salt if necessary, a sprinkling of sugar, the butter and, if you like, a squeeze of orange juice. Heat through and serve. Children seem to like this as much as carrots.

For 4–6

Tomato and Mozzarella Salad

4 tomatoes
1 Mozzarella cheese
basil or oregano
salt and freshly ground pepper
oil and vinegar

Slice the cheese into rounds and lay a slice of tomato on top of each, or lay in overlapping lines, alternating tomato and Mozzarella, on a dish. Sprinkle with fresh or dried basil or oregano. Serve straight away with oil, vinegar, salt and pepper.

☐ *This is a very Italian salad. Eat it as a first course.*

For 2

Plain Tomato Salad

1 lb firm, under- rather than over-ripe tomatoes
1 small onion
salt and pepper
2–3 tablespoons olive oil
sprinkling of fresh chopped parsley, basil or chives

You need not bother to peel them, but if you want a very delicate salad dip the tomatoes in boiling water as briefly as possible and skin them quickly. Slice them thinly across and lay the slices on a plate. Sprinkle lightly with salt. Treat the onions, also thinly sliced, in the same way.

When they have stood in the salt for $\frac{1}{2}$–1 hour, tip the plates and drain off the juices. Rinse the onions, dry them, and scatter them over the tomatoes. Sprinkle with parsley and chives or basil. Add the oil and a turn of pepper, and serve chilled. Don't let it stand too long or the tomatoes lose their firm texture.

For 4

To Peel and De-seed Tomatoes

Stuffed Vine Leaves

20–30 vine leaves, fresh, or bought ready for use at
    Greek or Cypriot shops
3 oz rice (6 oz cooked rice)
4 oz minced lamb, beef or pork, raw or cooked
1 small onion
pinch ground coriander (or fresh leaves)
pinch ground cumin
salt and freshly ground pepper
good squeeze of lemon
$\frac{1}{4}$–$\frac{1}{2}$ pint stock or tomato juice
olive oil

Put the kettle on. Put the tomatoes (without their stalks) in a deep bowl. When the kettle boils, pour the water over them. Scoop them out one at a time with a spoon and peel them as quickly as you can. If there are a great many to skin, do them in several batches, as standing in hot water makes them mushy.

If you only have one or two tomatoes to peel, and a gas cooker, stick them on a fork and hold them over a burner. Turn the flame up high and turn the tomato in it until the skin pops, singes and splits; it will then peel off quite easily.

To remove the seeds: cut the tomato in half and hold one half in the palm of your hand. Squeezing it slightly, give it a brisk shake and the seeds will flop out.

To draw out the excess moisture: if you want to make stuffed tomatoes you can get rid of some of the water by sprinkling the insides of the halves with salt and leaving them upside-down to drain for half an hour or so.

If you have fresh vine leaves, trim off the stalks and plunge them into boiling salted water for five minutes. Drain and let them cool while you fry the onion, finely chopped, in oil until it is quite brown. Boil the rice, unless you have some ready cooked. Brown the meat with the onions if you are using fresh meat; if using cold cooked meat, chop it finely. Mix the onion, meat, rice and spices, and add salt and pepper to taste. Put a teaspoon of the mixture on the rough side of each leaf, wrap neatly into a little parcel, lay them side by side in a flat flameproof dish (they don't need tying), squeeze lemon juice over and pour on the stock or tomato juice. Cover with a plate that fits right down on to the vine leaves, to stop them coming apart. Cook over a very low heat for half an hour. Serve cold.

☐ *These are good served with drinks before dinner, especially if you have your own vine, and can make them quite small, choosing leaves that make good wrappers — not too indented, and not too old and tough.*

Makes 20–30

Stuffed Peppers

4 medium peppers (round dumpy ones)
2 large onions
1 thick slice bread
$\frac{1}{2}$ lb minced pork or beef
1 clove garlic
a small bunch of parsley, $\frac{1}{2}$ teaspoon oregano or
  marjoram
1 egg yolk
1 dessertspoon tomato purée
2–3 tablespoons olive oil
salt, fresh ground black pepper
breadcrumbs

Slice the stalk off the peppers and scoop out the core and every seed. Plunge into boiling water with a drop of oil in for 3–5 minutes according to how thick they are. Remove, refresh in cold water and drain dry. Fry the finely chopped onions in olive oil until slightly brown. Soak the slice of bread in a little water. Crush the clove of garlic and add it with the meat and a handful of chopped parsley and oregano or marjoram to the onions. Brown, stirring for a few minutes, then remove the pan from the fire and add the egg yolk. Mix well then add the bread with the water squeezed out, tomato, salt and fresh ground pepper and mix very thoroughly. Stuff the peppers with this mixture with a teaspoon and put in an oiled baking dish. Sprinkle the tops with bread crumbs, pour a little olive oil over this and bake 40 minutes at Reg 5/375°. If the tops aren't brown finish off under the grill.

For 4

Stuffed Tomatoes

The mixture above is good for stuffed tomatoes and is enough for 3–4 large tomatoes. Cut off lids, scoop out seeds and pulp and use the pulp in the stuffing (add after meat is browned, sizzle till liquid is reduced to a thick purée). Stuff generously and replace lid. Smallish marrows can also be stuffed with this method.

Stuffed Cabbage

1 fine cabbage — Savoy is good for this
$\frac{1}{2}$ lb sausage meat or minced pork
4–5 chicken livers ($\frac{1}{2}$ lb)
1 thick slice bread, crusts removed and soaked
  in milk
2 egg yolks, salt and pepper
plenty of nutmeg or mace, thyme, parsley
a few dill seeds if liked
1 oz butter, 1 oz flour
$\frac{3}{4}$ pint stock
3–4 cloves, handful capers

Make a stuffing with the sausage meat or pork, finely chopped chicken livers, bread, crusts removed, soaked in milk and squeezed dry, egg yolks, herbs, seasonings and spices. Let it stand. Wash the cabbage well and drop it whole into a large pan of boiling salted water.

Let it boil 8–10 minutes, remove and drain it very carefully. Now open it out leaf by leaf. Lay a light layer of stuffing over each leaf, starting from the middle and carefully pressing them back into place to re-form the cabbage.

Tie it up (strips of silver foil or tape are good for this) and put it into a casserole in which you have previously made a thinnish sauce with the flour, butter and well-seasoned stock.

Stick the cabbage with 3 or 4 cloves, spoon some of the sauce over it, cover the pot and cook over a low heat for $1\frac{1}{2}$–2 hours adding more water if necessary, or bake at Reg 2/300° for 2–3 hours. To serve, remove the foil strips or tape, and throw a few capers into the sauce.

If you can spare it a tot of rough brandy poured over it at the last moment is delicious. Do not ignite it.

□ *The number of people it will feed depends on the size of the cabbage. This amount of stuffing can be used in a small cabbage or a large one.*

For 4–6

PUDDINGS

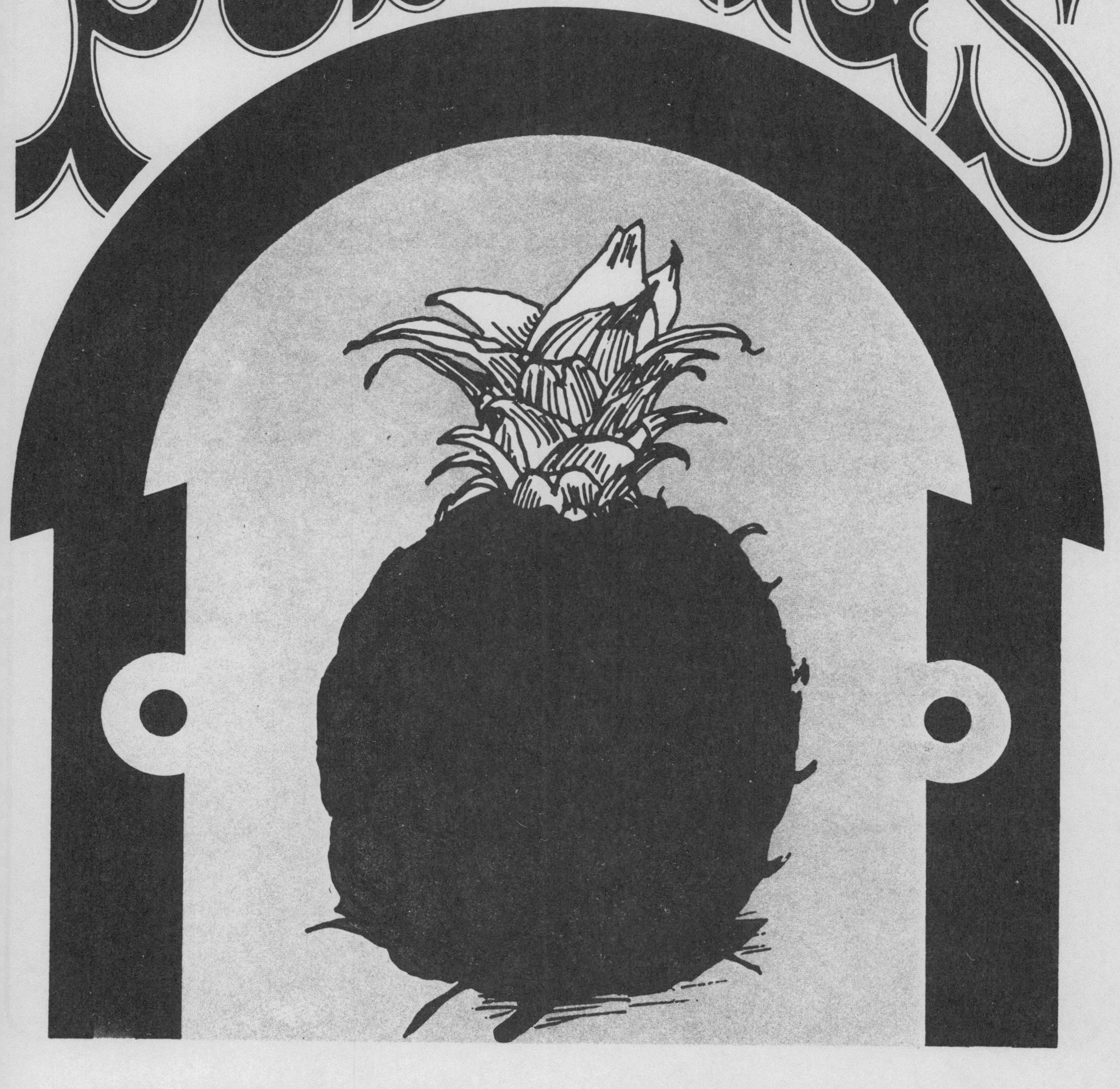

Puddings

This chapter concentrates mainly on puddings that children like, since many people now seem to want to go straight on to fresh fruit and cheese; but if your first course is nothing much, then a good pudding does help to salvage your reputation. One or two steamed puddings are included, and although they are a bit of a challenge to the modern stomach, they are comforting on a cold winter's day after a morning in the fresh air. Vanilla sugar is mentioned in several recipes; this is made by putting a vanilla pod into an airtight glass storage jar, and filling it up with caster sugar. Let it stay there, refilling with sugar when necessary, until it loses its aroma, which is only after several months. The flavour given by vanilla sugar is different and much better than the flavour of vanilla essence.

The sort of puddings you make depends very much on whether you are trying to fill people up or just to please them. Since most filling puddings contain large quantities of fattening things they are becoming less and less pleasing to more and more people, including the mothers who make them and see their hungry children beginning to bulge and remember menacing words about forming life-long over-eating patterns.

So our recipes are mainly for puddings that use fruit, with perhaps beaten eggs or a light pastry crust, ice-cream and mousses where the emphasis is on quality rather than quantity, pancakes which make a small amount of flour go a long way and the occasional luxurious pudding made with cream.

For a glimpse into the British heritage of puddings look at any run-of-the-mill cookery book of about 1890 and you will find recipe after rib-sticking recipe for steamed and boiled puddings, baked puddings, cabinet puddings, diplomat puddings. They are probably all very good, but because almost every family has at least one member who should be thinner we have mainly, out of kindness, left them out.

Baked Apple Dumplings

½ lb flour
2 oz butter
2 oz cooking fat } for the pastry
pinch of salt
water to mix
4 medium-sized apples, peeled and cored
½ oz butter
1 oz Demerara sugar
1 teaspoon grated lemon rind (optional)

Make the pastry and let it stand in a cool place for at least half an hour. Preheat the oven to Reg 5/375° Peel and core the apples; mash the butter, sugar, and lemon rind, and stuff the apples with the mixture. Divide the pastry into four and roll out into four thin circles on a floured board. Place an apple on the centre of each; damp the edges and neatly bring the pastry up round each apple, pinching it together and trimming off any excess. Place the apples, joined side down, on a greased baking sheet, decorate the tops with pastry leaves and stalks, brush with water and sprinkle generously with caster sugar.

Bake the apples for 30 minutes and serve hot with cream.

For 4

Apple Crumble (or Apricot, or Blackberry and Apple)

1½ lbs cooking apples or apricots
or 1½ lbs blackberries and apples
sugar to sweeten the fruit
2 oz soft brown sugar
2 oz butter
4 oz plain flour
pinch of cinnamon

Preheat the oven to Reg 3/325°. Put the prepared fruit into a casserole with enough sugar to sweeten, cover and stew gently in the oven until the juice begins to run, or the apples begin to soften — 20–30 minutes.

Meanwhile rub the flour, butter, sugar and cinnamon together until the mixture looks like breadcrumbs. Take the fruit out of the oven, turn the oven up to Reg 6/400° and sprinkle the crumble mixture over the fruit. Return to the oven, uncovered, for 20 minutes, or until crisp and golden on top.

Serve hot with cream.

For 4

Apple Strudel

For the pastry
12 oz flour
1 egg
½ teaspoon oil
a large pinch of salt
¼ pint lukewarm water
½ teaspoon white vinegar
½–1 oz melted butter for brushing

For the filling
2 lbs cooking apples
4 oz currants or sultanas
½ teaspoon cinnamon
3 oz caster sugar
2 oz ground almonds and 2 oz walnuts *or* 6 oz
   breadcrumbs and 3 oz butter
a teaspoon of grated lemon peel
1–2 oz butter for brushing

Sieve the flour into a bowl, make a well in the centre and add the egg, oil, salt, vinegar and enough lukewarm water to make a pliable, silky dough. Pummel, knead and beat the dough for 5–10 minutes. Allow to rest in a warm place, well covered with a damp cloth and a lid, for 30 minutes.

Peel, quarter and core the apples. Cut the quarters in half then slice them thinly, like cucumber. Mix the slices with the sugar, currants, cinnamon and roughly chopped walnuts. If you are using breadcrumbs fry them in butter.

Remove your rings and put half the warm strudel pastry on a well-floured tablecloth and roll it as thin as you can with a rolling pin. Then gradually pull it into an oblong shape, putting one floured hand right underneath with the fingers spread out, to ease the pastry evenly towards the edges (see diagram). Gradually pull and work the whole thing very gently into a thin sheet (you should be able to see your hand through it). When it is 2 to 3 feet by 18 inches to 2 feet and without too many holes, stop pulling. Cut off the thick edges and let it harden for about 15 minutes. Brush with butter, sprinkle with breadcrumbs or almonds and lay half the apple mixture over ⅔ of the pastry (the part with the fewest holes). Roll by lifting the cloth evenly at one side so the pastry wraps itself round the filling, and roll to the end (see diagram). Pinch the ends of the roll and cut off any extra pastry.

Make the second strudel in the same way.

Preheat the oven to Reg 8/450°. Lay the strudel in a crescent on a buttered baking tin and brush with the remaining butter. Bake at Reg 8/450° for 10 minutes and Reg 6/400° for 20 minutes. Brush with butter two or three times during baking. When it is cooked, dust with icing sugar and allow to cool or serve hot with cream.

☐ *Practice makes perfect. This is also good with cabbage or stoned cherries, stoned plums and cream cheese.*

For 16 (2 strudels)

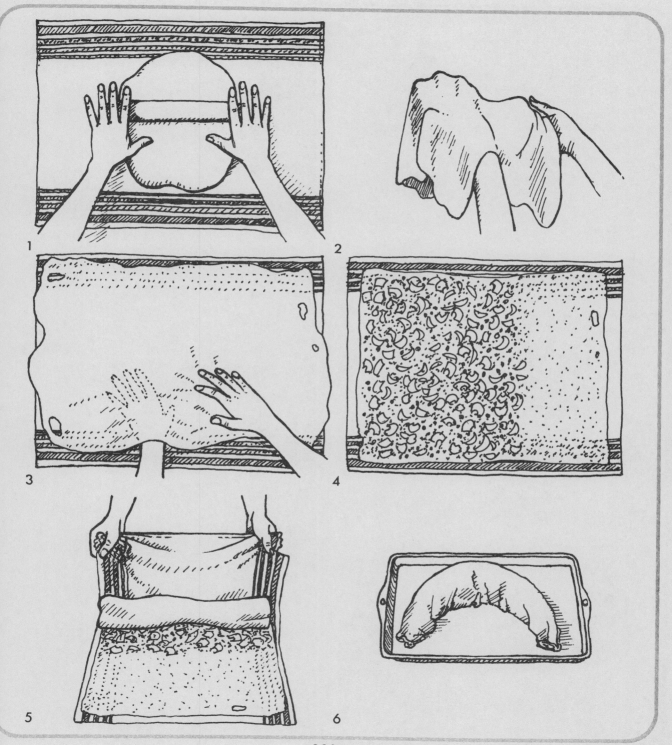

Apple Flan

2 lbs dessert apples (Golden Delicious are best)
½ small teaspoon powdered cinnamon
2 tablespoons brown sugar
2 tablespoons red wine vinegar
1 lb shortcrust pastry (page 255)

Preheat oven to Reg 5½/390°. Peel and slice the apples, and put them in a pan with the cinnamon, sugar and vinegar. Simmer covered, stirring occasionally, for half an hour; allow to cool. Line a seven-inch flan tin with a moveable base with two-thirds of the pastry. Fill with the apple mixture and cover with two-thirds of the remaining pastry. Decorate the top with a huge flower and bake in a moderate oven, Reg 5½/390°, for 30 minutes. Cover the top with sifted sugar when the pie has slightly cooled. The apples will be a wonderful golden brown and very spicy, and the vinegar flavour so delicate you could hardly tell.

For 5

Spiced Apple Pudding

1 lb apples (windfalls)
1 oz soft brown sugar (pale,
¼ teaspoon ground cinnamon
¼ teaspoon ground cloves
a pinch of nutmeg
8 oz self-raising flour
2 oz butter
4–6 oz caster sugar
grated rind and juice of 1 lemon
2 eggs
4 tablespoons milk

Preheat the oven to Reg 4/350°. Line a square 7″ cake tin with buttered greaseproof. Peel, core and slice the apples. Mix the brown sugar and spice. Rub the butter into the flour, add the caster sugar (judging the quantity according to the sourness of the apples), lemon rind and juice and eggs beaten together with the milk, beat well until the mixture is a soft dropping consistency. Spoon half the mixture into the cake tin. Arrange ⅓ of the apples over this. Cover with the remaining mixture, arrange the rest of the apple slices prettily on top, sprinkle with the spiced sugar. Bake for 1½ hours until cooked through. Cover the top with greaseproof paper if it is browning too quickly. Take it out of the tin and serve hot with cream or cold in slices like cake.

For 6 or more

Buttered Baked Apples

4 nice firm eating apples
4 thin slices bread
2 oz butter
3–4 oz sugar

Preheat oven to Reg 3/325°. Peel the apples very carefully and remove the cores. Butter a square gratin dish. Cut the crusts off the bread and lay the slices in the gratin dish. Stand an apple on each one. Fill the hole with sugar then put in a nob of butter. Bake the apples slowly, adding more sugar and butter two or three times, taking care the bread does not catch or burn. If it appears to be doing so, turn down the oven.

After 1 hour the apples should be soft (big ones may take longer).

Serve them in their dish, basted with their juice and sprinkled with sugar. They are baked a light brown, and the bread is crusted and golden.

For 4

Apple Charlotte

2 lbs cooking apples
8 oz breadcrumbs (brown or white)
4 oz sugar (brown or white)
a sprinkling of grated nutmeg
2 oz butter
2 slices lemon peel

Preheat the oven to Reg 4/350°. Peel and slice the apples. Mix half the sugar with the breadcrumbs in the bottom of a buttered pie dish and sprinkle with nutmeg. Pack in the apples with the remaining sugar, most of the butter and the lemon peel. Cover the top with the rest of the crumbs, dot the top liberally with butter and bake covered for 20 minutes to ½ hour. Then cook on uncovered for 20–30 minutes.

☐ *This pudding is very light.*

For 6–8

Fried Bananas

6 bananas, peeled and halved lengthwise
1 ½ oz butter
juice of half a lemon
Demerara sugar
1 tablespoon brandy, rum or liqueur
top of the milk or thin cream

Melt the butter in a large frying pan; as it foams put in the bananas. Brown them gently on each side for a few minutes, add the lemon juice and let it sizzle. Warm a spoonful of brandy or whatever, set light to it and pour, flaming, over the bananas. Sprinkle with Demerara sugar and serve at once, with cream if liked.

☐ *A good, quick last-minute pudding*.

For 4

Banana Soufflé

4 bananas
2 whole eggs, plus 2 whites
dash of rum
1 oz butter
1 ½ oz flour
½ pint milk
2 oz vanilla sugar

Butter a two-pint soufflé dish. Put three of the bananas in their skins into a moderate oven, Reg 4/350°, for about ten minutes, while you make a sauce with the butter, flour, milk and sugar. Remove the bananas and turn up the oven to Reg 7/425°.

While the sauce cools prepare the bananas by removing the skins, which have gone black, and pulping the fruit. Stir them into the sauce, and add the egg yolks and the rum, stirring all the time. Cut the remaining banana into cubes and stir it in.

Beat the egg whites to a firm snow and fold them into the sauce. Turn the mixture into the buttered soufflé dish, put it in the oven, turn down the heat to Reg 6/400° and cook for half an hour. Serve at once dusted with fine sugar.

For 4

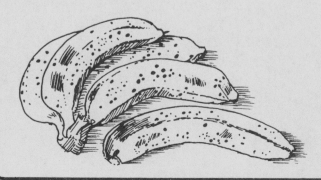

Blackberry or Blackcurrant Kissel

1½–2 lbs blackberries or blackcurrants
4 oz sugar
2 tablespoons cornflour
1 tablespoon brandy (optional)

Rhubarb Fool

1 lb rhubarb
½ pint egg custard
1 lb rhubarb
½ lemon
2 oz sugar
a little water

Simmer the fruit with a little water and the sugar, until soft enough to sieve. You should then obtain about a pint of juice-purée (make it up with a little water if there is not enough). Allow to cool a bit.

Mix the cornflour with a little water, add the brandy if you have any, add a little of the fruit juice and mix very well. Add the cornflour mixture to the rest of the fruit juice. Bring to the boil, stirring well, and simmer 2–3 minutes. Allow to cool a bit, stirring occasionally before pouring it into glass dishes. Serve very cold with cream. It should set, not hard, but as thick soft jelly.

For 4–6

Wash the rhubarb and cut it into square chunks. Cut the lemon in half lengthways and then into thick semi-circles, or long crescents, whichever you think looks prettier. Put them, with the rhubarb and sugar and a little water, into the top half of a double saucepan. Cook them over gently boiling water for 20 minutes to half an hour, until the rhubarb pieces are soft but not falling to pieces.

Sieve or liquidise the rhubarb when it is cold (first removing the lemon slices it was cooked with). Fold the custard in gently when it too is set and cool. (If you do it when hot it will curdle.)

If you are not feeling frugal you can add instead of the custard, ½ pint double cream whipped lightly but not too stiffly or it won't mix with the fruit.

Taste for sweetening. Serve cold.

For 4–6

Lemon Mousse

1 large lemon, rind and juice
½ lb cottage cheese
¼ pint single cream
2 oz caster sugar
½ oz powdered gelatine
¼ pint milk

Grate the lemon rind then squeeze the lemon.
Whisk the cream and cheese together well, or
liquidise. Stir in the rind and juice and add the
sugar. Heat the milk and dissolve the gelatine in
it. Leave it to cool but not to set, so that it
mixes homogeneously, otherwise the solids go to
the bottom and liquids to the top. Just before it
sets mix in quickly the cream and cheese and
leave to set. This needs something to eat with it,
like a compôte of fruit, or puréed apricots, plums,
blackberries, or biscuits.

For 4–5

Fruit Soufflé

6 oz any soft fruit, such as strawberries, raspberries, blackberries, peaches, apricots
3 large dessertspoons caster sugar
3 egg whites
a little butter

Try to use a white china or glass 6″ soufflé dish.
Butter it well. Preheat the oven to Reg 6/400°.
Make a purée of the fruit by sieving it, and add
the sugar.

Beat the egg whites very stiffly (an old fashioned
test is to see if a penny will stay on top without
sinking in — these days, use 2p). Mix gently but
well with the purée and turn it into the soufflé
dish. Flatten the top smooth and level so that
there are no peaks or ridges to go brown and
spoil its appearance. Bake in the centre of the
oven for exactly 13½ minutes, after which it
should be perfectly cooked. (All ovens vary
slightly so watch the result carefully the first time
you cook this dish in order that you can time it
accurately in future). It is good with cream.

☐ *This is very useful for using up egg whites and
squashy fruit.*

For 3–4

Compôte of Fruit

1 lb washed fresh fruit
½ pint water
4 oz sugar

Heat the sugar and water in a saucepan and when
the sugar has dissolved bring it to the boil and
carefully put in the fruit. It will not be covered by
the liquid so turn it over gently once or twice to coat
it. Return to the boil and then turn the heat down
as low as it will go, and cover the pan. Leave for ten
minutes for soft fruit, 15 minutes or more for apples
and pears; the fruit should be tender but still whole.
Remove it carefully with a perforated spoon and put
it in a glass or china bowl. Return the liquid to the
heat and boil, uncovered, to a thickish syrup. Allow
to cool, then pour it over the fruit.

☐ *Use plums, greengages, apricots, Morello cherries,*
peeled pears or apples, quartered or sliced.

For 4

Clafoutis

2 eggs
3 oz sugar
1½ oz flour
¼ pint double cream
½ pint milk
1 lb stoned black cherries
kirsch (optional)

Preheat oven to Reg 5/375°. Cream the eggs and
sugar in a basin, beating hard with an electric
beater or wire whisk. Add the flour all at once, beat
it in and add the cream, then the milk. Put the
cherries in a shallow earthenware oven dish, pour
over the batter and cook in the oven for 35 minutes.
The batter should be brown on top and halfway
between custard and cake inside. Eat it hot or cold
with cream.

This is really delicious but can be improved slightly
by the addition of a tiny glass of Kirsch just before
the cream. The whole thing is rather indigestible
but worth it.

☐ *You can use other fruit such as plums, apples and*
apricots, which are cheaper and more often available.

For 4–6

Bread and Butter Pudding

6 slices assorted bread and butter (white, brown or
    currant loaf, or a mixture of all three)
handful of currants, raisins or sultanas
2 eggs
1 tablespoon sugar (preferably vanilla)
¾–1 pint milk

Lay the bread, crusts cut off, in a buttered pie dish
in layers, with fruit in between. Beat the eggs with
the sugar and add the milk. Pour over the bread and
leave to soak for half an hour or so. Cook in a low
oven, Reg 1/275°, for one hour, loosely covered with
greaseproof paper and for a further half hour,
uncovered, to puff and brown.

Serve with cream and more sugar.

Batter Pudding

Batter (page 56)
2 tablespoons butter, lard or oil
4 oz raisins, sultanas or currants, or all three mixed
golden syrup and cream

Make the batter two hours before you need it.
Preheat the oven to Reg 9/475°. Put two tablespoons
of fat in a baking tin and heat in the oven for a few
minutes. Stir the washed, thoroughly drained and
dried fruit into the batter, pour it into the very hot
fat and return it to the oven. After five minutes
lower the heat to Reg 6/400°, and cook 35–40
minutes.

Serve hot with warmed treacle and top of the milk
or cream.

For 4–6

Egg Custard

1 large egg
2 tablespoons vanilla sugar
½ pint milk

Mix the egg and sugar in a basin. Heat the milk to
scalding point (almost boiling but not quite), pour
it on to the egg, whisking as you do so. Return the
mixture to the milk pan and heat gradually, without
boiling of course, over a low heat, stirring constantly
with a wooden spoon. When it has thickened enough
to coat the spoon, take it off the heat.

☐ *For steamed and other puddings.*

Hot Chocolate Sauce

4 ozs cooking chocolate
4 tablespoons single cream or top of the milk
2 tablespoons good strong black coffee

Melt the chocolate in the top of a double boiler,
stir in the hot coffee and cream and keep
stirring over hot water until you have a smooth
sauce.

☐ *For vanilla ice-cream.*

Rich Rice Pudding

2 oz rice (pudding rice, round, not long)
1 pint water
2 oz sugar
1 oz butter
1 pint milk
grating of nutmeg
a pinch of salt
1 bay leaf (or a little slice of lemon peel)
1–2 eggs, yolks and whites separated

Preheat the oven to Reg 3/325°. Cook the rice in the water until it is amost tender (about 10–13 minutes). Drain it well and put it, with the sugar, butter, heated milk, nutmeg, salt, bay leaf, in an ovenproof dish. Cover it with foil and bake in the oven for 2 hours. Stir once or twice to prevent a skin forming. Take it out, remove bay leaf or lemon peel, and beat in the egg yolks. Before serving whip the egg whites stiffly with a little sugar and fold into the pudding. Serve hot or cold, with strawberry or raspberry jam on each helping.

☐ *If you don't want to use the oven it can be cooked in a double saucepan, but watch the water level in the bottom half.*

For 4

Prune Pudding

½ lb prunes
4 egg whites
6 oz caster sugar
¼ teaspoon cream of tartar

Soak the prunes for 12 hours in cold water then stew them until tender (about 15 minutes). Remove the stones. Preheat the oven to Reg 6/400°. Strain, and stir the fruit for 5 minutes over a low heat until it is a purée, adding a little of their cooking liquid. Beat the egg whites till stiff. Stir in the sugar and the cream of tartar. Fold in the prunes, turn into a pudding dish and stand it in a tin of water. Bake for 15–20 minutes. Serve at once with whipped cream.

☐ *Very good if you like prunes and have a lot of egg whites. It is a sort of soufflé.*

For 4–6

Mont Blanc

1 lb chestnuts
½ lb caster sugar
½ pint of double cream

Shell the chestnuts and boil them in water, or ½ milk and ½ water, until they are soft. This takes about ½ hour. Make sure they don't boil dry and burn; while they are cooking they absorb a lot of the liquid. Drain them and put them, with most of the sugar, through a mouli-légumes or sieve them letting them fall as lightly as possible into the dish from which they will be served and ending up with a little mountain of sweet, airy chestnut. Whip the cream with a little more caster sugar, until it thickens a little, but not too stiffly, then spoon it over the chestnuts. It should look like a softly enveloping snow cap, hence the name of the dish. Decorate the peak with angelica and a cherry if you feel frivolous.

☐ *Suitable when chestnuts are cheap.*

For 6–8

Ricotta with Coffee

4 oz Ricotta (or cottage cheese)
2 tablespoons freshly ground coffee
1 teaspoon caster sugar
Cream (optional)

Sprinkle each person's helping of cheese with the sugar and ground coffee. That's all. Serve with cream if you have some.

For 2

Oeufs au Lait

4 small eggs
1 pint milk
2 strips lemon peel and 1–1½ oz sugar
or 1 oz vanilla sugar

Put the milk, the lemon peel and the sugar or the vanilla sugar in a saucepan and bring to the boil. When it boils pour it into a bowl on to the well-beaten eggs, and mix well. Strain the mixture into a gratin dish and bake, covered with foil, in a slow oven Reg 3/325° for 30 minutes. When the eggs are creamy allow them to cool. Chill the custard, and just before serving sprinkle the top with caster sugar to a depth of ⅛″–¼″ and push the dish under a very hot grill. When the sugar melts and caramelises, serve the pudding. The caramel will start to melt if you leave this standing for more than a few hours.

☐ *Luxurious but cheap. Like crème brulée but not so rich. The custard can be made well in advance if necessary.*

For 6

Coffee Granita

4 oz vanilla sugar
¾ pint hot, double strength coffee

Dissolve the sugar in the coffee, pour the mixture into the ice-making tray and freeze until mushy. Remove it to a bowl and beat with a fork. Return and freeze to sorbet consistency. Serve in glasses with a dollop of cream if you like.

For 4

Lemon Ice

8 oz sugar
juice of 2 lemons and grated rind of one
1½ pint milk
2 teaspoons gelatine crystals melted in 2 tablespoons
    water

Dissolve the sugar in the lemon juice. Add the milk
and gelatine, stirring well. Add the finely grated
rind of one lemon and freeze, covered, in the ice
compartment of your refrigerator, turned to its
coldest setting, for three hours. Stir the mixture
twice during the setting time.

For 6

Blackberry Water Ice

1 lb raw blackberries
4 oz sugar
¼ pint water
1 small egg white

Turn the refrigerator to its coldest setting. Make
a syrup by boiling the sugar and water for four
minutes. Allow it to cool. Sieve or mouli the blackberries and mix with the syrup. Beat the egg white
until it forms soft peaks and fold thoroughly into
the blackberry mixture. Put into a dish, cover and
freeze to a mush. Stir and freeze for a further half
hour. Stir again and freeze until set, about 2½–3
hours altogether.

☐ *This can also be made with raspberries or logan-
berries.*

For 4

Grapefruit Sherbet

12 oz caster sugar
2 large grapefruit
¾ pint water
squeeze lemon juice
2 egg whites
tiny pinch salt

Stir the sugar and the finely grated rind of one of
the grapefruit into the water in a thick saucepan.
Heat gradually, stirring; when the sugar has
dissolved, bring the mixture to the boil and boil
fast for five minutes. Allow to cool, stir in the
juice of the two grapefruits and a squeeze of lemon
juice, and put in the freezer tray in the refrigerator;
freeze to a mush.

Beat the egg whites to soft peaks with a little pinch
of salt; fold them into the mush and freeze at the
coldest setting on the refrigerator for half an hour.
Whip until the egg whites are spread evenly through
the mixture and freeze again for 2½–3 hours.

For 8

Caramelised Oranges

4 oranges
4 oz caster sugar
water

Peel the oranges over a plate with a very sharp knife, removing the peel and pithy skin at the same time. Slice carefully on the plate into thin slices, cut these in half, removing the pips and centre core.

Lay them on a dish like the scales of a fish. Caramelise the sugar with the orange juice collected on the plate and a couple of tablespoons of water. When the sugar turns golden brown watch it carefully darken to deep chestnut, then pour it in a thin layer over the sliced oranges.

Don't make this too far ahead of time because the caramel will lose its crispness.

For 4

Candied Oranges

6 large juicy seedless oranges
½ pint water
6 oz granulated sugar
liqueur (optional)

Use a very sharp stainless steel knife with a saw-edge to score each orange with long narrow cuts forming strips running from top to bottom of the fruit. Then peel these off with your knife, or a sharp potato peeler, as thinly as you can so that you have a heap of little pithless orange-peel matchsticks.

If you like a bland rather than a slightly bitter flavour, blanch the strips for one minute in boiling water and drain them well. Melt the sugar in the water and bring to the boil; poach the orange-peel strips in this syrup, uncovered, until tender, about 15 minutes. Put the oranges, stripped of every shred of pith and skin, on a dish, and pour the syrup over them; allow to cool. Arrange the shreds of peel in little mounds on top of each one. Every Italian restaurant seems to have these on the sweet trolley and they are always refreshing and delicious. You can add a liqueur such as Grand Marnier to the syrup if you want.

For 6

Orange Jellies

6 large oranges
1 packet orange jelly (to make 1 pint)

Cut the oranges across in halves and squeeze the juice into a jug. Strain and measure it and use it, made up with enough water, to make the orange jelly. Remove all the skin and pith from inside the orange halves so that each one makes a clean bowl, and pour in the hot, dissolved jelly. Leave to set, and when quite firm you can cut each half in two, so they look like orange slices miraculously made of jelly.

☐ *This is pure children's party food.*

For 6–12 children, depending on their size

Frosted Redcurrants 1

1 lb redcurrants on their stems
4 oz granulated sugar
½ pint water
caster sugar

Carefully pick over and wash the currants if you are not sure they are clean. Shake off all the water. Make a syrup by boiling the granulated sugar with water for five minutes. Keeping the syrup gently on the boil, dip the branches of redcurrants first into the syrup, shaking off the extra drips, then into the caster sugar, shaking again. Then put them on a large flat dish covered with a white paper doily. It is easy if the currants are held by the end of the stalk or hooked on to the prongs of a fork, but they must only be dipped into the syrup for a moment and flicked in and out of the caster sugar. Lay them out side by side and let them harden as they dry — drying in the sun is ideal. They can be kept in the refrigerator until they are needed. Children adore them and they make a lovely end to a summer dinner party. It is rather fiddly and takes a long time but is still rather fun to do.

Frosted Redcurrants 2

These are made as before but dipped into whipped egg whites instead of hot syrup. Turn them over from time to time as they dry. This is good if the currants are very ripe, but shop ones tend to be on the unripe side and less sweet as a result.

☐ *Serve ice-cold. Lovely to make on a fine summer's day.*

For 6

Strawberry Fool

½ pint double cream, as cold as possible
1 lb second-rate strawberries
6 oz caster sugar

Whisk the cream until it is softly thick, and gradually add five ounces of caster sugar. Whisk on until the cream stands in peaks, but is still soft; over-beating leaves you with a bowl full of butter.

Hull the strawberries, leaving a few of the best ones for decoration afterwards. Mash them to a pulp, the potato masher does this quickly, and add an ounce of caster sugar.

Fold the purée into the cream so that it is not really well mixed, and tip the whole thing into a pretty bowl or glass dish. Put the strawberries you kept for best on top and chill in the refrigerator.

☐ *This can be made just as well with raspberries. It is one of the great luxuries of high summer, both delicate and rich, and of a beautiful soft pink. It sounds extravagant but a little of it goes a long way, far further than plain strawberries and cream, and it makes use of fruit that may be past its best, which you could not eat whole.*

For 5–6

Summer Pudding

1 lb raspberries
½ lb redcurrants
½ lb blackcurrants
6–8 oz caster sugar
several slices white bread

Cook each kind of fruit separately with a few table-spoons of sugar and one tablespoon of water, to stop them catching on the pan before the juice starts to run out. They should be cooked as briefly as possible, the raspberries scarcely at all. Line a seven-inch pudding basin with medium slices of white bread, crusts removed, cutting them into wedge shapes to fit the sides of the bowl. Put in the redcurrants first, then the blackcurrants for the second layer and finally the raspberries, using all the fruit juice. On top put a layer of slices of bread (crusts removed as before), and cover with a saucer, slightly smaller in diameter than the pudding bowl. On this stand weights, which could be put inside a polythene bag in case the juice comes up over the top of the saucer. Leave overnight in the refrigerator and turn out carefully the following day.

☐ *This should be made the day before you want it.*

For 4–6

Sweet Pancakes

½ lb plain flour
¾ pint milk and water, half and half
1 large or 2 small eggs
1 tablespoon melted butter or oil
1 tablespoon sugar
¼ teaspoon salt

Make the pancake batter at least two hours, and preferably more, before using it, as the starch granules need time to expand and absorb the liquid to make a really good pancake.

Put the sifted flour in a large mixing bowl, make a well in the centre and gradually add the milk and water, working the flour in with a wooden spoon. When all the flour is smoothly incorporated into the liquid, add the beaten eggs, melted butter or oil, sugar and salt, and beat the mixture thoroughly. It should have the consistency of thin cream. Add more milk if necessary, and then let it stand.

Have ready:

a frying pan
4 oz lard, cut into cubes the size of a sugar lump
a coffee cup
a large pan of hot water covered with a plate
a dozen strips of greaseproof paper, 1 inch wide, and 3 inches longer than the diameter of the pan

The painstaking preparations make the cooking of the pancakes much faster and easier, so do not despair.

Heat the frying pan on a brisk heat, drop a lump of lard into it, and tip the pan from side to side so that the base is coated. Stir the batter and fill the coffee cup. Tilt the pan and pour the batter in at the highest point, rotating the pan to cover the base completely with a very thin layer of batter. It should set at once. Let it cook until it shifts when you shake the pan, then flip it over with a spatula, first making sure it is not sticking anywhere. Cook the other side, and slip the pancake on to the plate over the pan of hot water. Put a strip of paper **across** and continue cooking the pancakes and piling them up, with strips of paper in between, to prevent them from sticking together.

The pancakes are now ready to be filled or sprinkled with lemon and sugar. Experts flip the pancakes into the air to turn them and keep two pans going at once.

For 12–14 average pancakes

Orange Pancakes

8 thin pancakes, freshly made
2 oranges
2 oz granulated sugar
4 oz butter

Grate oranges finely all over and mix the peel with the sugar. Soften the butter and beat the sugar into it, gradually adding the juice of the oranges. This butter can then be wrapped and chilled in the refrigerator until you need it; it keeps several days.

Put the orange butter in a frying pan over a moderate heat. When it starts to bubble lay a pancake in the pan, spoon the butter over it and then fold in it half and half again with a palette knife. Put the folded, juicy pancake on a hot dish, and put another one into the slowly bubbling sauce. Repeat the spooning and folding process until all the pancakes are used up; pour any extra butter over the folded parcels of pancake and serve immediately. You can also make this with lemons, using more sugar.

For 4

Sweet Pancakes with Cream Cheese

12 freshly made very thin pancakes
8 oz cream cheese
1 egg yolk
2 oz caster sugar
2 oz raisins
2 oz chopped blanched almonds
1–2 oz butter

Put the cream cheese, beaten egg yolk and sugar in a bowl and beat together with a fork. Add the raisins and nuts and stir them in. Put a large dollop of the mixture in a strip in the middle of each pancake, and fold it over as if you were wrapping a parcel.

Heat the butter in the frying pan, drop in the little parcels, brown them all over and serve hot, sprinkled with caster sugar. You can serve cream with these.

☐ *These are very filling.*

For 6

Treacle Tart

for pastry:
6 oz self-raising flour
3 oz cooking fat
pinch salt
water to mix
4 oz fresh brown breadcrumbs
1 cup golden syrup

Make the pastry and let it stand in a cool place for at least half an hour. Preheat the oven to Reg 6/400°. Grease an eight-inch flan tin and line it with the pastry. Fill with breadcrumbs and pour the syrup over generously. Use the pastry trimmings to make a slender lattice over the syrup. Bake for 20–30 minutes and eat hot.

For 4–6

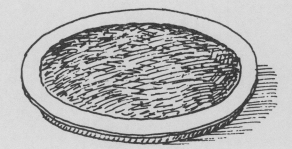

Treacle Sponge

for top of pudding
2–3 tablespoons golden syrup
juice of ½ lemon
½ teaspoon caraway seeds
small handful breadcrumbs

4 oz butter, 4 oz sugar
2 eggs, beaten
teaspoon grated lemon rind
5 oz self-raising flour
pinch of salt, milk to mix

Mix the syrup, lemon juice, caraway seeds and breadcrumbs in the bottom of a buttered two-pint pudding basin. Cream the butter and sugar together until fluffy, add the beaten eggs and the lemon rind and then the flour with a pinch of salt. Add a little milk to bring the mixture to a dropping consistency. Turn it into the basin, on top of the treacle and lemon juice mixture, cover well with a double layer of greased greaseproof paper and a cloth, or double aluminium foil, and steam for two hours, covered, in a large pan of water.

Serve, turned out, with more golden syrup, warmed, and cream if there is some available.

For 6

Six-Cup Pudding

Use an ordinary teacup that contains half a pint.
1 cup sugar
1 cup butter (7 oz)
1 beaten egg
1 cup raisins
1 cup currants
1 cup self-raising flour, or 1 cup plain flour and ½ teaspoon baking powder
1 teaspoon mixed spice
1 cup milk

Cream the sugar and butter together, add the egg, fruit, and then the flour, baking powder and spice. Moisten with milk, beating the mixture until it drops off the spoon. You may not need all the milk. Turn it into a greased basin, cover and steam for 2½ hours.

☐ *Serve this with home-made custard for a very good, thoroughly British, rib-sticking pudding.*

For 6–8

Little Chocolate Creams

4 oz bitter or cooking chocolate
2 egg yolks
½ pint creamy milk or ¼ pint milk and ¼ pint
   single cream

Preheat the oven to Reg 3/325°. Put the chocolate in a mixing bowl and stand this bowl in a saucepan of hot water — be sure the water will not come over the top of the bowl. Put over a medium heat and while the chocolate is melting beat the egg yolks and milk together to a froth, then beat them into the chocolate — still over the hot, but not boiling water. When they are very frothy and the chocolate is dissolved pour the mixture into little pots or ramequins standing in a tin of hot water. (Use a jug for doing this as pouring neatly from a bowl is almost impossible.) Put the pots in their tin of water into the oven and bake 35–40 minutes.

Allow to cool, chill and serve with cream.

□ *If you are making this for children, they may prefer it sweeter.*

For 4

Mrs Sylvester's Christmas Pudding with Beer (1910)

¾ lb sultanas, 1 lb raisins
2 oz Valencia almonds
1 lb currants
6 oz mixed peel
1 lb suet, 1 lb breadcrumbs
1 lemon and its grated peel
1 lb dark raw brown sugar
1 small nutmeg, grated
5 eggs, a little brandy
about ½ pint stout

Mix all the dry ingredients together. Beat the eggs and lemon juice and add to the mixture. Stand overnight. Add enough stout and brandy to make a good mixture. Fill four 1½ pint pudding basins and cover them with paper and cloth. Secure with string or rubber bands. Steam or boil for 7 hours. Change the papers or cloth and store in a cool dry place. Steam a further 3–4 hours on Christmas Day.

□ *It is a light but rich dark pudding. This fills 4 1½ pint pudding basins making 4 × 2 lb puddings.*

Each pudding for 6–8

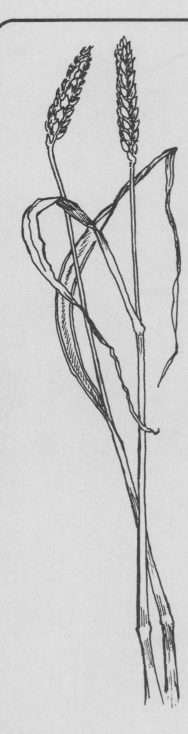

Cakes, Biscuits and Bread

Like suet puddings, huge great teas at tables spread with home-made cakes and scones and biscuits seem to be vanishing (much to the consternation of the people who make and sell flour). Children's teas now seem to be a form of supper, and after a ham salad or a hamburger it is hard to be enthusiastic about a many-layered chocolate gâteau. It is at weekends, especially if you come from the North, and are not on an almost perpetual diet, that all the delicious buns and tea-breads can be tried, and it makes a very cosy sight. You feel like a genuine mother or wife if there are home-made things for tea, and they are cheaper than bought ones, and contain only ingredients you have chosen yourself.

These recipes are all of a simple straightforward nature; there are no flights into the realms of mille-feuilles and sachertorte because the authors have never had time to get really familiar with the making of them, and feel it is better to leave the subject to those who love cake-making.

In all cakes and biscuits margarine can be used instead of butter; it is slightly cheaper and it creams faster, but the end products do lose a little in flavour.

If you want to bake your own bread it would be hard to find a recipe better than Elizabeth David's English Loaf, which uses no sugar and no fat in the making and is the most delicious straightforward loaf of bread imaginable. If you have difficulty in finding fresh yeast (it should be available through any baker that bakes his own bread, and most health food shops) try using freshly-bought dried yeast, giving it plenty of time to get working before you add it to your flour mixture. It likes a few grains of sugar to feed on, but does not need as much as is recommended on the packet, since using that amount might spoil the plain nature of the bread. Always buy special bread flour to make a loaf; ordinary commercial flour is finely milled specially for the making of pastry, cakes and so on, and is not good for bread. If you can find unbleached white flour it makes a loaf with a very good flavour.

Plain Sponge Cake

4 oz caster sugar
4 oz unsalted butter
4 oz self-raising flour, or 4 oz plain flour plus 1 ½
   teaspoons baking powder
2 eggs

Preheat the oven to Reg 5/375°. Butter and flour two eight-inch sandwich tins. Cream the sugar and butter together and when white and fluffy add the well-beaten eggs, a little at a time. Fold in the sifted flour thoroughly.

Spread half the mixture in each tin as lightly as you can, spreading it to the sides with a palette knife so that the finished cake will be flat rather than domed.

Bake in the top half of the oven for 15–20 minutes. Do not open the oven while the cakes are cooking or they may go sad. When they are cooked take them out and cool on a wire rack. Spread one half with whipped cream and the other with jam. Press the halves together so jam and cream are both in the middle.

Quick Sponge Cake

4 oz soft margarine
4 oz caster sugar
2 eggs
4 oz self-raising flour
1 level teaspoon baking powder

Preheat the oven to Reg 5/375°. Butter and flour two seven-inch Victoria sponge tins.

Sieve everything into a bowl and beat at top speed for 40 seconds. Turn the mixture into the prepared tins, flatten the top with a palette knife and bake for 15–20 minutes. Fill the middle with raspberry jam and cream, and sprinkle the top with sugar.

If the mixture is ready before the oven is up to full heat, put it in the refrigerator to check the action of the raising agent.

☐ *This mixture takes about 40 seconds to make with an electric beater. Don't be tempted to give it longer as overbeating toughens the cake. The trick is to use one of the specially soft margarines, which won't go solid even in the refrigerator.*
The sponge is made and cooked in less than half an hour.

Angels' Food

4 eggs
½ teaspoon cream of tartar
3 tablespoons cold water
12 oz caster sugar
scant ¼ pint boiling water
¾ teaspoon baking powder, pinch of salt
8 oz plain flour
a few drops of vanilla
grated rind ½ lemon

Preheat oven to Reg 2/300°. Butter and flour a cake tin 8″ across by 4″ deep. Beat the egg whites with the cream of tartar until they are stiff. In a separate bowl beat the egg yolks and cold water in the mixer for 3 minutes at least or by hand for 5 minutes. Gradually add the sugar, beating away, now gradually add the boiling water. The yolks should be going paler and paler. If you are using a mixer let it go on beating the mixture while you sieve flour, baking powder and salt. Add them gradually to the egg yolk mixture, add the vanilla and lemon rind, then gently fold in the beaten egg whites by hand. Turn the mixture into the cake-tin and bake for 1½ hours.

It rises like a soufflé, so do make sure the tin is large enough.

☐ *A light white fluffy cake. Ice it with Chocolate Icing*

Chocolate Icing

8 oz icing sugar
2 tablespoons hot water
2 ozs bitter chocolate
1 tablespoon butter

Sieve the icing sugar into a bowl. Soften the chocolate in the top of a double boiler, add the hot water and stir into the icing sugar in its bowl. While you stir, melt the butter, also in the (unwashed) top of the double boiler, collecting the rest of the chocolate. Stir the melted butter into the icing sugar for a minute or two — do this by hand or it will get too thick. Pour the icing over the top of the cake in bands, backwards and forwards, and smooth it over the sides with a spatula.

Enough for a large cake.

Marble Cake

15 oz self-raising flour
or 15 oz plain flour and 3 teaspoons baking
  powder
6 oz butter or margarine
15 oz caster sugar
4 eggs
¼ pint milk
4 oz bitter or cooking chocolate, grated
½ teaspoon cinnamon

Preheat the oven to Reg 5½/385°. Butter and flour a cake tin 8″ across by 4″ deep. Sieve the flour into a large bowl. In another bowl cream the sugar and butter together really well. When they are pale and creamy and the sugar has dissolved (and is no longer gritty) add the eggs, beating them in one at a time. Now add the milk and flour alternately, beating them in.

When you have a smooth light mixture, put a quarter of it back into the flour bowl and mix in the grated chocolate and cinnamon.

Put a layer of white mixture in the tin, then a layer of chocolate then more white, more chocolate and finish with white — don't try to get it even. Bake in the centre of the oven for 1 hour or more until cooked through.

Spicy Fruit Cake

about 2–3 cooking apples
4 oz butter
8 oz caster sugar
8 oz plain flour
1 teaspoon mixed powdered cloves and
  cinnamon
1 teaspoon bicarbonate of soda
6 oz mixed raisins and currants
a sprinkling of demerara sugar

Begin by making a purée, without sugar, of the apples. Peel and core them and cook them with a little water to soften and disintegrate. Leave the purée to get completely cold before using it. There should be about ⅓ pint.

Preheat the oven to Reg 4/350°. Cream the butter and sugar until pale and fluffy. Fold in the cold apple purée, sift in the flour, spices and bicarbonate of soda, add the currants and raisins. Butter a 7″ cake tin and bake for 1½ hours. Ten minutes before the end sprinkle with brown sugar on top.

□ *This is also very good if you undercook it by mistake. It should be fruity, spicy and crumbly.*

Dundee Cake

8 oz brown sugar (soft, dark)
8 oz butter, 4 eggs
4 oz each of sultanas, currants, raisins and
  candied peel
3 oz blanched almonds
4 oz cherries, halved
grated rind of 1 lemon and 1 orange
10 oz plain flour
a pinch of bicarbonate of soda
1 tablespoon whisky

Grease an 8″ cake tin and line with well-buttered greaseproof paper. Cream the sugar and butter together really well until fluffy and creamy (the sugar should melt completely). Add the eggs, beating each one in thoroughly before you add the next. Mix the currants, raisins, sultanas, peel chopped small, ¾ of the almonds coarsely chopped or broken, and the halved cherries in a bowl with 1 oz of flour and the grated orange and lemon rind. Preheat the oven to Reg 3½/335°. Fold in the flour, sieved with the bicarbonate of soda, then fold in the fruit. Stir in the whisky and turn the mixture into the tin. Smooth the top and decorate with the whole almonds. Bake for 2½ hours, turning the tin and covering the top when well-browned with dampened double greaseproof paper.

Makes an 8″ cake

Lardy Cake

1 lb bread dough (page 240)
3 oz lard, very cold from the fridge
3 oz sugar
4 oz mixed dried fruit mixed with 1–2 teaspoons
  mixed spice
For the glaze
1 oz sugar
1 tablespoon water

When the dough has had its first rising (after mixing and kneading, it is left in a warm place to rise and double in size), roll it out flat again into an oblong about ½″ thick. Cut the lard into small pieces and dot the dough with ⅓ of it, also ⅓ of the sugar, and ⅓ of the fruit and spice. Roll it up, turn it round and roll it out again. Repeat this procedure twice more, and finish by rolling it flat. Score it across with a sharp knife, and lay it in a shallow greased baking tin. Cover with a cloth. Allow it to rise again while you preheat the oven to Reg 9/475°. Bake 15 minutes then lower the heat to Reg 4/350° and bake a further 25–30 minutes.

Melt the sugar in the water and glaze the cake as soon as you take it out of the oven, but leave it in the tin until it is cool to reabsorb the lard which has run out of it during cooking. Sprinkle with granulated sugar while it cools.

Mace Cake

2½ oz margarine
7 oz caster sugar (vanilla sugar if possible)
¼ pint sour cream
2 eggs
8 oz plain flour
1 teaspoon baking powder
1 teaspoon bicarbonate of soda
¼ teaspoon salt, 1 teaspoon mace
For the topping
3 oz chopped nuts
1 oz sugar

Preheat the oven to Reg 4/350°. Cream the margarine and sugar thoroughly, then add the sour cream. Add the eggs and beat them in, then gradually add the flour, sieved with the rest of the dry ingredients. Turn the mixture into a buttered and floured 7″ square or round tin. Mix the topping into the top of the cake a bit and bake for ¾–1 hour.

Flap Jacks

8 oz rolled oats
7 oz butter
6 oz soft brown sugar
a pinch of salt
1 teaspoon ground ginger

Preheat the oven to Reg 4/350°. Warm the butter and beat it to a cream. Put the oats, salt, ground ginger and sugar in a bowl and stir well. Turn them into the bowl with the butter in it and mix thoroughly.

Butter a flat baking sheet, turn the mixture on to it and flatten it out to a cake ¼″ thick. Bake for 25 minutes. When cooked leave it in the tin for a few minutes, then turn it out and cut it into squares. They are dryer and more crumbly than flap-jacks made with golden syrup, but taste much better.

Makes plenty (about 12–18)

Plain Biscuit Mixture

4 oz unsalted butter
4 oz caster sugar
8 oz plain flour
1 small egg

Cream the sugar and butter together, add the beaten egg, stir in the sifted flour, mix to a firm dough. Ideally leave it to rest in the refrigerator, but if in a hurry carry on. Set the oven to Reg 5/375°. Roll the dough thinly and cut into shapes. At places like Fortnum & Mason they cut them into stars and moons, oakleaves and acorns. Place the shapes in a buttered and floured tin, brushing some with beaten egg, if liked. Put the tin near the top of the oven for ten minutes or until done. Leave to cool and crisp on the tin and then on a wire rack.

Variations: dip half of each biscuit (especially for acorns and oakleaves) into melted chocolate; or cover with white icing, flavoured with vanilla or almond essence.

You can add ginger or vanilla or chopped nuts to the mixture before baking.

☐ *This is so easy that children can make it by themselves.*

Scotch Cookies

1 egg
4 oz caster sugar
2 oz butter, softened
¼ pint milk
1 lb self-raising flour, or less

Preheat the oven to Reg 7½/435°. Cream the egg and sugar together, add the softened butter, beat it in, mix in the milk and then add enough flour to make the mixture the consistency of pastry. Roll out to quarter-inch thickness on a floured board, cut into two-inch circles with a glass or pastry-cutter and place on a buttered and floured baking-sheet. Bake just above the middle of the oven for 12 minutes; they will rise and go golden brown. Serve warm, sliced in half with butter and jam and cream. Next day they can be halved and toasted. Don't let anybody think that you were really trying to make scones.

☐ *This is a sort of hybrid, halfway between a biscuit and a scone.*

Makes 24

Madeleines

2 eggs and their weight in:
caster sugar (vanilla sugar if possible)
unsalted butter, softened
self-raising flour

juice of ½ lemon

Preheat the oven to Reg 5/375°. Separate the egg yolks from the whites. Beat the yolks and sugar together in a basin until white and fluffy. Add the butter softened to a creamy consistency, and beat away until the mixture is smooth. Beat in the flour and lemon juice and finally the egg whites, broken up with a fork but not beaten. Butter the madeleine tins which have shell-shaped indentations, or shallow jam tart tins and put a spoonful of the mixture, about the size of a walnut, in each well. Bake in the centre of the oven for 15–20 minutes. Beware — they can go from not cooked to burned in a very short time. They should be brown round the edges. Eat them the same day if you can; they are very crisp outside, light and soft inside.

Makes 24–30

Carolina Biscuits

½ lb margarine
6 oz pale soft brown sugar
1 egg white
1–2 teaspoons cinnamon
1 teaspoon ground ginger
pinch salt
10 oz flour

Preheat the oven to Reg 5/375° and grease two baking sheets. Beat the margarine with the sugar, egg white, spices and pinch of salt, using a wire whisk or electric beater. When it is thoroughly creamed add the flour and beat it in. Spread the mixture thinly on baking sheets with a spatula and bake 10–15 minutes to a nice golden brown. The mixture may seem very wet before cooking; spread it on the tins with well-floured hands if this is easier.

Cut the mixture in diamond shapes while it is hot. These biscuits should be thin, fragile and spicy.

Makes about 48

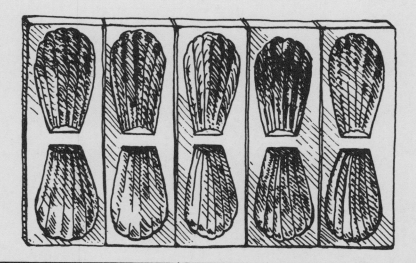

Dropscones

8 oz self-raising flour
½ teaspoon salt
1 oz caster sugar
1 beaten egg
just over ¼ pint milk, preferably sour, or buttermilk
lard to grease the griddle

Heat the griddle. Mix the dry ingredients in a bowl; make a well in the centre and add the egg and half the milk. Stir until the mixture is thick and smooth, then add the rest of the milk gradually, stirring all the time, until it is the consistency of cream. Pour into a jug.

Rub a piece of lard the size of a hazelnut quickly over the hot griddle on the point of a knife. Pour the batter on to the griddle in rounds about two inches across. Fry them till bubbles appear on the surface and the undersides are light brown. Flip them over with a palette knife and brown the other sides. Add more lard to the griddle and start again. As each batch is finished put it into a folded tea-towel to keep soft and warm.

Serve hot with plenty of butter.

Makes 15–20 scones

Midlothian Oatcakes

8 oz oatmeal (fine or coarse — porridge oats will do)
4 oz flour
½ teaspoon or more salt
1 teaspoon baking powder
water
3 oz butter, or half butter and half lard

Place the oatmeal in a basin. Sift in the flour, salt and baking powder. Rub in the fat and mix to a stiff dough with cold water. Turn the dough on to a board sprinkled with oatmeal, knead lightly and roll out to ⅛ inch thickness. Cut into rounds with a glass or teacup and bake in a moderate oven, Reg 4/350°, for 25 minutes. They should not brown, or only very slightly. Eat with butter for tea; they are also very good with cheese, at the end of a meal.

Makes about 20

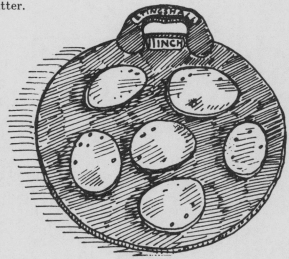

Cheese Straws

6 oz plain flour
salt, pepper, and a pinch cayenne
4 oz butter
1 egg yolk
4 oz finely grated Derby Sage cheese
1 tablespoon water

Preheat the oven to Reg 5/375°. Sift the flour with the seasoning into a mixing bowl, drop in the butter and cut it into the flour. Rub it in lightly and quickly with your fingertips until the mixture looks like breadcrumbs, Add the cheese and stir it in with a knife. Mix the egg yolk and water, add to the dry ingredients and mix quickly to a firm dough. Knead lightly until smooth and chill for half an hour before rolling it out to about ¼ inch thick. Cut into narrow strips about two inches long. Bake on a lightly greased baking sheet until cooked, 15–20 minutes; they will be a lovely freckled greeny colour.

☐ *This recipe is perfectly suitable for Cheddar or Cheshire cheese.*

Five-minute Ballater Scones

8 oz flour, 1 level teaspoon cream of tartar and ½ small teaspoon bicarbonate of soda, or use 8 oz self-raising flour plus a pinch of baking powder
1½ oz butter
¼ teaspoon salt
scant ¼ pint tepid milk (sour is good)

Preheat the oven to Reg 7½/435°. Sieve the flour, cream of tartar, bicarbonate of soda and salt into a bowl. Rub in the butter at top speed, stir in enough milk to make a slightly stiff dough, and knead the mixture lightly in the bowl. Roll out to half-inch thickness on a floured board and cut into two-inch rounds. Put them on a buttered baking sheet and place them just above the centre of the oven. When they are nicely puffed up and pale golden, after 10 to 15 minutes, take them out and brush the tops with milk. Eat them warm.

Makes 12 scones

Hot Cross Buns

½ oz fresh yeast (or ¼ oz dried yeast)
2 oz sugar
½ pint tepid milk and water
1 lb plain flour
1 teaspoon salt
½ teaspoon nutmeg
½ teaspoon cinnamon
4 oz currants
1 oz candied peel
1 egg, beaten
2 oz melted butter

For the crosses
1 oz fat
2 oz flour
water
For the glaze
2 tablespoons sugar
2 tablespoons water
2 tablespoons milk

Cream the yeast in a small bowl with a teaspoon of the sugar, stir in half the milk and water (tepid), sprinkle a little of the flour over the surface and leave in a warm place for about 20 minutes, when it should be covered in little bubbles as the yeast begins to grow. Sift into a large warm bowl the flour, salt, spices and sugar. Make a well in the centre and mix in the yeast liquid. Add the currants and peel, the beaten egg and melted butter. Mix with your hand adding enough tepid milk and water to make a dough. It will be very sticky at first, and softer than bread dough or pastry but firm enough to handle. Mix until it is smooth and leaves your hands and the bowl clean. If you *have* added too much liquid add more flour.

Leave in a warm place in the bowl, covered with a damp cloth, to rise until double in size. Knock it down and measure it off in about 1½ oz pieces, form into bun shapes and place on greased and floured baking sheets, with enough space round them for their increase in size during baking. Mix the fat, flour and water into pastry, roll it out and cut it into thin strips, brush with milk underneath each strip and lay in crosses on the buns (or if you have a steady hand, make the pastry runny by adding a bit more water and pour the crosses on, using a little jug). Other methods of making crosses are simply to cut the cross on the bun with a sharp knife, or lay it with strips of wet rice paper. But the runny pastry method looks the most professional. Heat the oven to Reg 7/425°, while the buns prove again in a warm place, when they will rise, and become smooth and puffy. This takes about 20 minutes. Make the oven steamy-hot, which buns like, by putting a tray of water in the bottom. Make the glaze by boiling the milk, water and sugar together for 1–2 minutes and keep it warm, with a pastry brush ready. Bake the buns for 15-20 minutes. Five minutes before the end brush with the glaze and return to oven.

Eat split in half, toasted, with butter,

☐ *These buns are traditionally eaten at Easter but are delicious sticky buns for any time of year.*

Makes 12–16 buns

Treacle Buns

4 oz butter
4 oz sugar
4 tablespoons golden syrup
10 oz self-raising flour
1 teaspoon ground ginger (optional)
2 teaspoons bicarbonate of soda and a little
   water

Preheat the oven to Reg 7/425°. Slightly warm the butter, sugar and syrup in a large basin over hot water. Beat to a cream, add the flour and ginger, and the bicarbonate of soda dissolved in a little cold water. Mix and work into a stiff dough, adding more flour if necessary. Pull off pieces the size of a small walnut. Roll into balls and bake on a well greased flat tin, keeping well apart, in the centre of the oven for 15 minutes.

The result will be flattish biscuity buns, crisp on the outside and soft inside, like Cornish fairings.

Makes 24–30 buns

Bread

FLOUR FOR BREAD MAKING
The flour used in white bread making should be strong flour that is made from especially hard-grained wheat. You can also make a good loaf with unbleached flour.

Plain flour of the sort that is used for making cakes and pastries, produces a perfectly good but rather soft and bland loaf.

THE CONDITIONS FOR BREAD MAKING
A warm kitchen is ideal for bread making. Yeast grows best in a warm but not hot atmosphere. Heat kills yeast and cold inhibits its growth.

Rising can be done almost anywhere warm — in the days before central heating, people used to take it to bed with them, but nowadays setting it down by a radiator or in a warmed airing cupboard is just as effective.

White Bread

2½ lbs flour
½ oz butter
1 oz yeast
2 dessertspoons coarse salt or 1 dessertspoon
   fine salt
1–1¼ pints tepid water

Making bread, like so many things, is easy when you know how. The more often you bake the better your bread will be. Once you are confident, this recipe can be altered according to how you like your bread — if you like it richer, add more butter, if you like it soft, add some milk to the water. You can sprinkle the top with sesame or poppy seeds, or glaze it with a strong salt and water solution (but don't drench it). If you are making a tin loaf add a little more liquid than you would for a round loaf so that you can press the dough well into the corners of the tin. For plaits, knots and twists, make a stiffer dough with less liquid or they will lose their shape. This recipe is for very plain everyday bread.

Warm the flour in its bowl. Make a well in the centre and if using fine salt, sprinkle it round the edge of the well. If using coarse salt, dissolve it in the water.

Cream the yeast with 2–3 tablespoons of tepid unsalted water and pour in the warm melted butter. Allow to stand for 5 or 10 minutes, Pour it into the middle of the flour, flick a little flour over it and then gradually add the liquid, mixing it thoroughly with your left hand as you pour with your right, until the dough is even and pliable.

Knead for 10 minutes. Cover the bowl with a damp cloth, a folded towel and a lid and allow to rise for 2 hours.

Shape into loaves on two floured baking sheets, sprinkle the tops with a little flour and rub it over, then slash them and put to rise again (prove) for ½–¾ hour. Preheat the oven to Reg 9/475°.

Bake the loaves at Reg 9/475° for ½ hour, move the tins so that all the bread has time on the top shelf and bake a further 30 minutes at Reg 5/375°. Tap the bottom crust of the loaf with your knuckles — if it sounds hollow and feels hard but springy, it is done. Allow to cool on racks. A pan of hot water set in the bottom of the oven during cooking makes a steamy atmosphere. which suits the bread.

Makes 4 loaves

Brown Bread

Add 1 oz more butter. Mix wholewheat flour and white flour in a proportion that suits you. Two-thirds wholewheat to one-third white is delicious, but if you want really healthy bread, use all wholewheat flour. It takes more liquid than plain flour, say about 1½ to 2 pints to 2½ lbs flour.

Barm Brack

1 lb plain flour
½ teaspoon powdered cinnamon
¼ teaspoon grated nutmeg
½ teaspoon salt
2 oz butter, 1 oz yeast
3 oz caster sugar
½ pint tepid milk
1 egg
8 oz sultanas
4 oz currants
2 oz mixed chopped candied peel

Sieve the flour, spices and salt into a warm bowl. Rub in the butter. Warm the milk; it should only be tepid. Mix the yeast with a teaspoon of the weighed amount of sugar and a teaspoon of the milk. Mix the rest of the sugar into the flour then pour in the yeast and the milk into which you have beaten the egg. Make a stiff batter and beat it very well. The best method for this is to sit down with the bowl between your knees and the wooden spoon held firmly in both hands, or use an electric mixer with a dough hook. The mixture should become very springy and stretchy.

Add the washed and dried fruit and the peel, mix it in well. Cover the bowl with a floured cloth and a towel and lid and put it in a warm place to rise for about 1½ hours until it is puffy and has doubled in size. Divide the dough and put it into two 7″ greased cake tins or 1 lb loaf tins. Allow to prove a further 30 minutes, and meanwhile preheat the oven to Reg 6/400°. Bake the loaves 40 minutes, turn them round, cover lightly with damp double greaseproof paper and bake 20 minutes more at Reg 4½/360°. Cool on a rack and eat fresh with butter.

☐ *This Irish yeast cake is a sort of superior currant loaf, and is eaten in slices spread with butter. When stale it is good toasted.*

Makes 2 loaves

Malt Bread

8 oz self raising flour
1 level teaspoon salt
1 level teaspoon bicarbonate of soda
3 oz sultanas
2 oz caster sugar
2 tablespoons (4 oz) golden syrup
2 tablespoons (4 oz) malt extract
¼ pint milk
1 egg, beaten

Preheat oven to Reg 5/375°. Sift the flour, bicarbonate and salt into a bowl. Stir in the sultanas and sugar. Melt the syrup and malt over gentle heat in a saucepan, then gradually blend in the milk. Make a well in the centre of the flour, pour in the syrup mixture and egg and mix well. It is a fairly wet mixture. Pour into a greased and floured 1 lb loaf tin. Bake for about 50 minutes or till golden and springy to touch. Cool on a wire rack. Keep in airtight tin for 2 days before using.

For 6–8

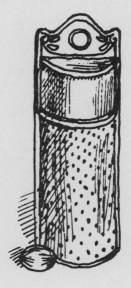

Moyna's Irish Bread

9 heaped tablespoons wholewheat flour (½ lb)
2 heaped tablespoons plain flour
1 level teaspoon brown sugar
1 heaped teaspoon salt
1 heaped teaspoon baking powder
½ pint sour milk or buttermilk

Preheat the oven to Reg 8½/460°. Mix the dry ingredients in a bowl; add enough sour milk to make a soft dough. It may take less than half a pint. Turn the mixture into a buttered and floured bread tin and bake 35–40 minutes. When it is cooked wrap it in a clean, damp tea-cloth and put it on a wire rack to cool. This prevents the crust from becoming too crumbly.

If you have not got any sour milk, add a little lemon juice to some fresh milk and stir it well.

☐ *This loaf should be crumbly and quite light. It is mixed in a couple of minutes and is a very good bread for tea.*

Cinnamon Toast

1 teaspoon ground cinnamon
3 teaspoons caster sugar
2 pieces hot buttered toast

Mix the sugar and cinnamon together and sprinkle on to the toast; eat straight away, hot and melting and spicy. Lovely for a winter tea.

For 2

Mrs Fitch's Walnut Bread

1 lb self-raising flour
1 level teaspoon salt
1 oz lard
4 oz walnut pieces
4 oz dates
3 oz sugar
1 egg
½ pint milk

Preheat oven to Reg 4½/360°. Sieve the flour and salt and rub in the lard. Chop the walnuts and dates and mix them into the rubbed flour together with the sugar. Beat the egg in the milk and mix it into the dry ingredients thoroughly, making a soft dough. You may not need all the liquid. Turn into a well-greased bread tin and bake in the oven for about an hour. Allow to cool and butter the slices like ordinary bread. Very good for tea.

STUFFINGS
SAUCES

Stuffings and Sauces

It is a bore making a stuffing when you are roasting a bird, but it is worth it when you find it later, a bonus as it were. Not only turkeys deserve this treatment; some fish and lots of vegetables take well to a stuffing, and so of course do chickens and boned shoulders and breasts of lamb and veal. Even a cut onion or lemon and a bunch of herbs help to keep a bird moist, but if you are going in for the real bona fide filling-stuffing you can choose from these categories, using a combination that suits the dish:

(1) To keep it moist: bacon, mushrooms, onions, celery, apples, prunes.

(2) To pad it out: breadcrumbs, rice, oats, cracked wheat, sausage meat.

(3) To bind it: stock, tomato purée, butter, olive oil, egg, wine, milk, suet.

(4) To flavour it: garlic, herbs, seasoning, spices, lemon peel or juice, pine nuts, chestnuts, almonds, raisins.

If you are stuffing vegetables, use part of the flesh that you remove to make room for the stuffing, and add minced beef, pork or lamb, chicken livers or diced bacon or ham.

Sauces were originally invented to disguise what the food was really like, and are now supposed to complement it. Certainly lots of dishes would be sadly lacking love if no sauce was made to go with them. The basic sauces are the very first things to be learned in domestic science lessons, and once you have béchamel, mayonnaise, hollandaise and basic tomato sauce under your belt, you can tackle almost anything. Sauces which use egg yolks to thicken them are the most difficult to handle because of the curdling, but with practice they go quite fast, and although fiddly and a bit extravagant, they add a great touch of luxury to simple food.

Marjoram Stuffing for Chicken

½ onion, finely chopped
2 thick slices white bread
1 ½ teaspoons chopped fresh marjoram, or 1 teaspoon
   dried
2 tablespoons softened butter
salt

Soften the onion in a little butter until transparent
but not brown. Cut the crusts off the bread and
grate to make fairly coarse crumbs. Mix these with
the onion and its butter, and the marjoram, salt and
softened butter. Stuff the bird with this mixture
and roast in the usual way.

Don't press the stuffing in too firmly as it should be
very light.

□ *In France this stuffing is often used with guinea-
fowl.*

For 4

Spinach Stuffing

1 lb spinach
1 clove garlic
¼ lb minced pork
salt and freshly ground pepper
1 small egg (optional)
½ oz butter

Cook the spinach and squeeze it dry. Purée it and
let it sit in a sieve while you sauté the minced pork
in the butter in a saucepan for a few minutes.
Pulverise the garlic clove and add it and the spinach
to the pork in the saucepan. Take it off the heat and
add salt, pepper and the beaten egg, or half of it
if the mixture appears to be getting too sloppy. It is
rather a wet stuffing anyway, but becomes firm in
the cooking.

□ *Excellent for boned shoulder or breast of lamb*

Stuffing for a Roast Chicken

The chicken's liver (only if pink or reddish), chopped
1 medium onion, chopped
2 oz bulgour (ground wheat), boiled in salted water
   5 minutes
1 oz softened butter
½ teaspoon grated lemon rind
salt and freshly ground pepper

Fry all the ingredients together for a few minutes;
stuff the mixture into the bird.

Chestnut and Apple Stuffing for Pork or Goose

½ lb chestnuts
2 shallots, or 1 small onion
1 small cooking apple
salt, pepper, sugar
parsley, thyme, or sage (whichever you like but
   only use one besides parsley)
single cream
1–2 oz butter

Slit the chestnuts with a knife, then cook them
either by baking in a little oil for 10 minutes
in a hot oven, or by boiling in water for 10
minutes. Shell them and remove the skin beneath
the shell by boiling them in fresh water for another
20 minutes when the chestnuts should also be
tender and pink inside instead of hard and yellow.
Mash them with a little single cream and season
with salt, pepper and a little sugar, so that
you have a purée.

Meanwhile, peel and chop the onion very finely
and soften in a small pan with some of the butter
for 15–20 minutes. Peel and grate the apple and
add it to the onion with more butter. Cook until
both are soft. Add them to the chestnut purée
with the chopped parsley and thyme leaves, or
a very few sage leaves. Mix well and taste for
seasoning, balancing sharpness and sweetness
to your liking. The consistency must be fairly
thick, or it will drip out in the cooking of the
meat.

□ *Use it to stuff a boned hand of pork or a goose.*

Aïoli

3–4 cloves garlic
2 egg yolks
¼ pint olive oil
salt and pepper
a few drops of vinegar or lemon juice

Make this exactly like mayonnaise but thoroughly pulverise the garlic cloves with salt and stir them into the egg yolks before you start to add the oil. Don't use much lemon or vinegar in the making of aïoli as it should be very thick.

☐ *For raw vegetables, fish soup, boiled vegetables, boiled chicken and cold chicken.*

Avgolemono Sauce

2 egg yolks
½ juicy lemon
½ pint water, stock, or water in which fish, vegetables or chicken have been cooked
salt, pepper

Beat the egg yolks, add the juice of the lemon, pour on the hot (not boiling) stock or water. Thicken very carefully in a small pan over the lowest flame, or in a double boiler. Stir all the time and watch that it doesn't boil (this is a slow job) or it will curdle. Add salt and pepper to taste.

☐ *For meat balls, broad beans, poached fish.*

Apple Sauce

2–4 apples, peeled, quartered and cored
1 tablespoon water
1 tablespoon white sugar
2 cloves
squeeze lemon juice
½ oz butter

Put all the ingredients in a pan and cook until the apple is tender. Remove the cloves. Beat to a smooth purée and serve hot.

☐ *For pork.*

Herb Butters

For serving with vegetables or grilled fish or meat. These herbs all make good fresh herb butters:
Mint: ideal for lamb, peas, new potatoes.
Parsley: for steak, fish or broad beans.
Tarragon: for potatoes, chicken or eggs.
Chives and parsley together: for steak, fish, lamb chops.
Rosemary: for lamb, pork, chicken, haricot beans.
Savory or Thyme: for grilled kidneys etc.

If you have a special chopping-bowl or a Mouli-Parsmint, chop the herbs in it, otherwise chop as finely as possible with a knife. Don't use more than one or two herbs, fresh and in generous amounts. For each person chop about one heaped teaspoon of herbs and mash it with a walnut of butter, a squeeze of lemon, salt and fresh ground pepper. Form into a one-inch roll in a piece of greaseproof paper, and put into the refrigerator to become firm. Place a half-inch slice of the roll on the food as you serve it.

Herb butters keep for up to a week in the refrigerator.

☐ *For serving with vegetables or grilled fish or meat.*

Béchamel Sauce

1 oz butter
1 oz flour
½ pint milk
salt, pepper

Heat the milk to just below boiling point (see note below on infusion). Melt the butter in a small saucepan over a moderate heat without browning. Tip in the flour and stir to amalgamate it with the butter. This mixture is called a white roux and should not be allowed to brown. When it starts to honeycomb, i.e. when small bubbles start to break all over the surface of the mixture, pour in one third of the milk, stirring vigorously until you have a smooth mixture. When it has thickened into a smooth paste add one third more milk. Stir again and when it has thickened gradually add the rest of the milk until you have a smooth sauce of the consistency you require. Season and cook very gently, stirring from time to time, for five minutes, to cook the flour. The best Béchamel is made with milk which you have previously infused with various flavourings to make it tastier. Simply put a small sliced onion, a bayleaf, a small bunch of parsley and a few peppercorns into the cold milk, bring it to boiling point, turn the heat right down and let the milk stand just not boiling over a very low flame for up to half an hour. Strain the milk before you make the sauce.

☐ *This makes ½ pint, medium thick sauce.*

Barbecue Sauce

1 onion, peeled and chopped
1 oz butter
1 small tin tomatoes (or 4 fresh, chopped peeled ones — or purée)
3 tablespoons wine vinegar
2 tablespoons Worcestershire sauce
2 teaspoons brown or demerara sugar
1 teaspoon made mustard
1 teaspoon paprika
1 teaspoon salt

Lightly fry the onion until transparent, add chopped tomatoes and all other ingredients. If using for spare ribs, bring to the boil before pouring sauce on to ribs and roasting. If using on already fried, grilled or barbecued meat, simmer a little while, for the sauce to amalgamate, before using.

☐ *Also good with epigrams, chops, kebabs*

Bread Sauce

½ pint milk
1 onion, peeled
5 cloves
2 blades of mace
2–3 slices of white bread, at least an inch thick
salt, pepper and a grating of nutmeg
walnut-sized knob of butter

Stick the cloves into the onion and put it in a small saucepan with the milk and blades of mace. Stand this on an asbestos mat over a very low heat, and let it infuse for up to one hour without boiling. Remove the onion and mace. Cut the crusts off the bread and crumble it into the milk, whisking with a fork. Season with salt, pepper and nutmeg, and if you like add the finely chopped onion with the cloves removed. Heat it without boiling and, just before serving, stir in the butter.

☐ *For roasted birds.*

Sauce Béarnaise

4 tablespoons wine vinegar
1 shallot
1 bayleaf
1 blade of mace
6 peppercorns
2 large egg yolks
4 oz fresh butter
1 heaped teaspoon of chopped tarragon, chervil and
    parsley, mixed
salt and freshly ground pepper

Reduce the vinegar with the spices to a tablespoon.
Work the yolks with a nut of the softened butter,
strain the vinegar over them, stir and thicken in a
bain-marie, gradually adding the rest of the butter
stirring constantly. Add the herbs and seasoning.

☐ *For grilled fish or meat.*

Breton Sauce

2 egg yolks
2 dessertspoons Dijon mustard
1 scant dessertspoon wine vinegar
2 oz very soft butter
2 tablespoons chopped fresh herbs (parsley,
    chives, chervil, tarragon)
salt, pepper

Mix the egg yolks with the mustard and vinegar.
Add the softened butter gradually (it must not
be runny but it must be soft enough to mix in
easily). The resultant sauce will be thick but not
quite as smooth as mayonnaise. Add the herbs,
and taste for salt and pepper, which you add if
needed. This sauce can curdle, and if it does, let
it get quite cold, then beat it.

☐ *For cold fish (especially mackerel) or cold meat.*

For 4

Black Butter

2 oz butter
1 tablespoon chopped parsley or chopped capers
1 teaspoon vinegar

Using a very small pan fry the parsley in the
butter; when the butter is dark nut brown, but not
black, stir in the vinegar and pour the sizzling
sauce immediately over whatever you are serving
it with.

If you prefer to use capers, omit the parsley and
put the capers in with the vinegar.

☐ *This is for brains, poached eggs, skate or liver.*

Cumberland Sauce

4 oranges
2 lemons
2 small shallots
1 dessertspoon fresh English or Dijon mustard
3 tablespoons cheap wine or wine vinegar
1 large glass cheap port
1 lb redcurrant jelly
salt and freshly ground pepper

Peel the oranges and lemons very thinly with a
potato peeler, so that the pieces of peel have no
pith. Cut the peel into tiny thin strips, cover them
with cold water in a small pan, bring to the boil and
then strain immediately. Peel and chop the shallots
very finely, put in a small pan, cover with cold water,
boil for a few minutes and strain. Mix the mustard,
wine, port and the juice of the lemons and of two of
the oranges. (Use more orange juice if they aren't
very juicy). Stir in the redcurrant jelly and dissolve
it slowly over a low heat. Add the peel and shallots
and a generous seasoning of salt and pepper. Simmer
20 minutes or more until it thickens a bit, pour into
small jars and keep in the fridge. It keeps a week or
two and makes a good Christmas present. It has a
very sweet spicy flavour.

☐ *For cold ham, duck, turkey or game.*

Cheese Sauce (Mornay Sauce)

1 oz butter
1 oz flour
½ pint hot milk
salt, pepper
1 teaspoon of made mustard or dusting of
   Cayenne pepper
1 oz or more grated cheese (Parmesan, Cheddar
   or Gruyère)

Make a white roux with the flour and butter
(just melt the butter stir in the flour and let it
bubble a minute or two, but do not let it start
to sizzle or change colour). Stirring carefully with
a small wooden spoon gradually incorporate the
hot milk. Let it return to the boil after each
addition of milk and stir it well to absorb the
flour before you add more. When all the milk is
combined smoothly with the roux add salt,
pepper and, if you like a sharp sauce, the mustard
or Cayenne. Let it simmer at least 5 minutes, to
cook the flour, before you add the cheese. When
all the cheese is melted the sauce is ready.

Chilli Mayonnaise

2 egg yolks
⅓ teaspoon or more chilli powder
salt, pepper
¼ pint olive oil or a little more
white wine vinegar

Mix the egg yolks with the chilli powder, salt and
pepper. Gradually add oil as you would if you
were making plain mayonnaise. When the mixture
becomes too thick, thin it with a little wine
vinegar.

☐ *This is a beautiful golden colour. Very good with
cold poached halibut, cod or other fish. Sprinkle the
flaked fish with a little lemon juice or vinegar and
oil, and serve the mayonnaise separately.*

Curry Sauce

1 small onion, chopped finely
thyme, bay leaf, mace
1½ oz butter
1 or more teaspoons curry powder
¼ pint of fish or chicken stock
¼ pint of milk
½ oz of flour
salt, pepper

In a saucepan make a Béchamel using 1 oz
of the butter, flour, stock, milk, salt and pepper.

Meanwhile cook the onion and herbs in the rest of
the butter without browning, then add the curry
powder. One teaspoon is not too strong, but add
more if you want a very definite flavour. Let it
sizzle a minute then stir the onion, etc., into the
sauce. Cook a further 10 minutes. Strain and
serve. This sauce should be fairly thin.

☐ *For fish or egg croquettes.*

For 4

Egg Sauce

½ pint well-flavoured thin Béchamel, made with
  half milk and half fish- or chicken-stock
2 hard-boiled eggs
salt and white pepper

Sieve the egg yolks into the Béchamel, chop the
whites and add these too. The Béchamel should be
of a creamy consistency so that the egg whites are
visible as a texture in the sauce. Season and serve
hot. This has become almost a joke because it smacks
of institutions, but made properly it is a good English
sauce of quality.

□ *A delicate sauce for chicken, fishcakes and steamed
cod, turbot or halibut.*

Sauce Gribiche

1 hard-boiled egg
a little chopped lemon peel
a tablespoon of chopped gherkin
oil
vinegar
salt, pepper

Mash the yolk of the egg, season and gradually
add as much vinegar as you would use for making
a vinaigrette, then gradually stir in the oil. Add
the finely chopped egg white, lemon peel and
gherkins.

□ *This sauce is good with cold meat, brawns, cold
cooked leeks and fish salad.*

Sauce Hollandaise

2 tablespoons white wine vinegar
1 tablespoon water
2–3 peppercorns
½ bayleaf
1 blade mace
1 large egg yolk
4–5 oz slightly salted butter

Cut the butter into small cubes and if it is very
hard let it soften a bit. Put the vinegar, water,
peppercorns, bayleaf and mace into a small
saucepan and reduce to half their quantity. Allow
to cool and remove peppercorns, bayleaf and mace.
Take a double saucepan, or a pan into which a
suitable bowl or basin will fit, and heat some water
in it to just below boiling point. In order to lessen
the risk of the sauce curdling keep the water below
the boil, and make sure it doesn't actually touch
the base of the bowl or pan in which the sauce is
cooking. Using the bowl or pan which is to go over
the water, mix the reduced vinegar and water with
the egg yolk and a cube of the soft butter. Place
it over the hot water and stirring all the time with
a wooden spoon, add the cubes of butter one at a
time, letting each one melt before you add another.
If the sauce shows signs of thickening too fast, or
curdling, remove it at once from the water. If it
is too thick add a few drops of water or the top of
the milk. Taste for salt. If it is too sharp add some
unsalted butter. It should be smooth and fairly
thick, and is served lukewarm.

□ *For serving with Oeufs Bénédictine and poached
fish (and asparagus).*

Horseradish Sauce

1–2 tablespoons grated horseradish
¼ teaspoon salt
½ teaspoon mustard powder
1 teaspoon white sugar
1 dessertspoon wine vinegar or lemon juice
2–3 tablespoons thin cream or top of the milk

Mix all well together. The grating of fresh horse-radish is far more of a torture than cutting up onions, but the result is really worth it. Beware if you start growing it in the garden; it must be confined, otherwise the whole garden will soon be covered with what is virtually an indestructible weed.

☐ *For hot or cold roast beef, or herrings.*

Mustard Sauce

¼ pint Hollandaise sauce
1–2 teaspoons made English mustard

Make the Hollandaise and when finished stir in one or two teaspoons freshly made mustard.

For 2

Mustard Sauce 2

½ pint double cream
1 teaspoon made mustard
salt and freshly ground pepper

Mix the ingredients together and pour over open filleted cooked fish.

☐ *These sauces are marvellous with fried or grilled herring, mackerel or sprats, and with tongue.*

For 4

Mayonnaise

1 egg yolk
scant ¼ pint olive oil
salt and white pepper
1 teaspoon lemon juice or white wine vinegar

Put the egg yolk, *not* straight out of the refrigerator, with the seasoning, into a bowl and beat it with a wooden fork or spoon. Put the oil into a jug with a narrow lip, or an oil bottle with a spout, so that you can drip it out in minute drops. Start adding the oil to the egg yolk a few drops at a time, beating continuously. When the mixture starts to thicken, add a few drops of vinegar or lemon juice, then continue trickling in the oil, adding a little more at a time as it gets thicker, until you are pouring it in a thin thread-like stream, and stirring all the time. Add more vinegar or lemon as necessary. If the egg yolk is small it may not take quarter of a pint of oil; when threads of oil appear in the lines left by the fork or spoon, be very cautious about adding more or it may curdle. When it is finished it can be thinned with cream, top of the milk or warm water to make a pouring consistency for egg mayonnaise etc. If you do curdle your mayonnaise, break a fresh egg yolk into a separate bowl, beat it, and add the curdled lot, *a little at a time,* until it is all worked in.

For 2–3

Green Mayonnaise

¼ pint very thick mayonnaise (this page)
handful of young spinach leaves
handful of watercress
4–5 sprigs parsley
fresh tarragon if available

Blanch all the greenery for two or three minutes in boiling salted water. Squeeze dry and pulverize. You should now have a dark green purée. Put it in a fine sieve to drain the water off.

Just before serving stir it carefully into the mayonnaise. It makes the most beautiful speckled, pale green sauce.

Mint Sauce

¼ pint wine vinegar
1½ oz Demerara sugar
1 tablespoon finely chopped mint

Bring the vinegar to the boil in a small pan, and dissolve the Demerara sugar in it. Put the mint in a bowl and pour on the boiling vinegar. Allow it to cool.

☐ *For lamb*

Pizzaiola Sauce

1 lb tomatoes, fresh or tinned, skinned and chopped
2 tablespoons oil
1 clove garlic, sliced
salt, pepper and a pinch of sugar
handful of parsley, chopped
½ handful of fresh basil or oregano, chopped

Heat the oil in a small frying pan and brown the garlic. Add the tomatoes, salt, pepper and sugar and cook, stirring, for 10–15 minutes. Add the freshly chopped herbs and serve.

☐ *For fish, pasta, steaks, chops, kebabs.*

Rouille

2 red pimentos, bottled or tinned will do
4 cloves garlic, peeled
1 slice white bread, crusts removed
salt to taste
2 tablespoons olive oil
2 tablespoons broth from fish soup

Cut up the peppers, remove the seeds and pound them with the garlic and crumbled bread and a little salt. Gradually add the oil and broth until you have a smooth sauce. It is hot because of the quantity of garlic, so if your cloves are very small use more.

☐ *For fish soup or boiled fish.*

Red Sauce

2 tablespoons fresh white breadcrumbs
2 tablespoons wine vinegar
2 cloves garlic
2 large ripe tomatoes, skinned and de-seeded
large pinch salt and paprika
6 tablespoons olive oil

Soak the breadcrumbs in the vinegar. Pound the garlic in a mortar and add the tomatoes and breadcrumbs. Season with salt and paprika and add the olive oil gradually, until the sauce is thick.

☐ *This is a Spanish sauce whose ingredients sound unlikely, but it is delicious, especially with cold fish or shellfish, hard-boiled eggs, or with a plain potato salad instead of dressing or mayonnaise.*

For 4

Salsa Verde

1 clove garlic
1 hard-boiled egg
2–3 anchovies
1 tablespoon capers
bunch parsley (preferably the flat kind)
2 teaspoons fresh white breadcrumbs
1 tablespoon wine vinegar
3–4 tablespoons olive oil

Cut a clove of garlic in half and score the cut side with a knife. Rub a bowl with the cut clove of garlic so that it is well-coated with the juice — you must press quite hard. Chop the hard-boiled egg, anchovies, capers and parsley quite finely and put them into the bowl. Soak the crumbs in the vinegar, drain them and stir them into the other ingredients. Now add olive oil, gradually stirring, until you have a smooth, soft sauce.

☐ *For boiled meat and fish. This sauce keeps well; if you leave out the egg it will keep indefinitely in a cool place.*

For 4

Sauce Soubise (onion sauce)

½ lb onions
2 tablespoons butter
2 tablespoons flour
½ pint creamy milk or light, good stock
salt, pepper and nutmeg
pinch of sugar

Peel and slice the onions finely and stew them gently in the butter in a saucepan for 10–15 minutes. They must not brown. Stir in the flour, cook for one minute, then gradually add the heated milk or stock, stirring as it thickens. Season and simmer for 15–20 minutes taking care not to let the sauce catch at the bottom. Sieve or liquidise the mixture, taste for seasoning and sugar and serve hot.

☐ *For roast lamb and lamb chops, and for Oeufs à la*

Tomato Sauce

2 onions
2 cloves garlic
2 tablespoons olive oil
1½ lbs tomatoes
½ glass red wine
sprigs of thyme and rosemary and a bayleaf
salt and freshly ground pepper

Chop the onions and garlic finely and soften them in the oil in a saucepan for about ten minutes without browning. Add the skinned roughly chopped tomatoes, seasoning, red wine and bundle of herbs. Simmer 45 minutes, uncovered.

☐ *For pasta, fried fish etc.*

For 6

Chilli Tomato Sauce

1 onion, finely chopped
2 red chilli peppers or 1 teaspoon chilli powder
   (more if liked)
1 lb tomatoes, skinned and chopped
3–4 cloves garlic, peeled and chopped finely
salt and freshly ground pepper
thyme, sage and parsley tied in a bunch
butter and oil

Heat a little butter and oil in a frying pan, add the onions and soften them. Stir in the chillies or chilli powder, fry for a minute or two and then add the tomatoes, garlic, seasoning and herbs.
Simmer uncovered until you have a thickish sauce, remove the herbs and sieve or liquidise.

Reheat in the same pan before serving. This can be ferociously or gently hot according to how much chilli you put in.

☐ *A hot sauce, excellent with fried chicken.*

Tomato Ketchup

6 lbs ripe tomatoes
½ lb onions
½ lb sugar
¼ oz paprika
pinch cayenne
1½ oz salt
1 fluid oz wine vinegar (chilli or tarragon)
spiced vinegar:
½ pint wine vinegar
small piece cinnamon bark
10 whole allspice
6 cloves
2–3 blades of mace
1–2 bayleaves
1 chilli pepper

Make the spiced vinegar: put the spices into the wine vinegar, bring it to the boil, take it off the heat and leave for two hours, covered. Then strain.

Slice the tomatoes and peel the onions; cook them covered until the tomato skins start to come away. Rub the pulp through a sieve, add sugar, salt, cayenne and paprika. Cook until the sauce thickens, then add the spiced vinegar and wine vinegar. Cook until the sauce thickens again to the consistency of thick cream.

Pour into hot bottles with sterilised tops and seal firmly. Leave to mature a month or two.

☐ *One pound of tomatoes makes about half a pint of ketchup, so this is only worth doing if you have masses of tomatoes and ready appetites for ketchup.*

Vinaigrette à l'oeuf

vinaigrette (above)
1 small onion or shallot, chopped finely
a few chives, chopped
1 soft-boiled egg

Add the onion, chives and the yolk of the soft-boiled egg to the vinaigrette. Chop the white and add this too.

Vinaigrette

4–5 tablespoons oil
½ teaspoon sea salt
several pinches freshly ground black pepper
1 teaspoon white sugar (optional)
2 teaspoons wine vinegar

Take a small bowl, mix the salt, pepper and sugar and add the oil. Then stir in the vinegar with a teaspoon; it should become thick and cloudy. Pour it over your green salad just as your serve it, and turn the leaves over until they glisten with oil. If you like garlic add a clove, first thoroughly pulverised with the salt, using the point of a stainless kitchen knife. If you only quite like it, put a few cubes of dried bread or rusk, thoroughly rubbed with cut cloves of garlic, into the bottom of the salad bowl. If you like a thick mustardy dressing, mix the vinegar with half a teaspoon of Dijon mustard and season this, leaving out the sugar, before you gradually add the oil.

☐ *For salads and cold vegetables.*

Walnut Sauce

2 oz shelled walnuts
juice of 1 lemon
2 tablespoons olive oil
2 tablespoons chopped parsley
½ teaspoon salt

Pound the walnuts in a pestle and mortar until they go creamy, add lemon juice and keep pounding. Add salt, gradually add oil until well mixed, and finally the parsley.

☐ *For use on hot ham, boiled bacon, or pasta.*

For 4

Miscellaneous Recipes

To Make and Bake a Fruit Flan

Preheat the oven to Reg 5½/390°. Press the pastry into an 8″ loose flan ring, previously buttered, on a baking sheet, also buttered. It is too crumbly and sticky to roll out. Arrange the fruit (sliced apples or halved stoned apricots or plums) prettily in the flan. Sprinkle with sugar and bake 10 minutes. Then lower heat and bake another 20 minutes at Reg 4½/360°. Allow to shrink and cool before sliding away the ring and lifting the tart with excruciating care on to a plate or dish. Glaze the top with syrup from in between the fruit, or with melted apricot jam.

Low Fat Pastry for Pies

½ lb self-raising flour
2 oz Nutter or butter
2 oz margarine (kosher is best)
a pinch of salt
ice-cold water

Sieve the flour and salt into a bowl.
Rub or grate the fat into the flour. Add just enough water to hold it together. It should be fairly crumbly and dry, and hard to handle. Roll out straight away. Bake at Reg 9/500° for 10 minutes, then at 4/350° for 20 minutes.

☐ *This recipe was invented for somebody on a diet that had to be completely free of animal fats. It turns out to be wonderful pastry.*

Beurre Manié

Mash together an equal amount of butter and flour and squeeze it in the palm of your hand to combine the two elements properly.

Use it to thicken stews and sauces at the end of the cooking.

Rich Sweet Flan Pastry

6 oz plain flour
2 oz slightly salted butter
2 oz cooking fat
1 oz granulated sugar
1 egg yolk
a few drops of cold water
a pinch of salt

Sieve the flour and salt into a mixing bowl. Chop the butter and fat into small pieces in the flour. Add the sugar and rub it all together very lightly with your finger tips until it is integrated. Blend in the egg yolk, using a knife, and then add just a few drops of water to make it the consistency of soft, light marzipan. Leave it in a cool place wrapped in greaseproof paper, cloth, or polythene for at least ¾ hour.

Basic Savoury Pancakes

4 oz plain flour
1 egg
½ pint milk
salt

Beat the egg thoroughly into the milk. Season the flour and stir in the milk and egg mixture gradually, to make a smooth lump-free batter.

Beat for several minutes with a wooden spoon with the bowl of the spoon turned over, so that the air in the hollow of the spoon gets into the batter, or beat with a balloon whisk or an electric beater. Allow to stand for two hours before using.

☐ *This mixture makes 6–8 pancakes; make it 2 hours before it is needed.*

255

Plain Pie or Flan Pastry

6 oz plain flour
1 ½ oz slightly salted butter
1 ½ oz cooking fat
½ teaspoon salt, cold water

Sieve the flour and salt into a bowl. Chop the butter and cooking fat into it with a knife and then rub it in, lifting your hands several inches above the bowl with each movement, so that the fat is cooled by the air as it falls into the bowl; this may sound far-fetched but it really helps keep the pastry cool and therefore light. When it looks like fine breadcrumbs, carefully add water as you mix the pastry with your other hand until you have a light firm dough. Knead it together lightly, to distribute the moisture evenly. Stand it in a cool place, wrapped or covered, for at least an hour, before rolling out.

Yorkshire Pudding

4 oz plain flour, salt
2 eggs, ½ pint milk
2–3 tablespoons oil or good dripping

Make the batter by sieving the flour and salt into a bowl, make a well in the centre and add the eggs, breaking the yolks with your spoon before you start stirring. Add the milk gradually, stirring in the flour little by little until half the milk is added; keep going until all the flour is taken up and the mixture is smooth. Then add the rest of the milk and beat for five or ten minutes. Stand the batter in a cool place for one hour. Preheat oven to Reg 9/475°. When the batter is ready, heat the oil or dripping in a baking tin, pour on the batter and cook five minutes at Reg 9/475° and 35–40 minutes at Reg 7/425°.

☐ *Batter to be made two hours in advance.*

For 6

To Clarify Butter

Clarified butter keeps better than ordinary butter and is used to seal up pâtés and home-made potted game and meat. It is also excellent for frying; it is the milk content in butter that makes it burn, and this is filtered out in the clarifying. It is also the nearest thing to ghee for making Indian curries.

It is not worth clarifying less than half a pound because you lose quite a lot on the way; more is worthwhile, since it keeps so well. Use the cheapest butter.

Melt the butter slowly in a thick saucepan, without browning. Turn off the heat, stir it and let it stand for a few minutes to settle. Line a sieve with a fine cloth squeezed out in hot water and stand it over a bowl. Pour in the butter and let it drip through. Allow to set and remove it from the bowl; pour away the water from underneath.

Clarified butter should be a lovely, even, semi-transparent yellow colour.

To Clarify Fat

The sort of fat which is left from a pot-au-feu or other lengthy boiling of meat is not very suitable for immediate use, as it is full of moisture and fragments of meat and vegetables.

To clarify it, put it in a pan with double its quantity of water. Bring it all to the boil, allow it to cool and the fat will form a solid disc above the water, with some of the pieces and fragments stuck underneath (the rest should be in the water). Scrape all the pieces off and melt the fat down again; pour it into a pot.

It is worth doing this with pork, beef or chicken fat.

Yoghurt

1 heaped teaspoon plain yoghurt
1 quart fresh milk (the amount of milk used makes
    the same amount of yoghurt)

Bring the milk to the boil over a high flame. When
it starts to rise in the pan take it off the heat and
allow to cool until you can keep your finger in while
you count ten (110°–120°). Put the starting teaspoon
of yoghurt in a bowl and stir in the milk. Put the
bowl in a warm place, wrapped in a folded towel,
and leave it undisturbed for six to eight hours.
Overnight is ideal. Unwrap the bowl. You should
now have yoghurt with water on top; if not put it
back for a while, otherwise pour off the water and
chill the yoghurt.

The first batch is not always as good as it might
be, because bought yoghurt has often been deep-
frozen, but using your own yoghurt as a starter will
make a good second batch — each subsequent
batch will become increasingly weak.

☐ *Also known as Persian Milk, yoghurt is a very
ancient food and is supposed to promote longevity.*

Eliza Acton's Fritter Batter

1 oz butter
½ pint cold water, or a little more
6 oz flour, plain
a pinch of salt
white of an egg

Put about 4 tablespoons of the water and the
butter in a small pan and bring to the boil. When
the butter has melted add the rest of the cold
water. Put the flour into a larger basin, and
mixing well all the time, pour in the tepid buttery
water. Stir well to get rid of all lumps, add the
salt, and leave to stand 1–2 hours. Just before
you want to make the fritters, whisk the egg
white very stiff and fold it into the batter.

This makes a very light delicate batter for
fritters.

For 6–8

Dripping for Toast

1 teaspoon Bovril, or an Oxo cube
a little hot water
dripping, from beef preferably

Dissolve the Bovril in a little hot water, just
enough to make it runny. Slightly melt the
dripping and mix the Bovril well in. Allow to set.

Use as a thick spread on thick hot toast.

☐ *This is slightly cheating, but in families where
dripping toast is popular, the brown jelly at the
bottom of the dripping bowl gets very quickly
snatched up, while the plain pure dull dripping is
left behind. This trick makes all the dripping taste
delicious, and is very nourishing and warming as
well.*

Fresh Mint Chutney

large bunch mint
1 teaspoon finely minced onion
1 teaspoon chopped green chilli
1 teaspoon chopped green ginger
a sliver of pounded garlic
a squeeze of lemon juice
Cayenne pepper
salt
3–4 tablespoons yoghurt

Scald the mint leaves, pound them, and mix with
the remaining ingredients except the yoghurt.
Stir it in and serve in a small pot.

☐ *Very good with curry, mutton or chicken
especially.*

Tomato Purée

2–3 lbs tomatoes
1 onion
3 whole cloves garlic
1 teaspoon dried basil
sugar
a little salt, several black peppercorns
1 tablespoon olive oil
1 oz butter

Soften the sliced onion in olive oil without browning. Cut the tomatoes in quarters and add them to the pan, mashing with a wooden spoon, then add the whole cloves of garlic, basil, salt and peppercorns. Simmer until you have a nice sauce (about 25–30 minutes). Pick out the cloves of garlic and peppercorns if you happen to see them, and sieve the rest. Return it to the pan and reduce it, stirring all the time to prevent it from sticking and burning, to a thick purée. (This will take some time.) Taste for seasoning and turn out into small sterilised jars (see note on sterilisation). Pour on a thin coating of oil and cover. If covered properly and stored in a cool dry place this should keep well and is very good used diluted with a bit of melted butter and water as a sauce for pasta or meat, or neat as an addition to Bolognese sauces or stews.

Sterilising Tomato Purée

Have ready a large pan of almost boiling water, and enough *hot* clean preserving jars (with rubber bands, glass discs and screwbands, or metal discs or screwbands) for your quantity of purée.

Bring the purée to the boil and pour it boiling into the jars, closing each one at once with lids and screwbands, and immersing them in hot water. Keep them from touching with a cloth pad. When all are done bring it to the boil and boil for 10 minutes. Remove jars, tighten bands if necessary, leave to cool and test for vacuum sealing after 12 hours.

Oven Method of Bottling Blackberries and Apples

apples, windfalls, peeled, cored and cut into
   sugar-lump sized chunks
blackberries, ripe and dry (no stalks)
2 cloves in each jar, if liked
the cores and peelings of apples
water, sugar
Kilner jars and tops (sold specially for bottling)

Make a light syrup from the apple peelings and cores (don't include any bruised or bad pieces), adding some blackberries. Do this as follows: Put the berries and peelings in to a pan and cover with water. Simmer for 1 hour. Strain through a jelly bag or fine sieve. Measure the resulting juice, add 8 oz sugar to every pint of juice and heat, stirring until the sugar dissolves.

As a rough guide, $1\frac{1}{2}$ pints of syrup should be enough to bottle 7 lbs of fruit. But this depends on how tightly you pack the fruit and how much the fruit shrinks, etc. This has to be borne in mind when packing the fruit. The proportion of apples to blackberries is a question of taste, about $\frac{1}{2}$ and $\frac{1}{2}$ is nice. Pack the jars as tightly as you can without squashing the fruit. Bang the jar on the table (put a cloth or newspaper under it first) to settle the fruit down and fill up to the top. Fill a spare jar with fruit for topping up. The fruit will shrink by $\frac{2}{3}$ or $\frac{1}{4}$ in the oven, so put one spare bottle for every 2 or 3. Place all the jars with lids on but not done up in the oven, preheated to Reg 1/275° and leave for 1 hour. Sterilize the rubber rings if you are using this method, by boiling them in water for 15 minutes. Bring the syrup to the boil (and keep it simmering) just before the hour is up. Have everything ready, for speed is essential, and everything is very hot. Put a thick layer of cloth on the table (or several layers of newspaper) for standing the jars on. Have the rings near and ready, the lids and the screw rings. Make sure they are the right sizes, and there are enough. Make sure the pan with the boiling syrup is easy to pour from. Put a kettle of water on to boil in case there isn't enough syrup. Have a good oven cloth for holding hot jars and have a spoon for filling up gaps. Take out a spare jar of fruit, and the first jar. Give it a bang to settle the fruit again and top it up from the spare bottle. Pour the boiling syrup up to the top of the jar. Put on the ring, making sure the surfaces are clear of fruit and juice or the seal won't work. Put on the lid, and screw up tight. Leave until the next day to test for success (the Kilner jars with tin lids and rubber seal joined on are much easier to use but must only be used once). Continue filling one jar at a time. This method depends on sealing by vacuum, which in this case is caused by the heated contents of the jars cooling and shrinking, which sucks the lids down tight on to the rubber seals. Therefore the hotter it is done, the greater the chance of success. Test the next day. You should be able to pick up the jar by the lid alone (unscrew the ring first). If it drops off — it is no good!

Pickled Cherries

Boil $\frac{1}{2}$ pint distilled vinegar together with a teaspoon of salt and 2 teaspoons of sugar for 15 minutes. Let it cool. Wash and dry 1 lb of firm sound cherries and remove the stalks. Pack them loosely in a jar with white peppercorns and sprigs of tarragon, pour on the cold pickle and cover. After 48 hours pour out the vinegar without moving the cherries, boil it up and let it cool. Refill the jars. Cover and store 2 weeks before eating with cold meats (especially game).

To make 1 lb

Seville Orange Marmalade

10 good Seville oranges
2 lemons
10 lbs sugar (preserving sugar is best because it
    dissolves well, but granulated will do)
9 pints water
a muslin bag to cook the pips in

To make a year's supply for an average small family
you need four times this amount, but 15 lbs is a
convenient quantity to cook, providing you have a
large preserving pan.

The oranges are only here for a short time in January
but it really is worth making your own marmalade;
it costs half as much as shop marmalade and is twice
as good. This method is spread over three days, but
doesn't take much time on the second and third
days.

1st day: halve and squeeze the juice from the ten
oranges and two lemons. Sieve the juice to retain
the pips. Shred the squeezed skins into large or
small matchsticks, whichever you prefer, or if you
are not fussy put them through the coarsest blade
of your mincer. Pour eight pints of cold water over
the peel and juice, and in a separate basin one pint
of cold water over the pips. Leave to soak for 24
hours.

2nd day: strain the pips and put them in the muslin
bag. Add their liquid to the peel and, in a preserving
pan, simmer the pips with the peel very gently until
the peel is quite tender. (Test by biting or by squeezing between finger and thumb). Do this in a pan
with a lid; it takes about $1\frac{1}{2}$ hours, but doesn't need
watching or stirring. When tender leave the whole
thing to soak another 24 hours.

3rd day: put fifteen clean 1 lb jam jars to heat in a
low oven. Remove the bag of pips, pressing it to
squeeze out all the juice which is an important
source of pectin. Bring the marmalade to the boil in
a large pan. Add the sugar, stirring well or it will
burn. Boil very fast after the sugar has dissolved
until setting point is reached, in 30–40 minutes.
Test for setting by letting a little marmalade cool
on a saucer or by holding up your spoon and waiting
for the drips to become large, slow and heavy.

Towards the end, take the pan off the heat while
you wait for the results of the testing. Overcooking
will produce a syrup that never sets, and undercooking produces a sloppy mess that won't keep,
but this marmalade sets beautifully and keeps two
or three years. When it is absolutely ready, turn
off the heat and allow to cool a little; it will soon
start setting in the pan, so have your jars ready.
Fill the jars, which should be standing on a board
or newspapers, wipe them clean, allow them to cool
and cover them carefully.

Makes 15 lbs

Bramble Jelly and Bramble Cheese

blackberries
water
sugar
Optional additions
1–2 cooking apples
or a handful of raisins
or 2 sweet geranium leaves

Stew the blackberries, plus the optional additions,
with a very little water (enough to cover the
bottom of the pan). Press them from time to
time with a wooden spoon to extract all the
juice. Stop when they have completely softened
and changed colour from black to purple.

For Jelly: Strain overnight through a cloth. You
will use only the juice.

For Cheese: Press through a sieve. You will use
the resulting purée, but leave out the pips.

For Jelly and Cheese: Measure the juice, or purée,
and for each pint of liquid take 1 lb sugar. Bring
liquid to the boil in a large pan, add the sugar,
stirring well to dissolve it. Continue cooking fast,
until setting point, about 20–30 minutes. Pour
into warm jars, allow to cool, cover and seal.

3 lbs blackberries makes 4–5 little pots.

Crabapple Jelly

crabapples
water
sugar
bowl
tea-towel
string
jam jars
covers

You can flavour this with cloves, ginger or cinnamon. Pick out any unsound or bruised crabapples, and wash the rest well. Leave the stalks on, put in a saucepan and just cover with water. Simmer covered until they are a pulpy mass (about 30 minutes) prodding with a wooden spoon occasionally. Add the cloves, ginger or cinnamon now, if wanted. Wet a clean tea-towel or similar cloth, in hot water and wring it out. Put it over a basin large enough to hold all the apple juice, pour the pulpy apples and juice into it, tie it tightly with string and hang it over the bowl on a convenient hook or nail. (Use the cup hooks on the dresser.) Let it drip about 12 hours.

Measure the liquid (it will be cloudy but never mind, it clears with the sugar), put it in a large pan and add 1 lb sugar per pint of juice. Stir over gentle heat until the sugar is melted. Then bring to a fierce boil, so it froths up high, which is why you need a large pan. Stir all the time, skimming, and test for jelling, by putting a little to cool on a saucer (when it wrinkles as you push it, it is ready) or when the drips are slow to leave the spoon if you hold it up over the pan. If you overboil, it will burn or go syrupy. If you underboil, it will be too runny and ferment. One pint can be ready in as little as ten minutes. Pour into clean hot jam jars, which should be waiting in the oven. Cover when cold.

Very good eaten with sugared petit suisse.

Fruit Syrups

1 lb preserving sugar to 1 pint juice
water

Put the fruit in a large china or earthenware basin with about $\frac{1}{2}$ pint water to 3 lbs fruit and mash it down a bit with a wooden spoon or steak-beater. Stand the bowl, covered with a large lid, in a pan of water and put it in a slowish oven Reg 1/275° for one to two hours, mashing from time to time.

When the fruit seems to have softened as much as possible, take it out of the oven and strain it through a double muslin or jelly-bag, overnight if possible.

Next day add $\frac{3}{4}$–1 lb preserving sugar to each pint of juice, depending on how sweet you want the syrup. Add a little bag of cloves or cinnamon, or a dash of brandy or lemon juice if you like. Heat gently, stirring, in a large pan until the sugar is dissolved — no longer, or it will set like jam. Cool.

Have ready some small sterilised bottles, with sterilised screw caps (15 minutes in boiling water does the trick). Fill them with the syrup to within $1\frac{1}{2}$–2 inches from the top and put on the screw tops. Without this space, the expanding hot liquid will burst the bottle when you sterilise it. Stand the bottles in a deep pan with a false bottom, a pressure cooker is ideal, and pour in water almost to the top of the bottles. Bring the water to the boil and keep boiling for 20–30 minutes. Take out the bottles and stand them on a wooden table or on folded newspapers, not on a cold surface or they will crack. When they have cooled tighten the screw tops if necessary and seal by dipping in melted wax, or with sticky tape.

Fruit syrup, as opposed to fruit squash, is incredibly expensive to buy and much nicer to drink. If there is a glut of any soft fruit such as blackberries, raspberries, blackcurrants, English grapes, strawberries, cherries etc., you can make your own. It will keep quite well until it is opened, after which it must be kept in the refrigerator.

It is very good in milk shakes or used as a sauce for a pudding, or of course as a base for a hot or cold drink.

German Green Tomato Pickle

5 lbs green tomatoes, small enough to eat whole
2 pints cheap malt vinegar
1 lb white sugar
6 cloves, 1 inch cinnamon stick, and a piece of
    nutmeg or 2–3 blades mace (½ teaspoon
    powdered)
1 pint white wine vinegar
pinch salt

Remove the stalks from the tomatoes and put them, with their skins still on, in a large pan with the malt vinegar. Bring slowly to the boil, stirring. Then strain, put the tomatoes in a china bowl, and throw the vinegar away.
Bring the sugar, spices, wine vinegar and salt to the boil, stirring to dissolve the sugar, and pour it over the tomatoes. Leave in the bowl for 24 hours; next day, remove the tomatoes, boil up the liquid again, leave it to cool and pour it again over the tomatoes. Leave it for another 24 hours. The following day, bring the tomatoes and the liquid to the boil together, remove the tomatoes, and reduce the liquid until it becomes slightly syrupy. Remove the spices. Put the tomatoes into clean hot jars, pour over the syrup, slightly cooled, cover and keep at least three months.

☐ *This takes three days to make and is ready to eat in three months. It is very sweet and delicious and looks beautiful, quite unlike anything you can buy at the grocer.*

Lemonade

5 lemons
1½ lbs granulated sugar
1 pint boiling water
½ oz citric acid

Thinly pare the lemons (no white) with a sharp knife or potato peeler, and pour one pint of boiling water on to this peel. Add the sugar and the juice of the lemons. Stir until the sugar dissolves, steep overnight and strain. Stir in the citric acid. Use diluted. This lemonade keeps for weeks in screw-top bottles in the refrigerator.

Makes 1½ pints concentrated juice

Coconut Ice

2 lbs sugar
just over ¼ pint milk
1 oz butter
8 oz desiccated coconut
pink colouring

Put the sugar, butter and milk in a heavy saucepan and bring them slowly to the boil, stirring to dissolve the sugar. Boil for four minutes stirring all the time. Remove from the heat, add the coconut, stir well and pour half into a greased tin, one inch deep. Colour the other half and pour into a separate tin. Mark into fingers when it is half set, and cut when cool. It sets quickly so you should work fast. It is very good for Christmas presents and bazaars.

Mr Hale's Method of Peeling Chestnuts

Put a tablespoon of vegetable oil in a roasting tin to warm in the oven. Score the chestnuts, cutting through to the inner skin, then place them in the tin and swirl around until they are coated in oil. Bake in the oven at Reg 5/375° for 15–20 minutes. The oil prevents burning and the skins are easy to remove.

Yorkshire Pudding

4 oz plain flour, salt
2 eggs, ½ pint milk
2–3 tablespoons oil or good dripping

Make the batter by sieving the flour and salt into a bowl, make a well in the centre and add the eggs, breaking the yolks with your spoon before you start stirring. Add the milk gradually, stirring in the flour little by little until half the milk is added; keep going until all the flour is taken up and the mixture is smooth. Then add the rest of the milk and beat for five or ten minutes. Stand the batter in a cool place for one hour. Preheat oven to Reg 9/475°. When the batter is ready, heat the oil or dripping in a baking tin, pour on the batter and cook five minutes at Reg 9/475° and 35–40 minutes at Reg 7/425°.

☐ *Batter to be made two hours in advance.*

For 6

Melba Toast

To eat with potted meat, pâté and of course caviar. It looks twice as expensive as ordinary toast and costs even less.

Make toast in the usual way with slices of bread about quarter of an inch thick. Cut off the crusts and slice each piece of toast carefully in half through the soft centre, making two slices from one, each toasted on one side only.

Turn the grill down to a moderate heat and toast the thin slices gently on their untoasted side. They will curl slightly, and should be served hot, in a crisp pile.

You can make this toast in advance and reheat in a low oven before serving.

Home-made Breadcrumbs

Collect all the left-over ends of loaves, making sure that none are going mouldy. Put them in a very low oven, or all day in the plate-warming drawer of your cooker, until they are completely dried and pale brown.

Lay a tea-towel on a firm table. Fold it neatly round the bread so that the crumbs cannot escape, and press a rolling pin all over it, crushing and crunching the bread. Hold a sieve over a baking tin and shake the crumbs through. Repeat the performance until the crusts are all fine crumbs. Store them in an airtight jar, and they will keep well.

To freshen a stale loaf

Useful for the end of a long Easter or Christmas holiday.

Hold the loaf (or part of a loaf) in the steam of a kettle for one or two minutes, then leave it in a hot oven, Reg 8/450°, for five minutes. When cool the crust will be as crisp as newly baked bread.

Cure for Indigestion

Boiled water, drunk as hot as possible.

Index

265

268